And Now on Radio 4

And Now on Radio 4

A 40th Birthday Celebration of the World's Best Radio Station

SIMON ELMES

BOOKS

Published by Random House Books 2007

2 4 6 8 10 9 7 5 3 1

Copyright © Simon Elmes 2007

Simon Elmes has asserted his right under the Copyright, Designs and Patents Act 1988 to be identified as the author of this work

First published in Great Britain in 2007 by
Random House Books
Random House, 20 Vauxhall Bridge Road,
London SW1V 2SA

www.rbooks.co.uk

Addresses for companies within The Random House Group Limited can be found at: www.randomhouse.co.uk/offices.htm

The Random House Group Limited Reg. No. 954009

A CIP catalogue record for this book is available from the British Library

ISBN 9781905211531

The Random House Group Limited makes every effort to ensure that the papers used in its books are made from trees that have been legally sourced from well-managed and credibly certified forests. Our paper procurement policy can be found at:
www.rbooks.co.uk/environment

Mixed Sources
Product group from well-managed
forests and other controlled sources
www.fsc.org   Cert no. TT-COC-2139
© 1996 Forest Stewardship Council
FSC

Typeset by SX Composing DTP, Rayleigh, Essex
Printed and bound in Great Britain by
William Clowes Ltd, Beccles, Suffolk

Contents

Preface

The working week begins on a Monday; the Christian week on a Sunday. For one weird practiser of druidry, the first day of the week is, I gather, Friday. However, the BBC has, for as long as anyone can remember, contrarily, started its weeks on a Saturday. Which means that big BBC events – like the inauguration of a new channel or, at a more mundane level, the first day of the week in *Radio Times* – fall very often on a Saturday.

There's something rather odd about this, really. A bit like what gets called these days 'a soft launch'. Not quite the roll-up-the-sleeves-and-get-down-to-it feel of a Monday morning. More a pull-up-a-chair-and-cop-this sort of event.

But Saturday September the 30th 1967 was just a bit more special. Transistor radios across the country were abuzz with the trails. *Radio Times* (price eightpence – eight *old* pence, well short of a shilling and, by twenty-first-century standards, a bargain at about 3p) had broken out into colour for the nonce. On the cover, a blonde babe dances obliquely amongst what looks a bit like an accident in a Smarties factory: a strange detritus of red, blue, orange and green discs. In her left hand she brandishes another red disc, inscribed in that so-fashionable curly-wurly writing that back in Beatlemania days meant *swinging*, *groovy* or indeed *dodgy* with two words: 'this week'. And on her pyramid-shaped snow-white mini-dress (in the same curly-wurly script) are the bright orange words: 'RADIO 1 ON 247'.

The minuscule silvery radio – as cool as some early-adopter 3G gizmo today – that she's about to trample under her dancing feet is a generational symbol. No longer was *sound* (or even '*steam*') *radio* synonymous with a hulking great ice-cream-shaped microphone the size of a small classroom-globe (technically, a Marconi-made 'Type A' type, dating from 1934). No, the sleek transistor was the image of radio cool that the corporation wanted to identify itself with that autumn week in 1967.

This was what we in the corporation call a 'Radio cover'. Since television got the lion's share of the sweeties, 'Radio covers' are rare phenomena in the *Radio Times* world. But September the 30th was indeed a big radio day, so it got its cover story. It was Radio 1's very first transmission, the day the world was greeted by Tony Blackburn, by those eagerly harmonising voices proclaiming 'Radio One is Onederful!' and at last introduced to the British listener 'The Swinging New Radio Service'. Don't you just love it?

But amongst the (slightly) hip new radio schedules for Saturday September the 30th (Tony Blackburn's *Daily Disc Delivery* was followed at – such BBC precision – 8.32 by Leslie Crowther with *Junior Choice*) there was an event that went barely noticed. *Radio Times* proclaimed it – well, they hardly could ignore it – but it wasn't exactly a cause for celebration, more a new arrangement, a redefinition, a change of designation. Or was it?

I'm talking of course about the other new radio services that first saw the light of day that September Saturday: Radio 2 – shedding its old Light Programme name and identity and fusing its schedules with the new baby (which explains why Leslie Crowther, then 'appearing in *Let Sleeping Wives Lie* at the Garrick Theatre, London', turns up as part of Radio 1); and, still on page 13 of that copy of *Radio Times*, the new Radio 3 – complete with, yes, *sport*.

Overpage on 14, with a whole side to itself, lies the subject of this book – the fourth new network born on Saturday September the 30th 1967: BBC Radio 4. Radio 4, epitome of all things British – the great voice of middle England – the tamper-with-at-your-peril network that's so often quoted (not always completely accurately) as representing the very best of the BBC. No fanfares or fandangos to launch this national treasure, no great unveiling or opening ceremony. No theme tune either. Just the Saturday edition of *Farming Today* opening up the network at 6.35 am.

In fact, that first Radio 4 day forty years ago is very familiar – but also very different from today's network. Many of the programme titles are similar or, surprisingly, identical to those of 2007: there's *From Our Own Correspondent* – FOOC if you're in the business – at 8.15, and a couple of hours later *The Daily Service*. (These days, though, Radio 4 is pretty ungodly on a Saturday morning.) There's comedy for Saturday lunchtime with *Round the Horne* and, at 3.15, the precursor of *Weekend Woman's Hour* called *Home for the Day*. There are a couple of plays, a book programme, some gardening news and *Desert Island Discs*: Roy Castle, the entertainer, was Roy Plomley's guest. So far, so very familiar.

There were fewer newses though, and, spreading its further-educational tentacles across what's regarded today as radio's morning primetime, at 11.35 am *Study Session*: Divertissement Français – *fifteen programmes for listeners with some knowledge of French*. The evening consisted of a curious concatenation of comedy – *Steptoe and Son* freshly bowdlerised for radio – and concert, as Albert and Harold's cart is followed incongruously on to the air by *Gala Night at the Opera* (from rag-and-bone men to *Carmen*, as it were; but also *Rigoletto*, *Rosenkavalier* and *Semiramide* . . .).

And just as the last applause from the audience in the Town Hall, Huddersfield is dying away, on strides Paul Daneman as Alexander the Great, to strut his stuff in fourth-century Greece as imagined by Terence Rattigan in *Adventure Story*, the first *Saturday Night Theatre* presentation of the new Radio 4.

Eclectic, I grant you, and eclecticism has always been a typical feature of the Radio 4 schedule. But coherent, perhaps not – and certainly very different in many ways from the layout of an average Radio 4 Saturday in the first decade of the twenty-first century.

And yet, as I hope to demonstrate most emphatically in the course of the following chapters, the ebb and flow of Radio 4 has, to a surprising degree, stayed wonderfully consistent across the decades: a bit like one of those speeded-up films of, say, a High Street across the years. We watch as a few buildings are pulled down and new ones spring up to replace them; the odd landmark is felled, the occasional tree planted, yet the main features – the roadways and the lamp-standards, the balconies above the shopfronts and the parish church on the corner – remain more-or-less unshifted, unaltered. Colours may change and detail may blur, but the intrinsic *streetness* of that High Street lives on. So, too, with Radio 4.

Professor Laurie Taylor (no longer 'of York University', as for decades *Stop the Week* described him, but now of London) has said that Radio 4 is 'like Marmite'

> Because Marmite *has* changed slightly: there *are* differences on the pack, there are differences in the advertising; there was a squeezy Marmite or something, wasn't there? (People got upset, and they said, 'Oh God we don't want that!' But Marmite now *plays* with that; it says 'some people hate us, some people love us' – plays that game rather well.) That's what Radio 4 is like: it does want change, but we don't want to see it, we don't want to notice it. And then it just somehow seems to *evolve*.

In these pages, with the help of Radio 4 luminaries like Laurie, I'll be shifting the curtain on some of the history of those forty years of surreptitious change. And, I hope, offering some glimpses of programmes forgotten or overlooked, celebrating some long-standing favourites, and bringing to life some of the many great names that have made their home on Radio 4, whose voices and style define that essence that is the world's most original and engaging radio station: unique – and uniquely British.

Here, though, I must enter a caveat. I've spent more than three of those four decades in the BBC, most of them fashioning programmes for Radio 4, and the prospect of endeavouring to be in any way comprehensive is I'm afraid impossible. Just consider the number of programmes that were broadcast on that very first Saturday alone – 47, if you count the news bulletins and weather forecasts – and then multiply that by 365 days, and then that figure by the 40 years of its existence and you begin to get an idea of the vastness of the flow of programmes that is

BBC Radio 4. It's the most densely packed schedule in the UK, certainly, and I'd hazard a fair bet that that applies to the rest of the world as well. James Boyle, the network's eighth controller, described the schedule as a 'medieval town plan' packed with tiny streets and alleys and buildings. He vowed to do as Baron Haussmann did to Paris, to open up some decent thoroughfares, regularise the crossroads, put a news bulletin on every corner, as it were, and if not to institute a US grid plan, then certainly to bring order to this warren of programmes.

He did what he said he'd do – and provoked a near riot in the process. Yet it's Boyle's schedule that – broadly speaking – is still with us nearly ten years later. But it's still complex, still has some wonderfully obscure start-times and still retains enough idiosyncrasy to make the task of capturing every favourite programme, every much-loved presenter quite impossible. So, to you who search the Index in vain for your own pet Radio 4 moment, I apologise now. This has, by necessity, to be a selective collection.

But then, as Margaret Howard was at pains to explain to me when I first set foot in the office of *Pick of the Week* many Picks ago, we're not trying to be comprehensive, just represent the best we can get – and that we can afford. In some respects, the same might be said for this book.

INTRODUCTION

Because the pictures are better

It was the pictures that did it. I was cowering in my bedroom, bawling my head off. In the sitting room my parents were contemplating sitting down to write to the BBC. And it was all because of the drill – you see, the drill was whining towards the forehead of our hero, our warrior-for-truth, closer, ever closer . . . how could he possibly escape? Then out of the roar surged the screaming climax of the 'Infernal Dance of King Kastchei' from Stravinsky's *Firebird* . . . and the exciting episode of John Darran's *Counterspy* ended for another week. How could it finish there? What would happen? It was utterly terrifying – at least to a seven-year-old.

It was – it is – the sheer power of sound and story to conjure a picture, a situation, to strap you into that chair with the drill about to gouge the flesh of your brow, plough into the bone and . . . The pictures, the feelings were inside me, pulled from my imagination by some powerful sound effects, a bit of convincing acting and a thrilling, demonic musical crescendo. Simple really. It was, and is, the magical and effortless power of radio, of sound, to conjure up a scene – a picture as vivid and as shocking as anything million-dollar Hollywood CGI can achieve, and with the minimum of resources.

Many years later, when I'd become a young audio engineer (in the BBC they're usually called Studio Managers), I was asked by an eminent World Service drama producer to cook up the sound effects for a production he was doing of James Elroy Flecker's 1922 play of eastern magic and exoticism, *Hassan*. Thus it was that I spent a whole nightshift not on 'the golden road to Samarkand' but in a gloomy studio, creating with a few sound effects discs the imaginative landscape of the play, including the 'vast steel curtain slowly descending' which the plot required. The thrill! I was a master chef, concocting an impossible Cecil B De Mille image in the minds of listeners the world over – and it was just so simple.

Because that's how radio works. It takes the minimum resources – a single voice speaking into a microphone, a sound that conjures a world of recaptured memories – and the mind of the listener fills in all the other details. No need for costly sets, armies of extras, gratuitous graphics. Radio pictures live in the head, not in the eye: and they can get much, much closer to how we feel than any number of flashy images on a screen in the corner of the room.

This book is testimony to that power, as expressed in its purest form on BBC Radio 4 by men and women in front of the microphone, by writers and actors who bring to life a whole imaginary universe populated by . . . well, a two-headed creature called Zaphod Beeblebrox and a paranoid android named Marvin for starters; or perhaps simply by a sequence of sounds – a distant church bell, a churring cicada maybe and a faraway house-martin that in an instant evoke the soft warm breeze of a summer's morning in the heart of Tuscany . . .

'As a writer, the wonderful thing about radio is the freedom of imagery you can plant in people's heads, things that are just quite simply impossible.' The speaker is Steve Punt, writer, comedian and star of *The Now Show* on Radio 4 who knows all about this incredibly cheap source of imaginative power:

> You can suddenly be anywhere: you can be talking about getting the Olympics ready and you can say 'I wonder whether they had this problem building the Pyramids?' and then: FX DESERT WINDS, bit of Egyptian music. And the guys who do the sound effects are just brilliant because you type in on the script, FX VAST WOODEN ROLLERS CARRYING BLOCKS OF SAND-STONE THROUGH THE EGYPTIAN DESERT, and in a single sentence suddenly the audience are picturing vast teams of slaves dragging blocks of stone across a desert.

But the wonder of radio is you don't even need the resources of skilled sound effects technicians. Take, for example, Alistair Cooke, one of the most exquisite of Radio 4's voices and the perfect radio story teller, who could reel in his audience like Hemingway's Old Man playing his great fish. Several times, in various Radio 4 programmes, I've had the chance to regale listeners with an incredible account by Cooke back in July 1945, when he described the crash of a B-25 bomber as it ploughed into the Empire State Building in New York. It was ten to ten on a foggy morning and the pilot had become disorientated. The facts were horrific enough – this was nearly sixty years before 9/11 – but Cooke's first-hand account of the hours it took stranded office workers to make their way down the staircases of what was then the city's tallest building was astounding. Looking up into the swirling fog, he imagined the scene he couldn't see, hundreds of feet above him on the seventy-ninth floor where the bomber had slammed into the structure, engulfing it in flames and sending one of the lifts crashing down the shaft. It was and is still a magisterial piece of radio writing – economic, evocative and – given that the fog prevented anybody on the ground getting any photographs that meant anything much – infinitely the best pictures available.

If further proof of radio's evocative power were needed, many years ago a letter, postmarked Ireland, landed on my desk at the BBC, thanking me for a documentary that I'd made for Radio 4, called *Forbidden Journey*. A young adventurer called Nick Crane, today a seasoned star of TV travel programmes like *Coast*, was making for me what was only his second radio programme, a secret journey through Soviet-occupied Afghanistan. In her letter, our Irish correspondent said she'd been by Nick's side every inch of the way as he crept past the border defences, and announced that she had already cancelled a dinner party she had arranged for the following week when the next episode was to be broadcast. She couldn't miss a moment, she said. Such is the power of radio to enthral . . . and modify social arrangements!

This strange ability of the very best radio to worm its way inside your head and transfix you isn't uncommon. Most producers I know have stories to tell of listeners late for work because they just had to wait till a particularly gripping story finished on Radio 4. Another, more famous, Nick – Nick Clarke – one of the network's most accomplished journalists (and coincidentally Alistair Cooke's biographer), with a warm and perfectly modulated voice ('sublime' Radio 4's controller Mark Damazer called it) made a programme with me in the last year of his life about his struggle with cancer. It was an incredibly painful, raw personal account by Nick and his wife Barbara, built round their audio diary, and it held listeners captive. Like I suspect hundreds or even thousands of listeners, a group of BBC colleagues, including the Chairman of the BBC, found themselves trapped in their cars by the story. As they bumped into each other on the stairs on their way to the office, they all discovered they'd been listening to the same unswitchoffable account. So much for those who speak slightingly of 'steam radio'.

If the most effective radio still has the power to stop us in our tracks, it has also an amazing ability to urge those behind the microphone to perform near miracles. In his *Forbidden Journey* documentary, for example, Nick Crane accomplished something few do outside the arena of war. He recorded what he thought might well be his last hours, as he struggled high in the mountains on the Afghan border to keep himself alive in snow that was almost burying him. It was by no means unique: Ted Edwards, virtually out of water, had done it during his 1983 crossing of the Arabian Empty Quarter which was also chronicled on Radio 4. Yet both kept recording. The fact that Radio 4 had given them a microphone meant they were somehow duty-bound to commit the moment to tape, even if it was their last.

Few who heard it will forget the legendary journalist James Cameron's dramatised account of open heart surgery *The Pump*, broadcast in the early days of the network (1973), or, from the mid-80s, Tony van den Bergh's graphic documentary, commentating, with only an epidural to ease the pain, on his own hip replacement operations. And May 1968, less than a year into the new network, found a tear-gassed David Jessel – later the TV champion of the wrongfully convicted – vividly painting radio pictures for *The World at One* of a hail of *pavés* as he struggled for breath during the student riots in Paris.

These were pure radio moments of the highest order, infinitely memorable, and which have helped give Radio 4 its deep-rooted place in Britain's psyche. 'I suppose it's got virtually everything on it that you want to listen to,' says Nigel Forde, erstwhile weekly 'instant' poet on *Midweek*, and last presenter of the long-running literary programme *Bookshelf*:

> It's got plays, it's got talks, it's got interviews, it's got current affairs, it's got news and – most of all I think – it's got surprises. All sorts of things that you never think you could make a programme out of, like 'doodling' – and suddenly, it's mind expanding. I get hooked and start listening perhaps to *Round Britain Quiz* or *Counterpoint* and then you hear a dreadful play, and then next day you hear a lovely play and it's just total surprise all the time.

As with Alistair Cooke's signature 'Gud evening', for the Radio 4 listener a part of the pleasure of the network lies in the familiarity of its voices and their words as much as in the many surprises that are packed into the average Radio 4 day. So John Ebdon, another voice of urbanity who died not so long ago, was defined across his many years of broadcasting from the BBC Sound Archives by the breathy, arch 'Haow do you dooah?' of his opening, and his invariable ending: '. . . and if you have been, thanks for listening.' It's these oft-repeated vocal idiosyncrasies and catchphrases that characterise the network's voices. (Margaret Howard's 'Hello again' and 'Goodbye now', bland though they look on the page today, were significant enough to be mercilessly lampooned by one Radio 4 wit.) And of course *Dead Ringers* has, over the years, had enormous fun attributing fantasy other-lives to the stalwarts of Radio 4 continuity like Charlotte Green and Brian Perkins, which, as you'll see later in this book, they absolutely adore.

If television is the home of instantly recognisable faces, Radio 4 is the domain of the voices millions clean their teeth to, (literally) set their watches by and nightly drift off to sleep with.

It's why for many listeners, Radio 4's voices become friends. 'It's something to do with the very slow ways in which voices wheedle their way into listeners' consciousness,' observes Laurie Taylor, bringing the trained eye of a sociologist to bear on the subject:

> People after a time find a voice is part of their household – somebody who is welcomed into their household. It fits inside the room, rather like their armchairs or rather like their favourite vases or their favourite ornaments. It seems to be part of the furniture. Now anyone who's going to be successful on Radio 4 is going to [take] a long time: you've got to sit there while people say, 'Don't like the shape of that; don't like the look of that, my word!' And then, after a few years' time, [you're] accepted. That is a huge distinction from television. Television, you come in, you have to make an instant impact – sort of overnight you can be a star – and then you can disappear completely in two years.

One of the first pieces of BBC jargon I learned on joining the corporation in August 1974 was 'continuity'. 'Continuity' refers both to the rolling sequences of presentation, introductions and publicity material broadcast before and after programmes (on television just as on radio) by the team of network continuity announcers, and to the place from which these announcements are made: the 'continuity studio', or 'Con'. But it's always seemed to me a most apt word when applied more broadly to Radio 4: from month to month, year to year and even decade to decade the Radio 4 ethos is one of continuity – change, certainly, but a broad continuity of purpose and of the way in which that purpose is realised in programmes and voices that remain recognisably Radio 4-shaped. As journalist Zoe Williams wrote recently, 'It's true that even the regional accents on [Radio 4] sound uncannily well-enunciated, which is odd; it's like a national costume that is made of felt or hemp but has nevertheless been incredibly well-tailored . . .'

What this book intends to do is take you on a journey through that distinctive, instantly recognisable Radio 4 world. I hope that through the programmes I've featured and the voices I talk about, as well as the generous contributions from the many Radio 4 people – presenters, producers, controllers – who've spared the time to talk to me, some sort of coherent picture of this phenomenon that is Radio 4 will emerge.

Since this book at no stage sets out to be a formal history of the network, I've decided to organise it much as our lives as Radio 4 listeners shape and are shaped by the network. So, it begins where Radio 4 begins early each morning, and ends just before 1 am with 'Sailing By', the *Shipping Forecast* and those valedictory words (plus the Queen) that take listeners into the night. At the same time, I've used various key moments across the day as an opportunity for time travel – a sort of radio time-shuttle – zooming effortlessly across forty years of history. Along the way I hope to show how the network has evolved, and to tell stories of programmes old and venerable, young and thriving, defunct and forgotten and – in the words of Richard Baker's old Radio 4 music programme – *These You Have Loved*.

Not everything in the media always goes smoothly and there are stories here of how it was often only just all right on the night. I'll be letting you inside a few trade secrets too (not least the insider's cheeky names for that Richard Baker programme just mentioned, *Kaleidoscope* and *Brain of Britain*). I hope to give you too a sense of what it's like to make your way through the (thankfully these days, automated) heavy bronze doors of Broadcasting House in London and into radio's venerable seventy-five-year-old home.

A radio studio is an odd place. It's a room with a table and chairs and a glass wall, but usually with little or no decoration, and most have no windows. It has nothing of the *magic* of radio about it, and yet, when voices speak into the waiting micro-phones and music swells from the spinning CD next door in the control cubicle, or waves of sound effects surge from the huge monitor loudspeakers, a whole world fills the room. As Piers Plowright, one of radio's most distinguished producers, says:

This is the central mystery of radio, isn't it, that it doesn't exist except as a series of sounds. But I do have this theory that all sound goes somewhere and is floating about. Like the post-horn, in the Baron Munchausen story [by eighteenth-century writer Rudolf Erich Raspe], that got frozen as the coachman was driving along, but once he put the horn down by the fire in the pub, suddenly all the tunes came out and filled the inn. Now that's a lovely image, in a way, for what might be happening to the vanished voices, and even a quite clinical place like a radio studio I think *must* carry something in its walls.

To help me drill into those walls and quarry out some of the mystery of radio, and of Radio 4 in particular, I have to thank the many, many colleagues and friends who, like Piers Plowright, have taught me everything I know about radio, and shaped the way I make programmes – from the late Noel Michelli who magicked a microphone out of a KitKat foil in the first week of my training, to Robin Cherry whose sound balances on my programmes remain absolute masterclasses in audio perfection.

The names are too numerous to list in total, but I must above all thank Jenny Abramsky, Director of Audio and Music and radio's greatest champion, who gave this book her blessing and without whom the medium – and in consequence British daily life – would be infinitely poorer. Graham Ellis, Controller of Radio Production, has been a wonderfully supportive departmental leader (and a great personal ally) as the BBC has negotiated the rigours of the past ten years of change; and thanks too to Mark Damazer, current incumbent of the Radio 4 controller's chair and thus holder of the 'best job in the BBC', who manfully continues the fight to keep the standards flying as high as ever.

I am completely, *grovellingly* indebted to the dozens of Radio 4 people who've submitted to my relentless questioning over the months – their words constitute much of the substance of this book. Big thanks, too, to Robert Robinson and Nigel Forde for permission to quote from their books and to Simon Rooks in the BBC's Sound Library and the staff of the Written Archive Centre at Caversham for their patience and courteous help as I rooted around in Radio 4's earliest days . . .

On a personal note to Helen Fry, Helen Boaden, Ian Gilham in World Service, Geoffrey Braithwaite of Schools Radio, Annie Howells and Alastair Wilson go special gratitude – you all helped me when I needed it most in my career – and of course thank you to the myriad presenters and friends who've so often been the public face of magical Radio 4 collaborations: Michael Rosen, Melvyn Bragg, Christina Dodwell, Lenny Henry, Miles Kington and many, many others; it's been a wonderful creative journey.

Finally, thanks must go to those close to me and to this project without whom it would never have seen the light of day: my editor at Random House Nigel Wilcockson and, in BBC Documentaries Unit, Rob Ketteridge.

And thank you not least to those at home, my now very grown-up children Jocelyn and John, both of whom are beginning to step gingerly on to the media ladder, and above all to my wife, Liz, faithful Radio 4 listener, who's had to be present at the often painful birth of too many programmes over the years and who's cheered me on every inch of the way.

The red light is flicking; the studio is about to go live. From the loudspeakers in the control cubicle 'cue-programme' is feeding the words of the announcer in Radio 4 Continuity. 'In half an hour, *The Archers*, but now on Radio 4 . . .' – We're on air . . .

CHAPTER ONE

5.15 am: Stand by: light coming . . .

On a farm in Herefordshire, it's breakfast time – pretty early breakfast, actually. The cows have yet to be milked, and for them, at a quarter past five, it's really quite late. Across the spring fields, dawn is still half an hour away, but from the kitchen comes the burble of a radio.

No time for radios, though, on Dudley Road in Birmingham where the City Hospital's A&E night staff clock in another hopelessly drunk youngster scooped from the pavement on Broad Street: they've got another two hours of this till they can get away to their beds. On the M62 west of Leeds, a constant stream of early-morning trucks and cars is churning past a farm that lies bang in the middle of the motorway – an island of sheep farming in the middle of this internally combusted stretch of the Pennines. Almost every cab of every lorry has music playing – as often as not it's Radio 1 or Radio 2 keeping the night at bay.

In west London the traffic is also ceaseless. An N207 night bus with eleven passengers aboard rounds the curve at Shepherd's Bush Green. As it turns to head west up the Uxbridge Road, past the end of Wood Lane, a few solitary pedestrians are striding purposefully towards the glowing mass of Television Centre just down the road. There, in the BBC's main newsroom, it's already midday-busy. The coffee machine in the *Today* programme offices is doing a brisk trade. Ten miles to the east, in the heart of London's West End, on the first floor of Broadcasting House (the BBC's famous ship-like HQ building dating from 1932), a BBC radio continuity announcer is going through the preparations for a new day.

But on Sunday, April the 23rd 2006, this early-morning routine represented something special: it was the end of an era.

Early one morning

For me, it was perhaps because in my family in Bristol we'd sung folk songs round the piano, that those opening notes of 'Early One Morning' always made a very powerful connection. On the other hand, there's no doubt that, lovely though the arrangement was and is, by 2006 the UK Theme was a relic of another broadcasting era. When the then controller Ian McIntyre and his Presentation Editor introduced it, the IRA was at its height and the Troubles in full swing. Even if Radio 4 was still predominantly the voice of England, and southern England at that, it was nevertheless transmitted throughout the United Kingdom, and the UK Theme was intended by McIntyre to symbolise the encompassing national embrace of his network.

I suppose, as usual, it was the pictures that did it for me. Each time I ever heard it, images of mist rising over a West-Country valley at dawn floated, unsummoned, into my mind . . . three bars of 'Early One Morning'; then 'Rule Britannia', gradually gathering energy, slides gently from its climax into a clever blend of 'Danny Boy' and 'Annie Laurie'. Up steps a foot-tapping 'Drunken Sailor' who weaves in and out of 'Greensleeves' with more dexterity than his state might allow. 'Men of Harlech' then stride in, dancing in and out of the rugged kilt-clad legs of 'Scotland the Brave' like some instant eightsome reel, only to modulate down through the melodic gears to

BBC Radio 4 was about to bid farewell to one of its longest-established traditions. 'Change for the Worse at Radio 4' thundered the *Daily Telegraph* when the network's controller announced the termination of the opening musical theme. For thirty-three years it had heralded every day's broadcasting on Radio 4 with its 'row of bright flags run out to salute the morning' as Gillian Reynolds called it. Britain's longest-serving and most erudite critic and commentator on radio was cross: 'I like early-morning Radio 4 the way it is, a slower wake-up to a tune that calls to mind all those bits of the British Isles that are seldom mentioned on *Today* or any other news programme.'

find that maid singing in the valley below once again. Finally, there is a reprise of 'Rule Britannia' rising resplendent like the dawn over the confection. 'Fritz Spiegl was clearly a very clever arranger and there were elements that were indeed charming, I quite liked it actually,' comments Damazer, 'but to hear it day after day after day was frustrating.'

The Theme was the work of Fritz Spiegl, a great lover of radio and of this country which he'd adopted as his own. Fritz was a Radio 4 regular, notably on *Start the Week*, but the day job was as a musician – he was principal flautist with the Royal Liverpool Philharmonic Orchestra. As a teenager, he'd fled Austria at the outbreak of war with his family, and often used his outsider's view of Britain to maintain a brilliant witty commentary on the country's foibles, linguistic and social. I remember our hilarious encounter on the Radio 4 book programme *Bookshelf* when he came in to talk about his latest of many publications. It wasn't a weighty tome, but a collection of typically very funny gems culled from Fleet Street's finest, called *Keep Taking the Tabloids*. I still treasure my battered copy for its lovely handwritten inscription: 'Greetings from "Balding, bespectacled F.S." etc to Youthful Dynamic *Bookshelf* producer Simon Elmes (see p. 15)'. The cryptic reference was to the tabloid practice of listing 'apparently unconnected facts . . . strung together and piled up in front of a person's name'.

Fritz died in 2003.

The so-called 'UK Theme' was first heard in 1973, when the then Presentation Editor (head of the announcing team and keeper of the sacred sound of Radio 4) Jim Black asked the musicologist, wit and famous champion of all things Liverpudlian Fritz Spiegl to assemble a musical salad that would embody something of the spirit of the four home nations, and act as herald to the day's broadcasting, a sort of musical cock-crow for 'Radio 4 UK' as it was known for a while.

However, in early 2006, Radio 4's still newish controller Mark Damazer decided he wanted to set the agenda in a much more brisk way at the beginning of each Radio 4 day. 'I'm a fairly early riser and I was increasingly frustrated,' he told me.

> I know that we do a lot of news and current affairs, but I feel that it is not an unnatural instinct to get up and want to have some fairly crisp summary of what the world looks like – the news world, the sports world, the weather world, the papers . . . and I thought that it was pretty peculiar that we didn't really get going till six; and a lot of the audience gets going before that. So I thought there was a programme need.

After thirty-three years, though, the UK Theme was out of tune with the style of early-morning broadcasting in this country. Indeed, with or without the UK Theme, Radio 4, with its daily open-up and closedown, is still an anomaly. Radios 1 and 2 have been 24/7 stations for a generation, News 24 on television rolls round the clock, as do the BBC's commercial competitors. Even Radio 3 has been running its *Through the Night* classical music programme for years. Radio 4's controller would dearly like to bring his network into line if the cash were available, but for the moment it's BBC World Service that holds the fort while Radio 4 sleeps.

So, on April the 23rd 2006, as those three bars of clarion-calling on the horns and trombones from the valley below rang out through that Herefordshire farm kitchen as they had done every morning since 1973, it was a sad day for many, not all of them old faithfuls of the network: 'Early one morning, just as the sun was rising . . .' signalling the start of transmission was broadcast for the last time on Radio 4. 'I had a soft spot for the UK Theme.' The wistful voice is that of Charlotte Green, senior announcer. 'It was my constant companion on that early shift when you were feeling a little bit isolated. It was just you and a studio manager in a dark, unwelcoming building and it became a friend in many ways. It wasn't too insistent, and that certainly served to wake *me* up in a rather gentle way: it wasn't in-your-face nationalism at all; it was rather subtle, actually. But I do miss it – I wish it was still there.'

Damazer, just like his nine predecessors, knows he has to keep modernising – carefully – the shape and sound of the network, even if it means slaughtering a few sacred cows like the UK Theme. 'What still slightly intellectually irritates me is this thing about patriotism,' he mutters. 'I am in my own way fiercely proud about many things about Britain; Radio 4 exemplifies many of the best things, and to have it judged around this piece of music I thought was a little excessive.' Questions in the House and an Early Day motion resulted, plus a national petition, and even a march on Broadcasting House in London:

> Good stunt, quite amusing. I judiciously sought sanctuary in a nearby hostelry with a Radio 4 presenter, expecting to come back via a side door, going through the polite mass of protesters; only to discover that the bus had drawn up with six, yes *six* people on it.

Radio 4 Earthquake, Not Many Hurt; it was Mark Damazer's first big run-in with the Radio 4 audience. It's not inappropriate to start a celebration of Radio 4 with a row, because the passionate relationship between us listeners and the station is born of the intimacy of the medium through which it exists. It makes us all friends of Laurie Taylor and Jenni Murray, of Peter Donaldson and Charlotte Green – and you'll find that, as this book unfolds, so do the many controversies and altercations that dot the forty years of its life. That 'Change for the Worse at Radio 4' headline stands ready-minted for any columnist who wants to take a pop at the slightest modification to 'our station' – and Radio 4 listeners, not least because we pay our licence-fees, do have a very proprietorial attitude to it. So if *Dead Ringers* makes out that Charlotte, when she's not so beautifully enunciating Mark Damazer's new 'pacy' 5.30 am *News Briefing*, turns into an off-microphone vamp, we all love to believe it . . . just for a moment.

Meanwhile, in the offices of the *Today* programme at Television Centre, reporter Mike Thomson is preparing another series of reports from Africa. Radio 4's flagship programme, one of the twin engines of the network (with *The Archers*) is in the final stages of preparation. 'All the night staff come in at about 8.00 pm, and then of course the mad thing about the *Today* programme is it suddenly starts getting really busy about quarter to five, five o' clock, when you're just starting to get near tx [transmission] time.' Mike, who's made a name for himself on *Today* unpicking complex stories from places like the Congo and North Korea, watches the programme team assembling today's edition, on air these days from 6.00 am.

> And if some of the news has changed, then of course you're absolutely at your tiredest. It's always been an oddity with it that just at that point where you start to think that it's not too long to go before going home, suddenly you've got to ratchet it up twenty paces and get stuck into the programme as it goes out.

Forty years ago, the pre-dawn bustle was more genteel, though the newsroom was no less busy – albeit a lot smokier and noisier – with manual typewriters being hammered rather than clicking keyboards. At the equivalent moment in 1967, *Today* ('Radio's breakfast-time look at life around the country and across the world, introduced by Jack de Manio') wouldn't be starting for another two hours (at 7.15 am) and would run, believe it or not, for two short sequences of half an hour or less – another world from the agenda-setting current affairs factory of today.

Continuity, and change

But I'm getting ahead of myself. *Today* still lies in front of us, on the next page, as it were, of the transmission schedule. For the moment, the Radio 4 show has barely begun, and over at Broadcasting House, the Radio 4 continuity suite is at this hour empty and silent because, since that last burst of the UK Theme and the concomitant birth the following day of *News Briefing*, Radio 4 has been opened up by a newsreader from Television Centre. As Gillian Reynolds observed in her perceptive article in the *Daily Telegraph*, Harriet Cass, who did the honours that Monday morning, 'was, as her union representative (or agent) may have noticed, hosting a sequence . . .' It's not only more efficient this way, they say, but, by avoiding costly overnight shifts, saves the network a stack of cash. However, it leaves old Radio 4 hands like Charlotte Green once again just a little wistful:

> For me there was a sense of excitement, if that doesn't sound too stupid. You were right there at the beginning with these very tried-and-trusted formulas, the *Shipping Forecast* and the Radio 4 theme tune. I really remember a sense of excitement – the day was starting afresh, the *Today* programme was coming up . . .

Now, Con announcers no longer sleep over. Their shifts at Broadcasting House begin at 9 o'clock, so they can join all the other workaday London commuters fighting the rigours of Oxford Circus underground station in the rush hour. It's a far cry from the days when a young Peter Donaldson, recently recruited from British Forces Broadcasting, joined the Presentation Department in 1974. 'There was a lot more fun than there seems to be now,' he says, 'fun and games and a certain degree of irresponsibility which you probably couldn't get away with now!' Peter worked initially for the new Radio 2, but soon graduated to Radio 4, where for many listeners he still is, even in retirement, the quintessential voice of the network. Back then, evening shifts were particularly diverting: 'Several of us would be in the BBC Club and one of us was supposed to be on duty, but there were coins tossed to see who would go and read the next summary . . . and the one after that and possibly the one after that!' 'The Club' in those days was a rather dingy suite of rooms in part of the Langham Hotel, opposite Broadcasting House, which, until it was sold in the 1980s, housed studios, the training department and rooms for overnight staff to grab some sleep – supernatural events permitting, that is. The Langham is one of the capital's legendary haunted buildings, and many announcers have tales of seeing things when overnighting in Room 333. Peter told me his colleague on Radio 2, James Alexander Gordon, had once thrown his boot right through the apparition, and . . .

on one occasion I experienced what I can only describe as a spectre in a corner of the room, in the shape of a man wearing an opera cloak, a greatcoat. There was a shimmering shape in the corner where no shimmering shape should have been. And I hadn't been drinking particularly that night! The room had got very cold, as all these stories tell you, and there was this spectre in the room. But I didn't chuck anything at it. I think I just plucked up the courage to say 'Aahooo who are you?'

Now, the ghosts of the BBC presence in the Langham have themselves been long swept away, and across the road the old continuity suites that Peter and Charlotte remember with such affection have also been demolished for the development of the gleaming New Broadcasting House. Perpetual change – new premises, new methods, new programmes – it's how broadcasting works, anticipating trends, following fashion, hungry to take advantage of every new technical trick in the book. Thus now, when he or she does eventually open up the studio, Radio 4's continuity announcer operates solo in a studio with a large computer, the pre-recorded shows held on a digital server somewhere. So much change, and yet so little.

Because although back in 1967, Neil Armstrong hadn't yet got anywhere near the moon's surface, the *tone* of Radio 4's programmes was already recognisably struck from the same mould as now. Glance at *Radio Times* and here's an interview with a man who's recorded the New Testament in Scouse dialect, a visit to the Atomic Energy Commission, *Gardeners' Question Time* comes from Ipswich; and, of course, on that first Radio 4 Saturday morning, at twenty-five to seven, there was *Farming Today*. These days it occupies an earlier weekday slot after *Prayer for the Day*, but Radio 4 has always woken up with agriculture and God.

while, down on the farm . . .

idio 4 it's a quarter to six, and time for *Farming*
Mark Holdstock.' But the Herefordshire farm
re we began this chapter is empty now. The
gone; they're down in the cowshed: *Farming*
ying to a deserted room. Yet, as I say, farming
(1   ay and its sister programme *On Your Farm*) has
a   pecial place in the Radio 4 world. Not for nothing
d   ings on in Borsetshire yield the network's biggest
a   ama (for all the Ambridge action, take the short
c   Hill to Chapter Nine). For years, too, early risers
w   greeted with the Fatstock Prices, whose arcane
incantation of hoggarts, gilts and gimmers and the rest captured
listeners' imaginations as truly as did North and South Utsire in
the *Shipping Forecast*. But those listeners who loved the
romance of the language of farming rarely if ever actually
mucked out a cowshed or dipped a flock of Swaledales, and
James Boyle was the controller who first realised that even
farmers didn't automatically set the alarm any more for *Farming
Today*.

Before he launched his new shape for Radio 4 in 1998, Boyle
undertook a massive programme of consultation and research
about who listened to what and when. The results revealed that
the network that he'd taken over did not entirely understand
how its audience lived their lives:

> *Today* wasn't coming on the air for half an hour after the new
> Radio Five Live – daft to give them the lead. And then, who is it
> who listens to *Farming Today* – do farmers really get up for farm-
> ing news? Then we found out that they didn't; but actually that it
> was something else altogether. It was an agribusiness programme.

Boyle – coming in from a life beyond the Broadcasting House
comfort zone (he'd worked in education and had led BBC Radio
Scotland) – understandably wondered why farmers, as opposed
to, say, accountants or orchestral musicians, had their own

magazine programme occupying a daily chunk of his airtime. And it did seem odd; arcane and odd, a relic of the days when Radio 4 was still a bran tub of programmes representing a particular sort of genteel life. By the time Boyle was appointed controller, urbanised Britain had been setting the pace for generations, but one foot, or at least a couple of toes, of his network still remained permanently planted in the soil: he was determined on change. Thus these days the daily agricultural bulletin has become a magazine programme devoted to the ins-and-outs of food production, of interest, naturally, to farmers but also to the wider Radio 4 audience that gets up just as the sun is rising. It's not even live any more, as I discovered to my surprise when I talked recently to the programme team in their bright new open-plan offices in the heart not of the Warwickshire countryside but of central Birmingham. These days, *Farming Today* is recorded the night before and shipped down the line into the BBC's Radio 4 computer vault ready for the announcer to retrieve at 5.45.

Of course, when a big agribusiness story envelops the whole of the UK and takes over virtually the entire news agenda, *Farming Today* is there to serve everyone, a lifeline to farmers and consumers alike, as in 2001 when on February the 21st, the programme announced:

> An outbreak of foot and mouth disease among twenty-seven pigs has been confirmed in Essex. The government says it's a virulent strain of the disease and it's spreading quickly. It's expected they'll impose a ban on livestock exports . . .

During the foot and mouth crisis, the work done by the pro-gramme and the specials that linked it with the consumer show *You and Yours* were a vindication of the new style of farming programme and gave the Birmingham agricultural unit and its hard-working team of young producers a prominence that their regular dawn beat normally precludes.

So 6.00 am approaches. The NFU man has done his stuff, the topic of badger-culling has yet again been aired to no very precise conclusion, the sun has risen, and in the *Today* office, last-minute cues are being amended; the team are assembled in studio S1. Reporter Mike Thomson is on a watching brief:

> As long as you're busy, you've got things to do, the adrenaline just kicks in. It's when you haven't got much to do but it could happen at any moment, you're thinking, 'Gotta keep alert, gotta keep watching the wires, gotta keep alert to what's happening.'

Around the country – in the cars and lorries streaming past the now-woken denizens of the island-farm in the middle of the M62, in the nurses' rest-room at Birmingham City Hospital – the night is over. (If, incidentally, you wondered why I chose these locations, they've all featured in recent Radio 4 'fly-on-the-wall' documentaries about contemporary Britain.)

In the Herefordshire farm kitchen, the radio takes one of its statutory deep breaths; six 'pips' echo across the empty kitchen. 'It's six o'clock on Monday April the 24th . . .' And throughout Britain, another Radio 4 day is just getting into its stride.

How things began

As we've seen, the Radio 4 that was born in September 1967 was both similar to and very different from the animal we're familiar with today. It's a paradox that will run like a leitmotiv throughout this book, but there's another refrain which it's also worth singing out loud right from the start: that's the fact that the broadcasting, social and technological environments of forty years ago were radically and very prosaically different from now. Some of these differences are obvious: no mobile phones, computers or internet; no CDs, no DVDs, not even VHS tapes or very much home videoing either. You might just have acquired a cassette tape recorder, but there were no Walkmans, no personal music players. Radiograms – great coffins containing record player and radio – were still fashionable, as were those starkly rectangular Murphy black-and-white TVs on a metallic pod and painted shiny lurid colours like red or orange; a coloured TV not a *colour* TV.

Other differences were less obvious: that run-of-the-mill monochrome TV cost '72 guineas' in 1967 – just over £75 – but by today's values, that's a staggering £820. No wonder people *rented* television sets by the million forty years ago. In 1967, colour television was only just beginning, with Britain leading the way in Europe (and Wimbledon the first big hit). In radio, FM (or VHF as it was almost always then known) was very patchy, stereo very limited. The BBC was only just phasing out the last 78rpm discs, and much of the corporation's equipment dated from the 1950s or even from the war. For the audience, there was officially only the BBC to listen to, and when you slept, so did the wireless. Radio 4, like the Home Service that preceded it, started crisp and new each morning with *Farming*

Today at 6.35; not even a theme tune in those days. At the other end of the day, nobody on any of the networks stayed up later than the Light Programme's Colin Berry whose goodnights were delivered at 2.02 am. Thereafter, if you wanted something to listen to, it was 208 metres Medium Wave for Radio Luxembourg . . . or the pirates.

Ah, the pirates. That was what brought about all the palaver at the BBC in the first place. Time for a little history and an excursion down the dial. In the mid-1960s, with the country head over heels in rock 'n' roll, and the Beatles making millions across the globe – even recognised by the Queen with an MBE – the BBC had still not got itself tuned in. Granted, there were problems with a record industry that was very protective of the amount of its so-called 'needletime' – literally the number of hours of records which it allowed the BBC to broadcast annually – but, for all its lively creativity, the BBC can be a lumbering bureaucratic giant at times. It was very, very slow to respond to the clear voice of youth. The popular music department had been set up in 1963, but its remit also covered folk, old-tyme dance and what was referred to as 'concert music'. Hardly hip. Yes, there were pop programmes on the Light, but we had to tune into some pretty odd things sometimes to catch what we ached for, as I did in November 1963 when the Beatles filled the midway music spot on *The Ken Dodd Show*.

Shortly afterwards, Radio Caroline, broadcasting from a ship near Harwich, anchored just beyond the three-mile limit of British territorial waters, took the matter into its own barely legal hands and started broadcasting pop. Real pop. A small avalanche of pirate stations followed – Radio Atlanta, Radio London and Radio Sutch off Whitstable (Whitstable?!) – not just in the south either: Radio Scotland flew the flag from the Clyde, Radio 270 broadcast from near Scarborough and Radio Caroline North from the Isle of Man. The pirates were romantic figures, transmitting from places with exotic names – Rough's Tower, Knock John Tower, Shivering Sands – often with transatlantic accents, and flouted the law by not paying the phonographic industry its copyright dues. 'Names mattered to listeners and the fact that the disc jockeys often used aliases added to their glamour,' comments Professor Asa Briggs, official chronicler of the BBC's history. It's the power of those radio pictures once again.

In fact, life on the pirate ships was very often less than glamorous, especially when storms started rolling in from the North Sea, but if you wanted to imagine Emperor Rosko in a cape and tricorn hat bestriding some jewelled record deck on which he spun his magic then that was fine.

The Government wasn't happy, though, naturally. These stations were flouting the law and Tony Benn, then Postmaster General and in charge of broadcasting in the UK, started drafting urgent legislation to close the pirates down. Meanwhile at the BBC, there was now a fair wind behind the ideas that had been hatching for something a lot more radical than *Easy Beat*, *Saturday Club* and *Swingalong* (where the Easy Beats and the Montanas had to rub shoulders with Chris Barber's jazz band and Mrs Mills at the piano). A new radio service, broadcast by the BBC, would offer a home for those ears no longer served by the pirates. But, as Briggs noted, names mattered. So what would it be called?

In May 1967, internal BBC minutes reveal that a decision had still not been taken. It's a familiar story – choosing titles, names, the *brand* so often ends up fraught, full of disagreement . . . and late. Thus for ages, the minutes of the Sound Broadcasting Committee (SBC), the BBC's top management grouping for radio in those days, refer to the future Radio 1 as the 'Popular Music Service' or 'Radio 247' (it would broadcast on 247 metres, Medium Wave). Making the early running in this steeplechase were 'Radio 67' (how wonderfully up to date that would have sounded on Jan 1, 1968), 'Radio Elizabeth' (monarchist tendency, I presume), 'Radio Skylark' (hmm) and, bizarrely, 'Radio Pam'. The committee rejected 'Radio 247' as, typically, it wasn't going to be on the same frequency throughout the country. By May new names, or rather *numbers*, were being mooted for all the BBC's radio networks with 'Radio One' [sic], or 'Light One' for the new service.

For his part, the controller of the Home Service, Gerard

Mansell, was concerned that 'the title "Radio Four" [sic] for the Home Service . . . would to the average listener, however erroneously, imply demotion'. In response, the Assistant Director of Sound Broadcasting counselled the committee that

> once the idea of the numbering of the networks had been accepted every effort must be made to destroy the idea that 'Radio One' was in some way superior to 'Radio Four'. The titles were a means of identification, not a merit rating.

Finally, all the kerfuffle was set aside, the British Radio Equipment Manufacturers' Association, whose members made the sets and spent long hours in consultation with the BBC, were happy and on September the 30th 1967, the Light Programme and Home Service ceased to exist and Radios 1, 2 and 4 were born. Radio 3, always a special case, did start broadcasting under its new name, but retained its local, politically hyper-sensitive muddle of subtitles: Third Programme, Music Programme, Sport Service and Study Session.

In fact, though the fanfares for the new Radio 1 were loud enough, BBC radio was rather in the doldrums in 1967. Today, when listening is still rising while television audiences fragment and dwindle as the entertainment choices on offer multiply, it's hard now to capture exactly what that pre-dawn moment felt like for the new Radio 4.

The Home Service was deeply respected – though not quite as much as the Third Programme which had been created twenty years earlier and occupied the cultural high ground in Britain. Stereo broadcasts, limited to the Third Programme, were still in their infancy – the SBC minutes repeatedly refer to a desire to extend the experiments with 'Stereophony' being stymied by lack of funds – and television was capturing most of the head-lines. *Cathy Come Home* had been the big drama headline-maker of 1966, while *Dr Who* and *Till Death Us Do Part* were in their prime on BBC1, and 1967 was also the year of the triumphant *Forsyte Saga* which prompted mass desertions from pubs and church services on Sunday nights. Also, there were the huge outside broadcast spectaculars, like the famous live scaling of Orkney's sandstone needle, the Old Man of Hoy, by Chris Bonington and a team of British mountaineers. BBC TV was in its pomp.

Naturally, on radio's big day, the headline-maker wasn't the new Radio 4; all the hoorahs were over the way on the Onederful new station. Yet as I've mentioned in the introduction, the seeds of Radio 4's future greatness are there in that earliest incarnation. A number of today's monuments are firmly in place (*Desert Island Discs*, *Gardeners' Question Time*, *Any Questions?* and *From Our Own Correspondent* amongst them) and – although one well-established programme, *Home This Afternoon* (see Chapter Seven), inherited from the Home Service, didn't stand the test of time – the early green shoots of change are beginning to break through: *The World at One* (always *WATO*, pronounced 'wotto', to insiders) is already a fixture while its sister programme, *The World This Weekend* had been launched just two weeks earlier. Curiously, in that busy-busy broadcasting summer of 1967, *Woman's Hour* had migrated across the waveband from its traditional Light Programme berth to the Home Service to take the space occupied by Schools programmes.

As this last detail suggests, the schedules were in fact a bit of a muddle. They lacked clarity, they lacked distinctiveness – programmes flitted from Light to Home and back again – and they were cluttered with odds and ends that today look thoroughly messy and inconvenient. Listeners to Radio 4 in 1967 were expected to look in *Radio Times* to decide what they wanted to hear and then make a date. The notions that are part of the scheduler's craft today, such as 'inheritance' (an audience that stays on at the end of one programme for the next) and 'prime time', were pretty foreign.

So, for much of its early life, Radio 4, for example on Saturday mornings, was stuffed full of worthy but staid fare: adult education programmes on science, art and languages (even an *Introduction to Chinese*) and that lunchtime favourite, the *Top Gear* of its day, *Motoring and the Motorist* (specimen items: 'What's in a Tyre?' and 'Medicaments and Motoring'). Also, a big surprise this for today's Radio 4 fans, there was lots of music, every day, from mid-afternoon interludes ('Jack Brymer, on a Personal Note') to *Music at Night*, every evening at 11.15.

As if this salad weren't bad enough, during term time there were acres of Schools programmes which, until they found their own separate home on Radio 4 FM in the 1970s, controllers loved to curse, blocking off as they did any possibility of constructing a coherent 'Radio 4 day'.

There was another thing that made the new Radio 4 feel as if it had an identity crisis, and that was the 'repeat-pattern', as it's called, of programmes from other networks. *Any Questions?* started life each week on Radio 2 on a Friday, only to be repeated on Radio 4 on a Saturday or Sunday lunchtime (they tried both). Additionally, those Saturday adult education programmes had their first outing over on Radio 3's *Study Session*. Comedy, too, had a peripatetic life, with Sunday lunchtime Light Programme and Radio 2 fixtures like *Round the Horne* and *The Clitheroe Kid* floating breezily from one network to the other without a qualm. The radio garden was badly overgrown, desperately in need of pruning, and crying out for a thorough tidy-up.

Two men took on the task.

One was the erudite and shrewd first controller of Radio 4, Gerard Mansell; the other, his successor, Tony Whitby, who took over in 1969 when Mansell became radio's Director of Programmes. Whitby had come from running television's famed current affairs programme *24 Hours* and was full of fresh ideas. His is the name that resonates like the chimes of Big Ben through this book, for it was he, with the encouraging breeze of Mansell's enthusiasm urging him on, who was essentially the architect of so much of what we today identify as 'Radio 4'.

Mansell, having safely negotiated Radio 4's translation from the Home Service, now had a bigger BBC toybox to play with: the wholesale realignment of all the radio services. It was a huge undertaking that involved, not unnaturally, the Director General, the BBC Chairman, the heads of dozens of departments and units, and many hundreds of hours of consultation and thousands of words of submissions and argument. Gerry

Mansell was at the sharpest of sharp ends, and Tony Whitby was just the man to join him in the endeavour. 'He was a breath of fresh air, a delightful man and a wonderful character,' remembers Rosemary Hart. A leading producer on the afternoon magazine programme *Home This Afternoon* and already a prominent member of radio's Documentaries and Talks department, Hart regularly met Whitby across the departmental table: 'People were extremely fond of him as well as admiring his talent. He sort of cut a swathe through this rather conservative attitude which people had.' That swathe that Whitby, under Mansell's leadership, cut through Radio 4 was as revolutionary – arguably more so – as the changes wrought thirty years later by his successor but six, James Boyle in 1998. 'Suddenly,' says Hart, 'programme ideas were opening up which nobody had thought of or even thought were quite appropriate for the Home Service!'

So, appearances are deceptive, and if calm continuity attended the launch of Radio 4 back in 1967, the revolution instigated by what was to become known as *Broadcasting in the Seventies* and the work of Gerry Mansell and his appointed controller Tony Whitby, were being dreamed of even as the champagne flutes were being washed up after the Radio 1 launch party.

CHAPTER TWO

6.00 am: 'You're listening to Today...'

It's pitch dark and already a wild night. Sue MacGregor is arriving in central London to begin her morning's stint presenting the *Today* programme. It's October the 16th 1987.

> And just as I drove into the car-park all the lights went out. And I thought 'Oh God, I've done something; there's a live wire somewhere!' And there were no lifts of course in Broadcasting House, so we climbed up to the office in the pitch dark.

The *Today* programme offices on the fourth floor were in more or less complete darkness; a power-cut had knocked out much of central London. In the corridors only the 'maintained' emergency lighting was running from the generators that had by now kicked in. It was the night of what came to be known as 'the great storm of 1987', the event that forever (and grossly unjustly) marked weather forecaster Michael Fish out for particular ridicule for denying that a hurricane was on the way. For Britons in the north of England, Scotland and Northern Ireland it was just a very windy night, but in the south it felt like the end of the world. For Sue MacGregor, John Humphrys and the rest of the *Today* team, it was a radio event to savour:

> Yes, because television disappeared for a while entirely. John and I had to move from the *Today* offices into the Sports department because, curiously, that was the only bit of Broadcasting House powered by the emergency generator. And we had relied on tickertape and faxes coming through with stories from the regions and none of this was working so that really was seat-of-the-pants stuff.

Illustrious corpses – having a laugh on Today

There are not, if truth be told, many deliberate laughs on *Today*. Rabbi Lionel Blue, of course, is the exception who has made a point, over many years, of deftly underlining his message on *Thought for the Day* with a gag. Generally, however, *Today* keeps a very straight face, as befits an agenda-setting news programme; not for them the jolly-jolly banter of other breakfast shows. Perhaps that's why, when something funny does happen, the audience, desperate to crack its face between worrying about the Palestinian situation and gun crime in Manchester, reacts so strongly. 'I think the adrenaline pumps; I think it's just that tension. It's a bit like being in school knowing you can't laugh at a teacher.' Garry Richardson, sports reporter whose views these are, is both right – and wrong – because Garry, for all his brilliant professionalism, is also game for a laugh. He's fond of recalling the occasion when the programme did a report on Britain's Cold War defences, which featured nuclear submarines keeping an ear out for signs that the country was under attack. One clue would apparently be the non-appearance of *Today*:

> And it finished: 'If the *Today* programme is there, the country's fine.' Then John Humphrys said: 'Seven twenty-five; here's Garry Richardson with the sport' . . . [I gave a long pause and] said, 'I'm just trying to frighten the lads on the sub!' Now a two-second pause on radio is like three hours, and I can imagine if they'd been listening to it under the North Sea there might have been a chuckle at that. No end of people mentioned it all day long.

James Boyle, eighth Radio 4 controller, took a long, hard look at the

For jaundiced listeners in the north of the UK, of course, it could have been seen as merely another instance of Radio 4 taking a very southern-English, metropolitan point of view, although in the end it did turn out to have been the biggest storm since 1703. 'And actually, in a funny sort of way,' concludes Sue, 'I think that cemented my relationship with John

network when he assumed the role in 1996: 'I used to listen to Garry and think "Actually this is the back page of a red-top. Why is he on?" It took me ages to see the obvious thing: he was just bringing that tremendous *bubble* and a bit of gossip, and he is equally important [to the mix].' He has also in his twenty-five years with the show developed a wonderful rapport with the top names in sport who will literally get out of bed to appear for him. Less dependable, though, are the celebrated *Today* racing tips, except, says Garry, oddly enough on one occasion when the regular tipster wasn't around: 'I went through the paper and there was a horse called David Junior, and my son's called David. I didn't know anything about the horse and I tipped it.'

It won at odds of 25–1.

The listeners have taken Garry, with his gentle Berkshire accent and self-effacing style, to their hearts – a sort of Everyman figure to whom they can easily relate. Like when his car radio was stolen while he was on air:

> John Timpson said, 'Here's Garry Richardson. He's not very happy this morning.' And I said, 'No. Whoever's stolen my car radio, I hope you're enjoying listening to me on it!' And do you know, I promise you for nearly a fortnight, everywhere I went people said, 'Oh, I heard about your car – any news on the radio?' I think it was because it was man-on-the-radio has had his car broken into, like man-on-the-street. I remember Brian Redhead said once, 'Here's Garry Richardson wearing a bright yellow jumper.' And I said, 'Yes, I'm like a fourteen-stone budgie' and people mentioned it all day long. So that was what fascinated people: you're a friend.
>
> ☞

Humphrys, because he decided I was OK after that! I suppose it was a bit like surviving in a lifeboat: you never forget your relationship with that person.'

As far as *Today* was concerned, however, despite the power-cuts, editorially it was just another dramatic day at the office. It was the sort of story *Today* has always thrived on – a big

In the catalogue of broadcasting sins, collapsing in fits of giggles on a serious programme like *Today* must be in the top three: 'It's like laughing in church, isn't it, or sniggering in the school assembly,' says senior newsreader Charlotte Green. 'You know you really, really shouldn't be doing it, but the more you say to yourself "I mustn't do this" the more it bubbles out of you.' And it does happen – not often – but when it does, it can be spectacular. First and foremost, you need the right catalyst: 'I am a great giggler,' Charlotte confesses. 'I've always been, and it doesn't take much to really set me off; and in the Newsroom they know it.' Being a true professional, however, she's perfected the art of keeping a straight face under fire; it takes other ingredients to break down the defences.

So here is Charlotte Green with the tale of the most celebrated *Today* programme corpse ever. Firstly, you need the right story:

> There's a Major-General, head of the armed forces in Papua-New Guinea, and the name was spelled T-U-A-T, pronounced 'twat'. And so one of the sub-editors decided to include the name deliberately in the story because he thought it would make me laugh. Well, you know, and *how*! It was just one of those awful things.

Presenting that morning were Sue MacGregor and Jim Naughtie ('all of us great gigglers actually,' says Charlotte).

> I knew this name was coming up and I tried to steel myself. I was really clenching everything, because the name came right at the end of the story. I think it actually ended with 'the head of the armed forces Major-General Jack Tuat'.

breaking news event that can be reported as it happens. Libby Purves was a *Today* presenter sitting alongside the great Brian Redhead in the 1980s:

> Oh my God, there's nothing like that feeling of being first up in the morning with a story to tell – oooh yay! Brian was a real news-hawk; he loved *stories*! And I remember there was a terrible train

For ultimate combustibility, next you need just a little devilment:

Then – again I think they'd done this deliberately – I had a story about a sperm whale that was stranded on a beach. And it was the juxtaposition of 'Jack Twat' and the story about the sperm whale: I just knew I was going to go. To make it worse, Sue looked at me, and it was fatal. She whispered, in a sense of wonderment, 'Jack *Twat*?' and I knew I was going to go; Jim started to laugh as well. So I start this story and my voice is going up and down like an opera singer on speed, and I knew I couldn't control it. I had to let go, and it all just burst out.

For the serious journalists of the *Today* programme, however, this joke was a three-stage rocket.

And then poor old Jim had to go into a story about a man called Finlay Spratt, who was something to do with the Prison Officers' Association in Northern Ireland. [He was area chairman.] And because we were all laughing so much, he called him 'Pratt'. So we went from 'Jack Twat' to 'Finlay Spratt' to 'Mr Pratt' in the space of about fifteen seconds and we all ended up almost under the table. It has to be and remains the funniest thing I've ever experienced in a studio. The atmosphere was extraordinary: all three of us had gone completely by the end of it. It was wonderful!

And of course the listeners loved it.

crash – a sleeper crash – down in the West Country and he was just sounding too gleeful. I nudged him between cues and I said 'Brian, people are DEAD. D-E-A-D' and he said 'Thank you', and he toned it down.

I suspect that on this particular occasion, the best *Today* was probably able to get was on-the-spot reports via a crackly line from a nearby phone box: the mobile era was yet to dawn. But the thirst to report such big stories, the competitive relish with which news people chase events, is a huge stimulus for change – and if once a scratchy short-wave circuit with Kampala or Kuala Lumpur was a wonder for listeners, these days we expect more of our current affairs.

I was reminded of this most forcibly when not so long ago *Today*'s intrepid sports reporter Garry Richardson found himself caught up in another weather-event that blocked his morning drive from Guildford to Television Centre. Calmly Garry presented his sports package complete with interviews from his home, with a microphone rigged, he tells me, under the stairs. It's another benchmark of how technology has driven huge changes in broadcasting across the last forty years, and one of the recurring themes of this book. Readers will no doubt remember that when reporter Andrew Gilligan, back in 2003, famously did his crack-of-dawn live 'two-way' with the *Today* studio about Iraq's weapons of mass destruction, it was not from studio S1 in Television Centre but (like Garry) from his home.

In fact, such has been the technological whirlwind over really very few years, that we now barely blink when, thanks to sat-phones, portable uplinks and mobiles, the *Ten o'Clock News* or *Today* are anchored, seamlessly, from almost anywhere, literally, in the world – to such an extent that, if *Today weren't* live from the heart of the action, questions would be asked. That's important because, as we've seen, Radio 4's news and current affairs, and *Today* in particular, lie at the very heart of the network. 'It's part of what defines Radio 4,' emphasises former *Today* editor and now head of all the BBC's network radio services, Jenny Abramsky.

> Of course there are some people who don't realise that it has the richness of its drama and its comedy, and its readings, and its ideas and all that amazing range of stuff that it does, but I think, in some ways, when we get the *Today* programme right it can encompass an extraordinary amount of what Radio 4 stands for.

Back in the early years of the network, *Today* viewed the world in less dramatic and event-driven terms. In 1967, Michael Green, later to become network controller and Deputy Managing Director of Radio, was a young reporter in Sheffield, and subsequently went to work for the BBC's main north of England home in Manchester. He remembers just how staid much of the coverage – even on the ground-breaking *World at One* – could be thirty, thirty-five years ago:

> Most journalism was studio-based. There was the occasional foray out – the *Today* programme did small packages [short recorded location reports] as did *The World at One* . . . but it was very much sort of *ex-cathedra* broadcasting. I think Radio 4 was very enclosed in Broadcasting House, largely, down here in London, didn't travel very far; certainly didn't get very much further than Watford – on a good day!

Green's career in the BBC was marked by journalistic achievements of the highest order, and he also played a big part in ridding Radio 4 of much of its studio-based stuffiness. He worked tirelessly too, both in Manchester and in London when he became controller, to rebalance the metropolitan, southern bias that has always beset Radio 4. On the gale-racked morning in October 1987, just as a relieved Sue MacGregor was finally removing her headphones, in the controller's office Green was grappling with a storm drama of his own. The Deputy Director General was at the door, and he wasn't happy.

> About half past nine John Birt came to my office and said, 'Why are we not still on the air?' And I said, 'Actually, John, there's nothing to say because the journalists can't get anywhere; all the roads are blocked. And furthermore, I think it's a story that is a real preoccupation to London and parts of the south-east, but anybody north of Watford couldn't care less'. And he profoundly disagreed with me; he said, 'If we had a rolling news thing now, this would be what you would be doing.'

The gleam in John Birt's eye that October morning was of

course what has become the very successful amalgam of sport and news, Radio Five Live. It was 'the moment when I became really aware that this was on the cards', says Michael Green.

> And of course John particularly wanted a rolling news service to include the four national Radio 4 sequences [*Today*, *The World at One*, *PM* and *The World Tonight*]. I said, 'Well, if you take away the sequences from Radio 4, you will kill it overnight. You will kill this network stone dead.' And fortunately good sense prevailed and another solution was found, and a good solution.

Yet it would take another six and a half years, a war – and another, much bigger battle between Green and Birt, over frequencies – before the first note of Five Live's theme music was heard, 'which in an odd way has liberated Radio 4, not having to worry about that any more'.

New beginnings

The pathway taken by news and current affairs over the last forty years on BBC radio – from the patrician bulletins of Alvar Lidell, who retired in 1969, to the inquisitorial *Today* and the demotic rolling sequences of *Five Live Breakfast* – is one way of measuring the loosening of social conventions – indeed broadcasting in all its forms is a fair mirror of the society it talks to. Yet, even by the standards of the time, the version of the *Today* programme presided over on Monday October the 2nd 1967, the first edition following the network's name change, by Jack de Manio, was out of kilter with the times. Elsewhere on the new Radio 4, the shape of things to come was already in place – William Hardcastle commanded a vigorous *World at One* and had just proudly unveiled its Sunday supplement, *The World This Weekend*. *Today*, on the other hand, was still firmly stuck – and would be pretty well until 1971 – in the genteel atmosphere that Michael Green remembers characterised much of the rest of the network.

Jack de Manio had been the voice of *Today* since 1958 and he possessed – like another broadcaster of the time, ITV's news-caster Reginald Bosanquet – a voice that sounded permanently slightly the worse for wear. Crisp, Jack never was, especially in his latter incarnation, after he'd left *Today*, on a cosy afternoon show called *Jack de Manio Precisely* that dragged on wearily until 1978. In his encyclopaedic and excellent history of the *Today* programme, *All Our Todays*, the distinguished radio critic and commentator Paul Donovan observes that 'Jack's world was one of chortles and snifters, in which a telephone was a blower and no evening was complete . . . without popping over the road for a quick one . . .' In fact, the only voice on Radio 4 that today bears any resemblance to Jack's is that of another broadcaster very much of the 'old school', Henry 'Blowers' Blofeld, the cataloguer of buses, cranes and pigeons on *Test Match Special*.

De Manio wasn't *Today*'s first presenter. That honour belonged to Alan Skempton, a staff announcer with the Home Service, who unveiled the very first 'collection of brief items . . . of . . . topical interest for the average, intelligent reader of the morning newspapers . . .' on the Home Service on October the 28th 1957. But there was no politics, virtually no current affairs worth speaking of, with despatches from foreign correspondents the sole nod to the real world of events. *Today* was, as the *Radio Times* billing was still describing it a decade after it began, a 'look at life' and a very, *very* long way from the agenda-setting programme of even just a few years later.

That Jack de Manio was famous for his gaffes is broadcasting legend, but the nature of those gaffes occasionally reveals a somewhat darker quality. His routine misreading of the clock was endearing, but more serious inaccuracies, particularly in his impromptu comments, forced him into public apology, and his unthinking club-bore references, for instance, to John Lennon's partner as 'Yoko Hama, or whatever her name is' nowadays sound little short of racism. To think that a small error thirty-five years later on the same programme could cost a reporter, the Director General and BBC Chairman their jobs . . .

A word here about something that's worth bearing in mind when considering the life of a radio station. Radio, by its very nature, is a relatively passive medium. It's classically something you absorb when doing something else, a 'secondary activity': i.e. great for doing the ironing to, or cleaning your teeth, or driving. So, since the beginning of time it seems, two of the most potent listening periods during the day occur when most of us are going *to* or coming *from* work, and, because the early morning remains still (more than twenty years after the birth of breakfast *TV*) radio's biggest moment in the day, hooking the audience over their tea and toast is a vital part of the scheduler's art, even on as high-minded a station as Radio 4.

It's also the moment in the day with – for most listeners – a natural sense of drama to it. How many of us have not felt just the slightest frisson as the clock-radio clicks into life and we're plunged, halfway through, into an overnight story of a ferry sinking . . . or a riot . . . or a murder . . . or someone famous who's died. Where is it? Will it affect me? Oh how sad – I was a real fan of hers . . . and the curtain goes up on another day's news. 'Getting breakfast right' is thus a key aim of any radio station boss or channel controller. Furthermore, the argument goes, get breakfast right and to an extent you'll fix the rest of the day, or the morning at least, because people tend to stick with a station once they've started – though this traditional wisdom is somewhat challenged these days by the constant advance of technology that allows much easier channel-hopping.

It was inevitable, then, even forty years ago, that 'something had to be done' about jolly Jack de Manio's far-back saloon bar style on *Today*. Tony Whitby, when he took over Radio 4 in 1969, set out on a mission of fundamental reshaping of the network, in line with the recommendations of the top-level enquiry called *Broadcasting in the Seventies* that completely reorganised the way BBC radio was run (see Interlude 2). Henceforth, the Radio 4 day would be constructed around five major news and current affairs sequences, of which the *Today* programme would be the foundation. *Today* would deliver the big audiences for the rest of the morning, with *WATO* refreshing them at lunchtime, and so on. The day set for the implementation of Whitby's revolution was as we've learned to expect a Saturday – April the 4th 1970 – but the current affairs makeover would have to wait until the new week began on Monday.

In a photo strip at the top of the Thursday page of *Radio Times* for that first week of the makeover, a parade of men's faces stare out, trumpeting the new current affairs backbone of the Radio 4 day: bushy-eyebrowed William Hardcastle (*The World at One* and *PM*), a young Gerald Priestland, earnest, eyes downcast, presenting the new *Newsdesk* at 7.00 pm, and on the right, a professorial, half-smiling Douglas Stuart, anchor of *The World Tonight*. The left-hand picture in this newsy gallery is Jack's: heavy-rimmed spectacles, and behind them heavy-rimmed eyes and an expression that could be slight surprise, or possibly an ironic lip-curl, it's hard to tell. At least he *looks* as though he fits with the new line-up – male, authoritative, engaged. The listing for *Today* has moved on too. Gone is the 'breakfast-time look at life' of the past, replaced by 'the world this morning: Britain at breakfast-time and the news from anywhere on earth'. Here was the modern *Today*, in fit shape for the new schedule.

But as we've seen, de Manio wasn't – or not completely. And here's the paradox; when the Radio Review Board, the successor body to the Sound Broadcasting Committee, considered *Today* shortly after the new schedule started, views were mixed. Head of Drama preferred John Timpson who had joined de Manio as co-presenter yet 'all acknowledged that [Jack] was that rare thing, a Radio character with a very large personal following'. On the other hand, there was a lot of tut-tutting about the way de Manio made jokes about the newsreaders. 'The sight of a live newsreader,' observed *Today*'s editor, 'seemed to have a strange effect on Jack de Manio.' To which Tony Whitby observed, darkly, that 'the problem . . . would eventually solve itself'.

When Jack left the programme about a year later, a grand broadcast departure was planned, complete with presentation clock – to remind him of his many misreadings of the time – but in the end Jack left with a whimper, as an urgent telegram circulated the day before his scheduled departure reveals:

VERY MUCH REGRET THAT JACK DE MANIO WILL NOT BE TAKING

HIS LEAVE OF THE TODAY PROGRAMME ON THE AIR TOMORROW.
HE IS IN HOSPITAL FOR A WEEK SO WILL MISS WHAT WOULD HAVE
BEEN HIS FINAL SHOW.

A fresh team

Libby Purves, presenter of *Midweek* for now nearly twenty-five
years, joined the BBC as a studio manager in 1971, just as Jack
de Manio was finding the *Today* seat too hot to stay in. By the
end of the year, he'd left and Robert Robinson had joined
Timpson to present the show. 'I was in London on my own and
I had shifts round Christmas,' Purves remembers, 'and I said,
"Look, is there any chance I could go into the *Today* studio,"
where they were doing a midnight New Year's Eve programme,
"Could I just go and watch them?"' *Today*'s future reporter and
presenter was transfixed:

> There were Timpson and Robinson, and I stood by the glass in my
> little corner, just looking through the glass at them and loving the
> nimbleness of it, the way that words alone could weave whatever
> it was they needed to weave, without that television business of
> looking at the camera and smirking and having your hair properly
> combed. I just loved that kind of *nimbleness*.

Words were the thing, and Robert Robinson's facility with
them, his curlicues of phraseology in particular, lent a very
particular – the Review Board thought 'too clever by half' –
quality to his presentation. Robinson, for his part, was phleg-
matic about the new job: 'We jogged along as a duo,' he writes
in his autobiography, 'sour as lemons when we arrived in the
office, grumbling that the stuff the overnight shift had prepared
for us was threadbare . . . No wonder they called us the Brothers
Grim.'

This newly evolved *Today*, though a major advance on de
Manio's, was still a far cry from the Humphrys / Naughtie /
Montague / Stourton / Quinn vehicle of thirty years later. It even

still had its keep-fit spot with the Green Goddess of her day, Eileen Fowler, finally ditched in 1974. When Robinson left in the same year, it's a programme in search of direction that's suggested by the roster of well-known media names who now take a whirl on the *Today* roundabout for varying lengths of engagement: Barry Norman (a good long spell), Des Lynam, Douglas Cameron (who defected to the new London commercial station LBC), Nancy Wise (from *WATO*), Michael Clayton, James ('Apollo') Burke and Malcolm Billings (later Radio 4's archaeology guru on *Origins*). Even Melvyn Bragg had a brief, arty go at *Today*, notes Paul Donovan.

In the middle of this period of exits and entrances, Libby Purves worked on *Today* as producer and reporter, and later as its first regular female presenter. She'd learned the art of live broadcasting in Oxford in that other burgeoning bit of the BBC (which had also been given its head as a result of *Broadcasting in the Seventies*), local radio. 'When you've been at the top of Magdalen [College] tower trying to do a commentary, and you've accidentally stuck the aerial of your check-set up your nose and so you've got a massive nosebleed and all the choristers are giggling and you have to keep talking, the *Today* programme wasn't that taxing!'

Owing to squabbles between day and night shifts, hours were at that time unconscionably – and by today's standards impermissibly – long.

> You did a 22-hour shift, the producer and Editor together. Technically you were supposed to have a couple of hours off to have a kip in the middle of the night; you could go over to the Langham where the ghosts are, and have a sleep. But you were so wired by that time that you couldn't usually get to sleep, so I used to play poker with the commissionaires down behind the desk.

Reading now about the battles on *Today* feels a bit like tales of skirmishes in the Hundred Years War; in the end, who did what to whom and when hardly matters now. Despite overnight tantrums and the revolving door for presenters, the programme went out, the news was covered, and a pattern for the day's broadcasting on Radio 4 was set, daily, week-in, week-out. Faster, smaller technology allowed greater flexibility and, in tandem, news coverage became closer to the people that made it; ordinary voices were widely heard on air. Tony Whitby's network was now starting its day more freshly, more connectedly than ever before.

Then catastrophe struck – not just some passing programme emergency but a real crisis for the network; and to most it was completely unexpected. An announcement was made that Tony Whitby had been taken ill and was in hospital. His Chief Assistant (deputy controller) and scheduler, Clare Lawson-Dick took charge. It was spring 1975 and when, a few weeks later, Whitby succumbed to the cancer that had laid him low so suddenly, Clare became his formal successor. She wasn't, though, by all accounts a charismatic figure, and although she'd been excellent at helping build the house that Tony designed, Clare was not the person to make it her own. A year later it was Ian McIntyre, the star of one of Whitby's new current affairs shows, *Analysis*, who landed the big job at Radio 4.

For news and current affairs, and for *Today* in particular, it was a disaster.

Cuts and crisis

Ian McIntyre is a man with a very precise style both in manner and in speech, with quick decisive movements, a light, clear, slightly nasal voice and a splendid grin. 'There were times thirty years ago when it was impossible to sit down to write a considered piece about certain subjects without actually hearing McIntyre's voice in your ear,' remembers radio critic Gillian Reynolds, 'that measured, careful voice looking at one side, then the other.' He brought to the controllership a brilliant mind combined with a ruthless rigour – his great word – in analysing the world about him. 'He had such very high standards,' remembers Monica Sims who became his successor at Radio 4. 'I was always rather scared of him. He was a real intellectual which I never was.' Not for nothing do some still consider

> ## Ten Controllers of BBC Radio 4
>
> **Gerard Mansell CBE**, Controller Home Service/Radio 4: 1965–1969
> **Anthony Whitby**, Controller 1969–1975
> **Clare Lawson-Dick OBE**, acting Controller, then Controller 1975–1976
> **Ian McIntyre**, Controller 1976–1978
> **Monica Sims OBE**, Controller 1978–1983
> **Sir David Hatch**, Controller 1983–1986
> **Michael Green**, Controller 1986–1996
> **James Boyle**, Controller 1996–2000
> **Helen Boaden**, Controller Radio 4 2000–2004
>   Controller BBC7 2002–2004
> **Mark Damazer**, Controller Radio 4, BBC7, 2004–

McIntyre the greatest presenter the *Analysis* programme has ever had (see Chapter Ten). Michael Green produced him on the show: 'I mean, I enjoyed working with him enormously. He's an incredibly bright bloke and had some very good ideas about what radio needs to do to stay cock o' the north if you like.'

But another of McIntyre's qualities when he was controller was a certain pugnacity. He was resolute, and up for a fight. It is perhaps inevitable, therefore, that opinions would be divided on his period in power. Piers Plowright, one of the corporation's greatest producers, then working in Drama Department, saw him in action when, later, McIntyre moved to run Radio 3. 'And the great day was an argument about some play that had gone out, and Ian was ruthless about it, and Ronnie [Mason, head of Radio Drama] got up and threw his chair across the room and stalked off. After that there were no more meetings for two or three weeks.' Generally, however, Plowright's sympathies lay with the controller:

For me, I learned a great deal from Ian McIntyre, nearly all good. I learned first of all his favourite word 'rigour'; and this idea of 'Don't tell us things we know. I don't want to see things that are written in newspapers already or in books. There must be something new about this.'

So, unhappy with the way current affairs were serving Radio 4, Ian McIntyre decided to take an axe to them. He halved the length of the *PM* programme and scythed into *Today*, acquiring about this time the inevitable nickname 'Mack the Knife'. The cuts caused outrage, yet Michael Green for one still has some sympathy with another of the basic motives for McIntyre's radical move – underfunding: 'The *Today* programme was run by a couple of lads and, you know, it really was thinly extruded – the journalism – across the outlets. And that for him told on air: he thought it just didn't have enough gravitas, enough authority.'

However, the makeweights that the controller commissioned to fill the missing bits of current affairs were under-resourced and unimaginative, snippets of programming from the sound archive and from Radio 4 Presentation department. So now, *Serendipity* followed *PM*. Much more controversially to the millions tuning in over their cornflakes, *Up to the Hour*, with its inappropriately chirpy classical French theme tune and staff announcer replacing stars like John Timpson, inserted itself into *Today*. 'Well, I was of course in the News and Current Affairs camp,' grins Jenny Abramsky unsurprisingly, from her seat behind the newsroom barricades.

Peter Donaldson, already a stalwart of Radio 4's presentation team and always a playful character, did what he could, he says, to avoid having to present *Up to the Hour*, 'and then was told that I *had* to do it, but I could do it "my way". But I was then told the night before that I had to play it straight. Which, of course, is like a red rag to a bullock . . . sorry to a bull!' What Donaldson did next was to bring the wrangle between the power of News and the authority of the controller's office to some sort of a head.

We just had a bit of fun the next morning. I called myself 'Donald Peterson' and said 'Good morning. This is Donald Peterson to take you *Up to the Hour*, drive you out to work or send you round the dial to Radio 2. And if you're staying, you're very brave and welcome to *Up to the Hour*!'

With a disingenuous grin and all the hindsight in the world, Peter adds: 'And I think I compounded things by saying that it was twenty-to-eight, instead of twenty-to-seven and saying, "Oh, that must have been wishful thinking on my part!" Just a bit of mischief!' Jenny Abramsky, tuned-in at the time, naturally also enjoyed it:

I do remember switching on that radio and hearing Peter Donaldson say, 'Hello, this is Donald Peterson!' [big laugh] And I do remember him being summoned and being accused of disloyalty to the network – I mean 'disloyalty to the network'! It was absolutely amazing!

The mood in the *Today* offices on the fourth floor of Broadcasting House was militant. 'In the lifts, in the corridors, everybody was with Peter,' remembers Libby Purves. 'I think even Ian McIntyre, who had set up this ridiculous load of old floor-sweepings wasting half an hour of our *Today* time every day, I think he knew we'd all have been out – it would have been one out, all out for Peter.'

It was Donaldson and his colleagues in the newsroom who had the last laugh.

I was called in for a Recorded Interview, and told I must go straight home. Do not pass 'Go'; do not do anything; almost go straight to gaol. And needless to say it appeared in the *Guardian* Diary the next day; so I was hauled in again for another interview, accused of leaking it to the press. I hadn't, but I said, 'You can't make someone go home, and think . . .' The *Today* programme sent me a wonderful card, and two bottles of champagne, one vintage, saying 'Thank you very much. Don't do it again because we want to hear you in the future!'

The incident spelled the beginning of the end for the *Up to the Hour* experiment. Michael Green, longest serving of all Radio

4's controllers, who had his own fair share of struggles over the years, takes a more philosophical view of the battle for *Today*.

> In an odd way I think, although it was *deeply* painful at the time, and *Up to the Hour* was a terrible mistake (and we've all made them haven't we?), in an odd way I think the fallout of that meant that Radio 4, the *Today* programme and the other strands were revalued. More investment went into them over the period and I think they became the stronger for it.

For Jenny Abramsky the ill wind blew a lot of good. She found herself the beneficiary of a wholesale reorganisation in the senior management of radio, in the course of which she became editor of afternoon current affairs. Ian McIntyre took over the controllership of Radio 3 and Monica Sims assumed his seat at Radio 4. 'I thought what he had done in many ways had been very good, and I was quite lucky to come after him,' she says. Monica had been editor of *Woman's Hour* before she had made a very successful and happy move to run children's television. She was clearly the person to calm everything down after the turbulence surrounding Ian's controllership.

> But I think it was a shame that he and the News and Current Affairs department didn't get on because I think the standards he wanted to import were very necessary. And in fact I think a lot of them were adopted, though the people concerned were probably not going to accept that the changes had been made because of him. But that's a matter of style I think rather than substance.

Today's Today *is born*

Today was returned to its former length, along with *PM*, and reporter Libby Purves joined the morning team as presenter alongside Brian Redhead who had by now started a double act with John Timpson. The call, when it came, arrived by a very odd route.

I was interviewing some druids down at Stonehenge, as you do, and I had a message, through a druid actually, to ring the office. And they said 'Would you consider presenting the programme next week with John Sergeant? He's the only one left before Brian Redhead comes back and he says he's not doing it on his own.' So I said, 'Okeydoke. I'll go and present it with John Sergeant.'

So Libby moved from being a reporter among the druids to the presenter's chair; and stayed. A third voice had joined the duo of John Timpson and Brian Redhead.

The idea was that I would be with each of them either end of the week. So I did four days a week, they each did three and on Wednesdays they were the team together. And so for three and half years I was the bolster between Timpson and Redhead.

Much has been written about the golden years of Brian Redhead (joined 1975) and John Timpson on *Today*, and I shall only offer here some personal views from people who were involved in the programme in their heyday. For a more detailed view of Brian Redhead the man, see page 38.

The relationship between Timpson, the genial lover of East Anglia, and Redhead the hearty northerner was tricky, but then, I guess any partnership forged in the early hours of the morning, over not quite enough sleep and too much coffee is likely to have its spikes, even for the most accommodating of characters. 'I don't think it matters enormously, though it helps, when the audience feels that the presenters don't actually want to kill each other!' The speaker is John Humphrys, one of *Today*'s current stars, who in 2007 received the radio industry's highest accolade, a Sony Radio Academy Gold award for News Journalist of the Year.

But I don't want them to feel necessarily that they're sleeping with each other; I think they want to feel that they get on all right and that they're able to do their job together as well as possible. And for that you simply need to have at least a working relationship.

Brian Redhead – a word in the ear

Brian Redhead was, until his untimely death in January 1994, without equivocation one of Radio 4's greatest voices, to be spoken of in the same breath as Alistair Cooke – warm, full of character and with a huge sense of fun. Though to many he epitomised the *Today* programme in perhaps its richest period, dropping as he liked to say 'a word in the ear of the nation', my own first memory of Brian on air, as also for the radio critic and writer Gillian Reynolds, was in the Saturday night programme he presented originally for the Home Service and then for Radio 4, *A Word in Edgeways*. 'I adored *Word in Edgeways*,' she recalls.

> It would come on at ten past ten, and I would extend everything I had to do in the kitchen, even the job I hated most – I had a horrid wooden draining board and I used to scrub it down with bleach. So, for years, every time I thought of *Word in Edgeways* I had this scent of bleach in my nose.

A Word in Edgeways was a discussion programme. Nothing particularly exciting, unusual or memorable in that. Radio 4 has been full of them throughout its forty years. Deceptively simple in format, a really outstanding discussion is in fact a miracle of preparation, meticulous casting and masterly chairing. That's why *Edgeways* was so memorable. You can find a full memoir of the programme in Chapter Eleven.

Redhead loved the sense of challenge and getting to grips with people and ideas that *Edgeways* offered; indeed he was an indomitable enthusiast in all things. A Radio 4 biography of him

Yes, it's a team; but in the end they are solo performers. We're not Torvill and Dean!

He for one thoroughly rejects the very notion of 'early-morning chemistry' on the show: you don't, he says, have to be 'pitch-perfect and all that. You'll think I'm sounding very

broadcast after his death ends with a list of epithets describing him from friends, family and colleagues. Just count the number of times the word '*enthusiastic*' crops up: 'without malice, full of curiosity, enthusiastic, bouncy, irrepressible, enthusiastic, opinionated, big-'eaded, committed, mercurial, slightly barmy, enthusiastic, reckless, warm, enthusiastic, childish, loving, enthusiastic, aggressive, ebullient, infuriating, sincere and gentle, cultivated, fluent . . .'

Along with the enthusiasm went a certain aggressiveness – 'a very combative man, not merely intellectually, but there was a sort of physicality in Brian – quite pugilistic' commented Michael Green, and from Gillian Reynolds: 'He could be a terrible bully and he was very antagonistic the first time I met him.'

> I'd heard him a lot on the radio, seen him on television a lot and then thought 'Oh, you cocky little thing! You're not going to bully me around.' So I just stood up to him and shouted back at him and he roared with laughter and we were great friends after that.

David Hatch, who at one point in his long BBC career ran the BBC's Manchester centre, was also a *Word in Edgeways* fan: 'He was a northerner, yes, he was proud of being a northerner, but he didn't throw the north in your face.' So when moves were afoot to start broadcasting half the *Today* programme from Manchester, Redhead was the obvious choice as presenter:

> The liveliest person I've ever known at five o' clock in the morning! Brian was never quiet, always ebullient, throwing stuff about, lovely to everybody whether they be the Prime Minister or not. He was just
>
> ☞

negative about this, but I do think that more is made of all this than should be!'

Even so, the mix of big events, early-morning starts and the sheer excitement of being able to address the world's leaders one-to-one (not to mention that a sizeable chunk of the country is tuned in at the time) mean that sparks can fly. 'Timpson and

a gorgeous, very educated man. Tony Whitby used to say he wanted people on Radio 4 with 'well-stocked minds' and Brian had a well-stocked mind.

When the Manchester *Today* experiment was closed after a couple of years, Brian came south to present the programme, though he continued to live in his beloved Macclesfield. John Timpson, who was of course already an old hand when the bearded northerner appeared by his side, was somewhat taken aback by his appearance, observing in Redhead's radio-biography that he'd have looked 'more at home sitting beside a fishpond with a curly hat on and a fishing rod – he was the walking image of every garden gnome you have ever seen'. Also on the other side of the studio table at that time was Libby Purves:

He was ever so bumptious, old Brian. And he did name-drop wonderfully. 'I was talking to this woman the other day – it was the Queen, actually . . .' was one of his. And 'I told Lord Carrington about it and he was as shocked as I was' – he did do all that. But he had this glee and this gusto.

It was a habit that led former *Guardian* colleague Simon Hoggart to dub him 'the most solipsistic man I've ever met, before or since', taking the sting out of it by adding, 'That's not the same as egocentric or self-centred; he was a generous man and generous in spirit. But somehow life was a reflection of Brian Redhead back to Brian Redhead and to all those around him.' From his position on the *Today* sports desk, Garry Richardson noted other subtle Redhead characteristics:

Redhead . . . didn't actually like each other all that much at first,' Libby Purves told me. 'They *became* the perfect duo in the end.' Though, as with so many who work in news, they too were capable of displaying plenty of journalistic rivalry:

They were very, very competitive guys, both of them, bless their hearts; I mean they would count up who had the most cues to read

You always knew whether he thought the people that he'd interviewed had come up to scratch because Brian would always go 'Thank you very much! Come again.' And he'd put his hand up in the air. If he didn't do that – just said 'Thank you' – you knew that he thought that they hadn't been a good interviewee. But if he said 'Thank you *very mooch*! Come again' you knew that was the invitation back and Brian had approved.

Into the midst of this muscular enjoyment of life and ideas came a bolt of disaster that changed Brian's life for ever: in 1982, his son William was killed in a car crash in France shortly before he was to go to university. John Cole, ex-*Guardian* and ex-BBC colleague of Redhead's, described the 'bleakness' of his mood thereafter; and in the wake of William's death, Brian turned to religion, presenting acclaimed documentary series on Radio 4 for the religious affairs department: *The Christian Centuries* and *The Good Book*. He continued of course on *Today* and maintained his combative and energetic presence until shortly before his death. 'I was very fond of him,' adds Libby Purves, 'and I'll tell you something about Brian; he was always up for doing something better!'

Many will remember as I do the almost physical shock of hearing that this warm, enquiring yet essentially jolly presence that had helped us ease our way into so many mornings had died suddenly and unexpectedly from septicaemia and general organ failure, following undetected peritonitis. It was January the 24th 1994; Brian Redhead was just sixty-four.

in the morning. And I just used to be rolling around with laughter because I was young and I wasn't particularly competitive. And I'd say, 'For God's sake, you're fifty, man! How important can it be if I have eight cues and you have seven in the hour?'

'The perfect duo' of Redhead and Timpson that Libby Purves refers to was, it's acknowledged, a very particular professional relationship born as much of their differences, according to Sue MacGregor, as of a shared culture.

> They didn't have a great deal in common off-air – I think politically they were quite different but they both said that they both knew what the other was thinking. It was like a marriage on air. And in a kind of way I think the best partnerships on *Today* are like that. So I was very lucky. Although it wasn't easy at first to work with Brian.

By the time Sue joined the team in 1984, *Today* was unquestionably the heavy-duty start to the Radio 4 day, the wispiness and approximations of Jack de Manio firmly part of the programme's – and the network's – history. The show was even, according to one newspaper report, the morning listening at Buckingham Palace, a thought to send just the slightest shiver through the professional calm of *Today*'s sports anchor and another early-eighties recruit, Garry Richardson: 'It said the Queen tunes in at ten past seven and the Queen Mother at seven-twenty. And I suddenly thought, "My goodness! The Queen's probably listening to this!"' But it wasn't the royal seal that confirmed the programme's new found national status. By now it was the object of huge professional admiration for the way it covered the expanding and complex current affairs agenda. 'A rather busy time,' recalls Radio 4's present and tenth controller, Mark Damazer, then laying the early foundations of an illustrious career in news:

> Falklands war, Mrs Thatcher, the Cold War steaming rather strongly, cruise missiles, Greenham Common, the miners' strike, Britain and the unions falling out, a big crisis in NATO with the Russian pipeline, Sabra and Shatila [Palestinian refugee camps attacked by Lebanese militias], and of course the Northern Ireland hunger strikes and some terrorism. So really pretty big stuff; and [on *Today* we had] Redhead and Timpson and Sue – Radio 4 seemed to me to be vibrant; its news and current affairs coverage was thrillingly good compared to the allegedly

magnificent, Olympian World Service. Radio 4 was streets ahead, and you didn't have to be very bright to know it.

Damazer had just swapped a job in World Service for the zippier ambience of breakfast TV, which at the time many felt would sound *Today*'s death knell: 'I mean, where are we now? Twenty-three years on, they've got real viewers and good luck to them, but, I mean, they're not in the game, relatively speaking. Well, that's fantastic! That's absolutely wonderful!'

In the early 1980s, the world Damazer describes was in every sense *Today*'s oyster; and above all China – then difficult of access and little understood in the west – was one of those places where reporters ached to be the first to do the big, curtain-raising special. For *Today* it was Libby Purves who was at the front of the queue at the check-in desk. 'And it was the first live broadcast *in* China because they even recorded the news there so that they could make sure it was the right news that was read!' In these days of instant communications from almost anywhere, of mobile phone calls even from the summit of Everest, the sort of high-wire act that *Today*'s China editions represented is difficult to express; perhaps typically, Purves recalls, the team decided to go one better and do, as it were, somersaults on the wire and without a safety net: 'I said, "Good morning from China." John Timpson was in Dublin with the Pope, and Brian Redhead was with the Liberal Party conference in Margate; and so we had a three-wayer!'

John Humphrys may play down the importance of presenter chemistry, but for listeners, the pairing of Brian Redhead and John Timpson brought a really congenial, yet acute ambience. Abrasiveness was always available – Brian Redhead gained huge headlines for a number of run-ins with Tory politicians, notably in 1987 when Nigel Lawson, then Chancellor of the Exchequer, intimated that Redhead was a Labour supporter. Redhead's resilient response has gone down in legend: 'Do you think we should have a one-minute silence now in this interview – one, for you to apologise for daring to suggest you know how I vote and secondly, perhaps, in memory of monetarism which you've now discarded?' On the other hand,

'Timpson wasn't really a news person,' reflects Libby Purves, 'not at heart.'

Timpson's voice was a particularly felicitous match for Redhead's – people often forget that it's the *sound* of a radio programme sometimes as much as what it's saying that draws listeners in. 'I used to try never to be too shrill or too bossy as a woman,' observes Sue MacGregor, 'and I was always conscious that you were talking to people when they were feeling at their most fragile. Some of us were feeling pretty fragile too, having got up at a God-awful hour!' For announcer Charlotte Green (herself voted Britain's favourite voice in *Radio Times*) – and for me too – Sue's style is very special: 'It's a voice that I could listen to all day and every day – it has a soothing quality, there is an intimate quality there as well, but there's also intelligence and authority and a *little* bit of steel.'

Three years after Sue joined the team, the established sound of *Today* was about to be disrupted. There was a new editor, Jenny Abramsky, and Timpson greeted her with some news; he wanted to retire: 'Which is what he did. So I set about finding somebody to replace him. I found one John Humphrys.' Humphrys was very different from the genial Timpson, who, let's not forget, had joined a gentler, de Manio-led programme at the start of the 1970s. Yet Humphrys, for all his contemporary cheap press reputation as the '*Today* programme rottweiler', found the new appointment a little daunting – he'd not done much live interviewing and had spent much of his recent life as a foreign correspondent:

> I was entirely intimidated – intimidated partly by the reputation of the programme and partly by the reputation of Brian Redhead who was a great journalist and broadcaster. Possibly at his peak, he was the best broadcaster in the country, not least in his ability to talk to people as though in a one-to-one conversation, which is a very rare ability. Brian had it. I was intimidated by all that, so I suppose that my main emotion was fear.

Despite that, one could only with difficulty see either Redhead or Humphrys being comfortable with a 'junior partner' role.

The new twosome was never going to be the same as Redhead and Timpson. 'I don't know that Brian and I had any particular chemistry,' Humphrys says; but there's no doubt that they made it work.

> The fact is – particularly on the *Today* programme, having to get up in the morning – you do not establish, by and large, a close relationship with your colleague, because one of you is working. If you're not working the following morning, the other one is, so you don't go out for a nice long boozy dinner. Certainly I had one or two fairly serious bust-ups with Brian, when his illness was getting worse and we didn't know it. It was not easy at times with Brian, but nonetheless I counted him a friend.

For Sue MacGregor too, until her much lamented retirement from the show in 2002, the furnace of reporting disasters-at-dawn was hot enough to anneal any awkwardness she'd felt working in a team.

> It took me a long time to feel comfortable with John for instance, because I think John . . . would almost rather be on his own a lot of the time in the studio. But we accommodated to each other and then I think we became very fond of each other. So I miss working with him – and with Jim [Naughtie] who I like very much.

Tough times

In the modern era, for all Jim Naughtie's brilliance as a broadcaster (his wonderful election specials are a Radio 4 fixture), it's John Humphrys who has become the ultimate *Today* inquisitor, the asker of the hardest questions, the man whose mere encounters, let alone run-ins, with politicians make instant headlines and provide boundless copy for the diary columns. It was John Humphrys with whom reporter Andrew Gilligan had his notorious 6.07 am two-way about the 'Dodgy Dossier', which eventually resulted in the Hutton Enquiry and the departure not only of Gilligan but of the BBC's Director General, Greg Dyke, and its Chairman, Gavyn Davies. But the intense pressure from government that the programme came under in 2003 was nothing new. 'I think Greg thought the battle over Kelly and Blair and Iraq was a government behaving in a way no other government had ever behaved,' remembers Jenny Abramsky:

> . . . I mean, please! There are those of us who lived through the years of Mrs Thatcher! I remember one particular time when a senior minister came in to do a *Today* programme discussion and he walked up to Julian [Holland, the editor] and went like this [rubbing gesture]: 'I'm just rubbing off the bias.' To do that to the editor of the *Today* programme was an extraordinarily intimidating thing.

On the other hand, the close attention paid to *Today* by the Thatcher government, painful at times though it may have been for the production team, certainly gave the show a kudos unimaginable in the days when Radio 4 was born: not every radio programme can count the Prime Minister as a regular listener. It was a measure, says Abramsky, not without pride, of the fact that *Today* now regularly *led* the news agenda; it had what she calls 'that *absolute* immediacy'. Deeply embedded in her memory is the day when, with the Russian leader Mikhail Gorbachev about to visit London for top-level talks, the programme reported that there had been an earthquake in Armenia and he was cancelling the trip. The phone rang in the editor's office; the voice at the other end was Margaret Thatcher's:

> She said, 'I quite understand why he's not coming', and we were able to just put her on the air. Just little things like that because you're there, you're just there. And that was absolutely critical, and of course it's what the *Today* programme is about today.

Dealing fairly, yet firmly, with the pressures is part of having such a significant place in the public debate. Abramsky says:

If you believe that part of your role is to validly question and challenge government to be answerable to your audiences, then there are going to be times when it is uncomfortable for government; and therefore they're going to get upset with you. But that's part of the way we've built a trust with our audience, and if we didn't do that I don't think we'd be loved in the way we are.

However, the furore over the Gilligan report, which engulfed the programme and the BBC in 2003, caused deep heartache and soul-searching in the corporation. Too many words have already been uttered about the rights and wrongs of what did or didn't happen during this period, and I don't intend to rehearse them again here. However, no account of the vibrant life and times of *Today* can leave arguably its darkest hour undiscussed. 'Hutton was really extraordinary because it was like watching a slow car-crash.' The observer is Helen Boaden, now the BBC's Director of News, but who on May the 29th was controller of Radio 4 when the firestorm ignited. Coincidentally, Boaden's memories also illustrate the compartmentalised nature of the BBC where News Division and Radio 4, despite being conjoined twins, still sometimes don't speak to one another:

And although it happened on Radio 4, it happened in a news programme so, as it were, happened in another bit of the BBC. In fact getting any information about it at all was extremely difficult; so it was slightly peculiar as an experience. And as it got worse, more and more peculiar! It did feel as though we were living in the most strange and curious times possible. Little did I realise that the consequence of that would be that I would be moved from Radio 4 to run BBC News.

Jenny Abramsky, Director of Radio, had worked at every level of BBC news and current affairs, and had, as a young producer, followed very closely the process that led to President Nixon's resignation in 1974. Now she found herself very close to the seat of another fire:

This is probably a very dangerous analogy: the break-in at Watergate didn't bring down Nixon; it was what went on subsequently. And it was very similar in one sense, I think, in terms of what happened with Hutton. I mean, I believe very strongly that the *Today* programme were right to do the story. I also believe very, very strongly that it was very important that they got every bit of their facts right. You can't be mostly right – you have to be *all* right; and I think that equally is very, very important. There will always be times when out of good faith we get something not 100 per cent right and the critical thing is to be able to recognise that and sort it, and move on.

For all the hand-wringing that followed the Hutton Report, both of these immensely powerful BBC figures are very aware of the public benchmark that the painful process provided. Helen Boaden says:

I think what was really interesting was that it just did remind people that radio, and particularly the *Today* programme, is such a force to be reckoned with. I mean it played so powerfully against what media trainers would tell you, you know: radio can pack a punch! It's just a shame it was that particular punch!

To which Jenny Abramsky, as radio's chief executive, adds:

I think it is one of the things that is defining about this country, that radio is still such a powerful medium. I remember the then Press Councillor of the United States explaining to the new ambassador that the difference between the USA and the UK was that in the USA the most important programme to go on was a television programme; in the UK it was a radio programme. It is probably the most consumed news and current affairs pro-gramme in the UK, and it is still broadcast in what is primetime for radio. So I think it is a terrific thing that it is still there.

An unrehearsed intellectual adventure

'Radio went through a bad patch, generally, in the early 60s, I think, when clearly television was on a roll,' says Michael Green, later one of the greatest of Radio 4's controllers. He had graduated in 1964, and after a spell in Swiss broadcasting became a print journalist in Sheffield, moving to the local radio station there in 1967, just as the new networks were coming into being.

> The BBC was investing huge amounts of money in developing television and I think radio was rather shunted off into the sidings and was allowed to kind of drift along. I think the pirates and the need to create something under the BBC umbrella for young listeners kind of drove much broader change.

Some would date the change from the realisation in 1964 that TV now occupied the high ground of children's broadcasting, and that the time-honoured and much-cherished *Children's Hour* on radio should be axed. Certainly, the arrival of *The World at One* in 1965 under the controllership of the far-sighted Gerard Mansell (see Chapter Six) marked a vital new departure, as in comedy did the recruitment of the young David Hatch from the Cambridge Footlights. Whatever the early rumblings of the thunderstorm to come, the only real public sign of a change in the weather was the wave of protest that attended the death of *Children's Hour*. Michael Green, young and keen-eared, heard the thunder coming 'and one had a sense I think that radio was suddenly kind of *reviewed* in the round. People said, "Well what is this animal going to be, going forward? Do we sort of lie back and surrender, or do we actually try to create a new radio for the future?"'

However, despite the angular new logo at the top of its listings in *Radio Times* in September 1967, the new Radio 4, as we saw in Chapter One, was identical to the Home Service it had replaced. In fact, the new network looked as inviting as cold porridge, particularly when compared to the starry picture-led pages of the TV listings. But, says Michael Green, at least the name was different.

> I think that the 'Home Service' has an element of cosiness, a bit Home Counties, very much of London and the south east, rather than for the nation as a whole. And although no one would doubt that the creation of Radios 1 to 4 at the time wasn't the most imaginative series of *titles* one might have come up with, it felt much more part of the future than the past. 'Radio 4' was just more modern; and the programmes that started to be commissioned as a result of that change I think reflected that.

That's slightly to get ahead of ourselves. The big changes would take two and a half years to take shape, and for the moment, the cobwebby network ploughed on under its new name as if nothing was different. But it was.

It started with an internal BBC enquiry, by the Marriott Working Group, whose 1968 report, catchily entitled *Radio Reorganisation: Working Group on the Future of Radio*, consulted widely and considered a vast array of options for all the BBC's stations, including the very new Radio 1. As we saw in the first Interlude, the networks were then a mish-mash of mixed programming, cross-network repeats, even (in the case of the early Radios 1 and 2) shared services, with a distinct lack of identity. Now cash was tight, minority services like the Third Programme were very costly and streamlining was essential. The working group considered many options, and when it came to judging what the Radio 4 of the future might look like, they were remarkably prescient. Quoting the report, the BBC's historian Asa Briggs, puts it like this:

> *Cleared of school broadcasting* . . . Radio 4 would be essentially a *spoken word* programme, with *most stress* . . . *on daily*

journalism. It would not exclude radio drama and daily serials, however, and in the evenings it would carry *some of the entertainment programmes at present carried by Radio 2, comedy, quizzes and games, popular discussions like* Any Questions? and *some mainstream classical music.*

Radio 4 was, you'll remember, a network that still had vast swathes of Schools programmes camped all over its schedules during term time (and wouldn't be able to sidestep them till technology found a way). Above all, the controller of the network had numerous music slots (classical, naturally) to fill: *Invitation to Music*, regular evening concerts and, before closedown each day, *Music at Night* which despatched listeners off to sleep. It was clear that any new formulation of Radio 4 would, if nothing else, have to significantly change the balance of programming.

Marriott was one of a number of enquiries and papers that undertook the close scrutiny of how BBC Radio was organised: submissions were sought from all quarters, and several different scenarios, some of them frighteningly radical, were discussed. Finally, after much deliberation, the outcome was delivered in the version officially approved by the BBC's Board of Governors and the Director General, and with radio's Managing Director Ian Trethowan and Radio 4's controller Gerard Mansell as its godfathers; published in July 1969, it was entitled *Broadcasting in the Seventies*.

The document proposed a pattern for BBC Radio in the future that would be 'more logical, more attractive and solvent'. The realignment of services would include the dispersal of the old English regions and the closure of some house bands and orchestras. Mixed programming on networks would be replaced by more specialised services, and Radio 4 would take over Radio 3's documentary output. News and current affairs would henceforth become the backbone of Radio 4 with four 'main news and magazine periods – breakfast time, lunch time, early evening and late evening'. It is interesting to note that a theme emerging in early discussions – the creation of a dedicated radio news channel – was not in the end part of *Broadcasting in the Seventies*;

though, as we'll see throughout this book, it was a recurring dream of many who led the BBC, that took until March 1994 and the first utterance of Radio Five Live, to become a reality.

For Jenny Abramsky, whose career path has taken her from playing tapes as a studio manager, via the creation of that news-and-sport network, to the very top of the radio industry in the UK as head of all the BBC's network radio services, the report was nothing short of revolutionary.

> It was one of the most far-sighted documents, because from *Broadcasting in the Seventies* you got Radios 1, 2, 3 and 4 as very clear propositions when they were going to face the coming of commercial radio, and actually creating a portfolio of services for the BBC. In one sense our television colleagues are only now waking up to the fact that that's what they have to do. That was an incredibly far-sighted document, but it was not seen as that when we were there.

Which was to put it mildly. The document fell on listeners and broadcasters like Hitler's incendiary bombs on the City of London. The firestorm was immense. Nine months of public and internal protest ensued, with editorials, petitions and many doom-laden prophecies of the end of radio broadcasting as we knew it. The writer and broadcaster Michael Rosen, who today presents Radio 4's magazine about the English language, *Word of Mouth*, was back then one of the élite squad of newly arrived BBC General Trainees. His placement was in the Radio Drama Department, hotbed of resistance to the plans, where great meetings were called:

> So I go along, and I'm sitting there and various people get up including the great [producer] Raymond Raikes, who wore the most amazing suits that have ever been seen: hand-made three-piece suits, beautiful pinstripes and huge trousers, just enormous; they were like parachutes, incredible! And he had this wonderful fruity voice. I remember him standing up and saying, 'This is the loss of the duty of the BBC . . .' and so on: huge great florid speeches.

And then, amid all the anger, Michael noted something that both encapsulates the curious essence of radio celebrity, where the voice not the appearance is the star's indelible signature, and in a sense epitomises the passing of the old order:

> Suddenly I hear another voice, and someone stands up and says, 'I've never felt so betrayed in all my life.' And I think, 'I know that voice, I know that voice . . . Who was it?' It was Uncle David. David Davis.

Davis had been the masterly, fatherly voice of the defunct *Children's Hour* who'd washed up in Drama when his unit had been summarily closed five years or so earlier. David's was a mesmerising voice (he was always known professionally by his first name) and when, many years later, I too met him and he sat down at his grand piano at home and played again the programme's signature tune, it was like meeting a Hollywood legend. Michael Rosen was equally captivated during his own encounter with the broadcaster:

> There was Uncle David, sitting amongst these people and the great Raymond Raikes and his beautiful suits. Uncle David was there. But a lot of the time he was asleep. He would come to the meetings and he would look quite brightly for a moment, and then suddenly [snort] and the head would go down, and he would just sit there asleep. And in a sense he represents in my mind the transition. People talk about how the Home Service became Radio 4; well, what it conjures up is Uncle David playing his piano in his room (because the BBC couldn't bear to sack him) and turning up at meetings, on the one hand to protest and on the other to go to sleep.

David Davis's battles though were over. He'd resisted the closure of the programme that was his life's work, *Children's Hour*, and had lost. For others, the fight for what they saw as the soul of BBC radio went on. At the other end of a BBC career, Jenny Abramsky, who joined the BBC right in middle of the storm, was watching:

There still were petitions going against *Broadcasting in the Seventies*: people were coming around and saying this was going to be the death of radio, the death of the intellectual heart of radio, the BBC was going to renege, was going to dumb down . . . It's a joke when you look back at it now.

With the huge wave of protest rolling on inside and outside the BBC, the controller, appointed in October 1969 to implement the changes, had a sensitive job to do. He was the remarkable man we met in the first Interlude, Anthony Whitby. Tony Whitby, who 'combined intelligence, enthusiasm and charm' according to Asa Briggs, was recruited from television, but had been a radio producer earlier in his career and had also gained senior management experience as BBC Secretary, working to the Chairman and Board of Governors. 'Tony Whitby, in my view, was the best controller of Radio 4, ever, not least because he helped me and inspired me to work for the channel; I thought he was brilliant, but he *took charge* of the channel and he decided on what programmes and where they would be.' The opinion is that of David Hatch who, fourteen years later, would himself be sitting in the controller's chair, but who, when Whitby took over from Gerry Mansell, was a young executive producer in Light Entertainment Department.

Eventually, many editorials, union meetings, questions in Parliament and letters to *The Times* later, the row over *Broadcasting in the Seventies* began to die down. Working at an incredible pace over the last weeks of 1969, Whitby set about implementing the recommendations and devising actual programmes. The sharpening up of the network's current affairs output, which would eventually clear out the gentleman's clubbery of Jack de Manio's *Today*, was the main thrust of the plan. The *PM* programme, dominant sound of Radio 4's drivetime ever since, was perhaps the most prominent of Whitby's raft of new shows, sweeping away the gentle *Home This Afternoon* magazine (see Chapter Seven). But Whitby's wind of change, driven on by *Broadcasting in the Seventies*, blew throughout the whole schedule.

Even a cursory look at the memos issuing from Whitby's

office in those first months, and preserved at the BBC's Written Archive Centre near Reading, reveal the deep thought – and the pace of thinking – that he was pouring into the whole shape of his new Radio 4. His deadline was terrifying: a bare four months, with Christmas in between, to redesign a whole network. 'I am brooding deeply . . .' he writes more than once, and invitations for ideas for new programmes are vigorously underlined: 'I urgently need offers. That means before Christmas, if possible,' he writes to a slew of current affairs editors and their producers on December the 15th 1969. Then again, 'I want bids urgently' he says in outlining his plans for a 'personal anthology audience show' (still with us as *With Great Pleasure*, see Chapter Eleven).

'I would like urgently any offers,' he notes, 'which would fit into a series with the working title "Love Affair" . . .' – and under the provisionally named 'Stories of Our Time', here he is again inviting proposals for documentary programmes for Thursday evenings at 8.00 pm: 'a single human situation told in narrative style'. *It's My Story* is the contemporary incarnation of this on Radio 4, and is still on Thursday evenings at 8.00 pm. Truly Whitby's work was revolutionary.

'Tony was quite small, wore blue television-type suits, blue shirts, always a tie; he was smart . . .' recalled David Hatch.

> He was a serious news guy; quite forbidding in that he was very, very intelligent but he wasn't fierce. I always said about Tony that if you went in and took a beating from him – which you could do when you did something that was rubbish – he still let you walk out of his room walking tall; he put you together again before you went out. I learned that from him.

Indeed in so many ways, it was Tony Whitby, with the *Broadcasting in the Seventies* gale filling his sails and driving him through the squalls, who carved out of his producers' and editors' imaginations the BBC Radio 4 that we have even now, four decades later: contemporary, reflective and interested in the way the world works, but fun too. Here, in his inaugural week – beginning on Saturday April the 4th 1970 – were the first editions of *Analysis* (analytical current affairs), *From the Grass Roots* (a regional take on politics), *Now Read On* (a book programme carefully scheduled to anticipate 'books that come out on a Thursday'), *The World and How We See It* (an ancestor of *Feedback*), *This Island Now* (on 'the present plight and future shape of town and country' in the face of new technology), *Start the Week* ('meet people for whom this is a special week'), *Week Ending* ('taking a look at the previous week's news with a slightly jaundiced view' according to David Hatch writing in *Radio Times*) and, not least, the new current affairs programme for listeners to drive home to, *PM* ('. . . that sums up your day – and starts off your evening'). Quite a line-up in little more than four months.

Taking a lead role in Tony Whitby's revolution at Light Entertainment HQ near Bond Street, David Hatch experienced at first hand how Whitby nurtured both his new shows, like *Week Ending*, and the producers who made them:

> It went out at 11.30 on a Friday night, and he would ring me at midnight and he would say, 'Right, let's go through it David. Now, I thought the opening was good, didn't like the second item; why did you do that?' and he did that for I suppose the first ten weeks of the programme. I got used to my controller ringing me at home about the programme. Now that I thought was what a controller should be about.

At the other end of the country, another brilliant young producer destined, like David, to reach the top of the radio tree, and equally in tune with Tony Whitby's new contemporary mood, was a young Michael Green, by now a producer in Manchester: in the BBC Archive I found an early enthusiastic note of his to the controller suggesting *Now We're the Boss*, a documentary about workers' co-operatives, with a handwritten 'Yes, in principle' in blue Biro in the margin.

Michael's regular show was the late-evening weekly debate programme chaired by Brian Redhead, called *A Word in Edgeways* (see page 294).

Brian used to say that *A Word in Edgeways* was 'an unrehearsed intellectual adventure' and that what mattered was getting not from A to Z but getting from A to C *interestingly*. And the 'unrehearsed intellectual adventure' I suppose characterised the new Radio 4 in some way. Because Radio 4, in particular I think, had been *rehearsed*, it was prescriptive, things were written down, people read their lines. The idea of discursive broadcasting, of ad-hoc broadcasting, of spontaneous broadcasting if you like, where people came into a studio and weren't *quite* sure what the script was going to be, seemed to me really what the new Radio 4 was about.

CHAPTER THREE

9.00 am: Start, Stop, Mid *and* Pick

The Radio 4 day is littered with elephant traps. Not that it looks that way from where the listener sits. For us at the receiving end, all we hear is a smooth flow of programmes, news bulletins, continuity announcements and trailers, but in the gleaming new fourth floor offices in Broadcasting House where the controller and his staff sit, the opportunities to put a foot wrong seem many and various.

Contemplate, therefore, The Radio 4 Junction. Because, dear reader, we have reached one. This isn't 'junction' as in Clapham or Crewe or even *Up The*. The Radio 4 junction is the point at which one programme ends, and, after a few well-chosen words from the announcer, the next begins. Now junctions are part of the reality of a complicated network like Radio 4; there are dozens of them, littered across the schedule, and each is an opportunity for the listener to change his or her mind about the station: 'Do I *really* want to stay with the musical joys of *Counterpoint* when I've just spent the last half hour being riveted by world events on *The World at One*? Certainly, plenty of people say, 'Yes'.

Maximising the number of people who say 'Yes' at crucial moments in the Radio 4 day is part of the scheduler's art, but no junction comes more vital than the one that has just hoved into view, potentially handing over the millions who've been hanging on Jim, John, Sarah or whomsoever's words in *Today*, to the next programme.

So, it's 9.00 am, and James Naughtie has signed off, just squeezing in one last word ahead of the Greenwich Time Signal. Once again, he's managed not to 'crash' (speak over) the pips; a cardinal sin at Radio 4. Famously, on her very last edition, the meticulous Sue MacGregor was so overcome by emotion that she managed to crash them rather spectacularly ('a hanging offence' she called it, whereas in France, oddly, they don't care two hoots and do it all the time, but let that pass).

Anyway, now the Radio 4 newsreader is heard: 'BBC Radio News at nine o'clock.' In technical terms, *Today* has 'done the handover': no continuity announcer has infiltrated him- or herself. In a network as finely crafted as Radio 4, such details matter a lot. 'Radio 4 is about boundaries and about marking out your day,' says James Boyle who, when he took over in 1996, spent more time than any controller since Tony Whitby reshaping the Radio 4 day to follow more closely the twists and turns of listeners' lives.

> And one of the things that shocked me when I took over was that there were elementary broadcasting mistakes being made from programme to programme, as with things like 'Well, that's all from us. Goodbye' – people were closing down the network. I don't know how much time I spent saying to people, 'Stop saying goodbye! We're not going anywhere! Just say "I hope you enjoyed . . ." Say anything, but don't say "Goodbye" and close my network!'

In lots of tiny ways throughout the day, Boyle re-engineered these 'sets of points' along the track of Radio 4; for instance, Suzanne Charlton and her weather forecast are today enveloped in the warm embrace of *PM*'s Eddie Mair: two junctions taken out of circuit there. And at the *Today* end of the day, handing directly to the News means there is only one excursion to Continuity before, say, Andrew Marr appears to launch us into another forty-five minutes of compelling listening.

Chat lines

Meanwhile, the stars whom Andrew, Libby or Melvyn are about to entertain on air have left the unstructured banter and unmentioned tension of a pre-transmission chat, and are now

John Ebdon: 'Thanks for listening'

Although nowadays you'd be hard put to slip a cue-sheet between the end of the *Today* programme and the nine o'clock news, it was not ever thus. Most mornings until 1998, *Today* ground to a halt at 8.45, to be replaced by *Yesterday in Parliament*. Except, that is, on Mondays when, following a Parliamentless Sunday, there were no proceedings to report. As if suddenly excused games, or let off a particularly gruesome detention, the Radio 4 audience loved it and, for twenty-six years, one man in particular gave the network's listeners their Monday morning treat. His greeting was a legendary 'How do you do?', and his name was John Ebdon.

In fact, looking at that ultra-formal opening, it seems rather bald on the page. When John Ebdon spoke it, it was filled with a nasal disdain, as if he were raising his eyes and his nose in tandem. His programme was tiny – less than fifteen minutes every third week – and yet when he died in 2005, the fulsome obituaries were testimony to the affection in which Radio 4 listeners held him.

So what, exactly, was his technique? Why did Ebdon forge such a place in listeners' imaginations? The simple answer was that he was funny. Not just him of course, though he was, quite; but it was his illustrations that most – though not all – loved. John's goldmine was the BBC Sound Archive, and for those twenty-six years, he was to be found, every third week, in Listening Room 1, on the look-out for daft voices, silly sayings, slips of the tongue. Like the woman who stoutly announced that Shakespeare was dubbed 'the *bird* of Avon', or the weather forecaster who predicted 'overnight mist and *frog*'.

John's targets were bouncy-voiced schoolmarms being ever so

ensconced around the baize-covered studio table. In the now empty Green Room, a litter of half-empty BBC cups sit forlornly on a couple of trays – BBC 'hospitality' has always felt a bit like Utility furniture looked after the war; that's to say, always serviceable, yet rarely good. Just a moment ago, this room was full of buzz and adrenaline – the producer slipping in and out with some instruction for the studio crew, proud about something, or antique backwoodsmen haltingly describing some ancient craft or lore. What he'd then do was weave a persona for the voice: so a plummy observation would be heralded by a big intake of breath (vocal technique was John's forte; after all, he'd been an actor and won prizes at RADA) and then something like 'As the archdeacon pointed out to a newly appointed curate just the other day . . .' and the clip would follow, the voice sounding, in John's phrase, as if someone had stuffed 'a handful of marbles into their ecclesiastical mouths'. There were those who objected to his mocking way with legitimate recordings; and yet for all his acerbic tongue and languorous, camp waspishness, he was very gentle, and the comedy never really mean.

I worked alongside John for a number of years, though I never produced his programme, and his was a familiar figure in his olive-green suit, rangily striding out along the windowless inner corridors of Broadcasting House – or hunched over that pile of recordings, 'rooting around in the archives like a demented truffle hound', as John described it in his final talk: two hours' solid listening, he confessed, might yield a mere eight seconds on air.

John Ebdon was born in 1923 of a Swiss mother and English father and served in the RAF during the war, suffering damage to his eyes in an explosion which caused him to abandon a career under the stage's bright lights. Later, he turned to religion, though ultimately deciding against ordination; his faith was always strong, however, and the eccentricities of church ritual underpinned many of his programmes.

☞

a message whispered to the broadcast assistant from a guest about a post-show taxi, or a surprise visit from the controller. Even for the calmest of programmes, there's always that sense of anticipation and anxiety, because, let's face it, early morning is, for most of us, not the moment we'd necessarily choose to give our very best performance. Yet performance is what the Radio 4 audience is offered at nine o'clock through

John loved language – indeed he'd found it a defence mechanism at school when he was terribly bullied by other boys – and like that other suave radio voice, Kenneth Horne, John Ebdon loved to use double-entendre in his script, so mumps was an affliction that produced painful swellings 'and not only round the ears – far from it, if you know what I mean'. And he could really make you laugh out loud – as one irate (but amused) listener wrote to him, 'Damn and blast you Mr Ebdon! I laughed so much I drove the Bentley into the back of a bus!'.

Take this classic Ebdon line, where the punchline is held back right to the end: 'One of the delightful things about being a broadcaster is that people write letters to you, and I can't tell you how much I enjoy receiving them. [PAUSE] Specially the ones with stamps on.' The breath-control, the pauses – he actually wrote PAUSE THREE SECONDS on his typescript – all were carefully planned to make the joke work, all part of the formula.

In fact, John's formula never changed – every edition would begin with the announcement from Continuity:

most of the week, in the form of live and lively structured conversation.

Indeed, these days, *Start the Week, Midweek* and *In Our Time* are technically known as 'conversation strands'. Not chat-shows, you notice. Conversations are more structured and managed, the best carefully conceived around a premise, thought through, and illustrated if necessary with suitable clips, all confected into a very carefully woven argument. Radio 4 conversation programmes are rarely, then, just chat; we listeners demand more. On *In Our Time*, one the most successful 9.00 am shows, for example, the production team will have been working on the subject of the programme for days and weeks. Long before Melvyn Bragg receives his briefing notes, the subject and angle have been plotted, as well as the cast of appropriate intellects ready to pick their way through nuclear fusion, Romanticism or Greek philosophy for three quarters of

> And here once again is John Ebdon who, after further researches into
> the Sound Archives, comes to no serious conclusion

and continue with the trademark opening 'How do you do' ('Oh, he really does say it!' squealed one listener to John after he'd greeted her thus one day). Also part of the enduring formula was Perseus. Perseus was John's cat who would purr and miaow at appropriate moments in the programmes, often to express controversial views that might have been libellous or given offence. Perseus, though, wasn't a fiction, and when he died in 1978, the event even made the Radio 4 news.

When nearing his own end and afflicted with cancer, John penned a moving and uplifting farewell which concludes: 'Whilst the act of dying itself leaves me with some misgivings, death itself holds no fears for me. When all is said and done, I shall merely move into another room in the Lord's mansion. In any case, as Peter Pan mused, "To die will be a very big adventure."' Sadly, on this occasion, he was unable to close with his time-honoured last line: '. . . and if you have been, thanks for listening. Goodbye.'

an hour – live. 'And actually,' says Bragg, emerging from the studio at ten o'clock, 'I like to know more, believe it or not!'

I get these papers for *In Our Time* on Friday evening and occasionally – as this week – a book as well, and I think, 'Oh, good! There's plenty to do for the next few days; there's plenty to think about.' I also very much like talking to people who really, absolutely, know their stuff – and I've got to believe that listeners like that, too. They know they're in the hands of simply the best people we can get in the United Kingdom to talk about that subject.

These programmes, then, are nowadays far from being the 'chatathons' or 'plug-fests' frequently rubbished by newspaper columnists; who, some twenty or so years ago, when *Start the Week* and *Midweek* were complemented by Saturday night's

Ringing the changes

When in 2006, a new phone-in show appeared, more or less unheralded in the Radio 4 schedules, nobody was particularly excited. A programme trail announced 'Radio 4's new late-night phone-in programme *Down the Line*' and that was about it. But Radio 4-land was appalled: the overnight phone-log that records calls to the Duty Office was overwhelmed with protests at the poor quality of the debate. In reality listeners had been hoaxed: *Down the Line* was a brilliant spoof by Paul Whitehouse and friends; a parody of the radio phone-in that was so close to the real thing that it was, for many, achingly funny.

So embedded, though, is the culture of the phone-in these days, even in the crafted texture of Radio 4, that *Down the Line* caused a stir only because it wasn't as intellectually rigorous as we Radio 4 listeners demand. After all, the first big Radio 4 phone-in host had been none other than the grand and bow-tied figure of Sir Robin Day, who had anchored *It's Your Line* with breathy excitement from early in Tony Whitby's new schedule. It was indeed the interactivity of its day.

It's Your Line, 'a new-style "live" current affairs programme' according to *Radio Times*, wasn't the sort of freestyle phone-in that's familiar today on stations such as Radio Five Live. 'Listeners will be able to "grill" leading public figures over the air,' explained *RT*, and on

Stop the Week, reported that the three shows were known in the trade as 'Pluggers (*Start the Week*), Nutters *(Midweek)* and Wankers (*Stop the Week*)'. And it's true there was a time when the Monday show was very often stacked with fairly unvarnished promotional chat around some book fresh in the shops that week. These days, new books are still a backbone (together with forthcoming lectures and events), but the discussion is all. In fact, with polymath Andrew Marr in the hotseat, and before him Jeremy Paxman, *Start the Week* is a very different animal from the jolly discussion that greeted the world as part of Tony Whitby's new schedule on April the 6th 1970.

that first edition on Tuesday the 13th 1970 under Sir Robin's grill was the tough-talking ex-Communist union leader Hugh Scanlon, who'd often been in conflict with Harold Wilson's government. He was also utterly used to speaking his mind and in public – not a bad booking for a first show. Also firmly in Tony Whitby's mind was the fact that commercial radio was only just over the UK broadcasting horizon, and they'd be relying on this cheap form of programming to sustain their hours of output for little outlay.

It's Your Line attracted very good audiences for an evening show, but by 1973, with commercial competition almost upon the BBC, it was realised that even bigger audiences could be garnered in the morning. So Tuesday evenings were for *It's Your Line*, and Tuesday mornings were chosen for a new phone-in that, in one guise or another, lasted until Nick Ross finally replaced the receiver on *Call Nick Ross* in 1997. Its first incarnation was as *Tuesday Call*, with Sue MacGregor, then also presenting *Woman's Hour* – indeed, *Tuesday Call* also shared a production team with the daily show. So if five past nine on a Monday was Richard Baker's starring moment of the week, Tuesday at 9.05 am kicked off with Sue and the phones: 'And we did that for years. And when *Woman's Hour* stopped running it, they personalised it to *Call Nick Ross*. But actually in my day it was the subject that was important, not the person sitting in the studio manning the phone!'

☞

A *fresh* Start

At five past nine, *Radio Times* for that day proudly announces, 'New Series: *Start the Week with Richard Baker*. Ken Sykora, Gordon Clyde, George Luce and who knows who take a lively look round and meet some of the people for whom this is a special week'. Not a very loud fanfare for the inauguration of a broadcasting landmark, still running thirty-seven years later. In fact, this first Monday page of Whitby's bright and reformed network is hardly designed to get anyone tuning in. Certainly the typeface is a great deal brighter than it was, but the dense

Another, less successful phone-in on Fridays – imaginatively titled *Friday Call* – was also launched. An internal memo of congratulations about the Tuesday show records appreciation of the 'admirable Sue MacGregor' and the team: 'they really sound . . . to be doing a grand job'. Though 'perhaps masterly silence about my *Friday Call* views would be wiser! Hopefully it will improve . . .' It didn't, and died.

'We did all sorts of subjects,' says Sue, but on September the 3rd 1985 the topic – and guest – was a first for the programme: the now Princess Royal. 'She didn't know what questions she was going to get,' Sue told me, 'but they were all pretty respectful. She was a great participator.' And in more ways than one. Just before the show went live, Sue's monitor, with all the callers' details and questions went blank. Princess Anne to the rescue: 'She had a screen, and she turned hers round [the problem was only with Sue's screen]. Very on the ball. And she coped . . . she was very good.'

Nick Ross took over the *Tuesday Call* slot in November 1986, with a mandate to make it 'very topical, cresting the wave of the issues people would be talking about that morning on the Clapham or Sauchiehall Street omnibus, intelligent and informed.' More like, in fact, the old *It's Your Line*, though geared very closely to the headline stories of the week.

In February 1994, Ian McKellen was Nick Ross's guest. The subject was homosexuality and was dealt with calmly and with dignity by both guest and host in the face of outrage and insult from the

columns are relieved only by a mugshot of Ian McKellen (starring in the evening's *World Theatre*), and have to share their space with details of foreign radio stations. It's scarcely credible now that, while the 1970 *Radio Times* didn't have one centimetre of ITV coverage, it thought it still worth noting that you could catch Stravinsky's 'Les Noces' from Oslo or, from the Netherlands, Mahler's Tenth. Unbelievable.

It doesn't, however, bother to list the overseas alternatives to *Start the Week*. Perhaps unsurprisingly, the new programme bore many of the hallmarks of a show that several of those involved had just been working on, *Home This Afternoon*

audience: 'Homosexuality is a terrible sin,' they cried; 'an abomination...absolutely dreadful...corrupts the young...should be outlawed,' screamed another. It was one of the most thrilling broadcast slanging-matches I've ever heard, and may have done not a little to change the prevailing climate about gay issues amongst the middle-England listenership of Radio 4.

Sue meanwhile was scooping the world.

> It's Your World was a co-broadcast with the BBC World Service, and we got Gyorgy Arbatov, who was a Russian equivalent of cabinet minister, three weeks after the Chernobyl explosion in Ukraine. And even Gorbachev had not yet given a press conference, so we were getting the first official Soviet reaction to the explosion.

Controversialists have, since the early days of commercial radio, found a niche in the phone-in world. Brian Hayes and the BBC's Robbie Vincent made their reputations for despatching tiresome callers with refreshing directness on their local London shows; but such has never been the way of Radio 4's phone-ins. Hence the public uproar when Gary Bellamy started getting argumentative with his spoof callers and fake guests on Down the Line; the tone just *wasn't* Radio 4.

Which was, of course, the point. The joke was on us.

(see Chapter Seven), now despatched to radio-elysium. Among the familiar names were presenter Ken Sykora, guitarist and jazz musician, and producer Jack Singleton. Joining them were another musician and writer, Gordon Clyde, and George Luce. Now there's a name to stir the memories of 1960s telly addicts, one of a long tradition of weathermen-turned-presenters, who ended up anchoring *You and Yours*. And the items on board to start that first Monday morning sound pretty familiar *Home This Afternoon* territory too, including Wordsworth's poetry, pigeons, tax changes in Sweden and a cookery spot with Zena Skinner. It was clearly a general magazine programme, much as its afternoon predecessor had been.

Yet, unlike *Home This Afternoon*, *Start the Week* immediately looked towards a modern age with its billed presenter, Richard Baker; it was a *personality* show. From the perspective of today, Baker is an old-fashioned rather than a starry figure, but forty years ago he had a huge public profile: he was the face of BBC television news – the first face in fact, back in 1954 – and of classical music on the box, where he always did the pomp and circumstance stuff at the *Last Night of the Proms*. The fact that Radio 4 was actually using a TV star to present its new series, and named him in the title no less, was more or less unprecedented.

So too was the length of the programme. Radio 4 has always been a segmented network, with short programmes and longer shows, but few extend to an hour. *Start the Week* was a full hour *and ten minutes*, a real rollercoaster of a magazine that anticipated (in more ways than one) what controller David Hatch was to do nearly fifteen years later in the middle of the morning, in a programme called *Rollercoaster* – presented by, yes, one Richard Baker (see Chapter Five).

So where was the audience for this new 9.00 am programme to be found? Jack de Manio had packed his bags and left the *Today* studio twenty minutes earlier, replaced by opera-singer-turned-personality David Franklin, he of the basso-profundo voice. Franklin (always known by colleagues as 'Bill') was a regular team-member on the *My Music* quiz and given to amusing anecdotes from the world of grand opera, and here he was this bright April morning, with a quarter-hour talk entitled 'Must You Learn to Sing?' Thus there were several diversionary junctions for the listener to negotiate between Jack de Manio's farewell and Richard Baker's cheery greeting on *Start the Week*. On other mornings, the switch-off factor was even more acute, as *Yesterday in Parliament* occupied the slot up to 9 am. It would take twenty-eight years for controller James Boyle, in one of his most controversial, yet astute, moves, to straighten out that bad bend in the Radio 4 roadway and take *Today* up to the 9 am news.

So the *Start the Week* journey began. The first edition was a strange affair, with *Radio Times* promising an interview with *Los Picaflores* (the Hummingbirds), a now more or less completely forgotten group of religiously orientated singers, but whose 1970 UK tour drew big crowds. Then there was an item about 'the anniversary of the Declaration of Arbroath, when Scotland's independence was asserted in a letter to the Pope'. Riveting stuff.

Despite this slightly stodgy-sounding mix, Gerry Mansell, Director of Programmes was soon reporting to the Radio Review Board (which each week gathered together all the senior people in radio), that he was 'agreeably impressed by its sureness of touch, confidence and style', and one departmental head observed that 'in his own experience . . . it provided an appropriate accompaniment to morning domestic chores . . .'

As time went on, the seventy-minute show shrank to an hour and, a year later, a man joined the regulars who was to carve out a firm if not entirely comfortable niche in the programme's history. He was another musician (Radio 4 seems with hindsight to have been beset with musicians making careers in talk programmes) – a pianist, architect and witty journalist called Kenneth Robinson. Robinson died a decade and a half ago, and was ditched by *Start the Week* more than twenty years back, so his is probably not a name that will spring immediately to listeners' minds, though you may just recall him from the telly, where he used to present *Points of View* (along, curiously, with three other Robinsons over the years, Robert, Anne and Tony).

Kenneth was *STW*'s great controversialist – and for anyone who puts people's backs up at nine in the morning on Radio 4, it's a bit like stripping in the middle of Trafalgar Square: there are bound to be a lot of people around to notice. Just think in more recent times of the spat between Joan Rivers and Darcus Howe on *Midweek* in 2005 (of which more anon). Kenneth had one of those rather nasal insinuating voices, and he used pauses . . . to make his witty and often bad-tempered points. He was the grumpy old man *de ses jours* who could be relied on to make a spiky comment that could wound (he once reduced the ever-poised Angela Rippon to tears) – but he also, singing witty numbers at the piano, managed regularly to raise a laugh with this listener, for one.

In fact, *Start the Week* in those early years was a very *active* show: knockabout stuff. Esther Rantzen was another regular, and warm-voiced Welsh-woman Mavis Nicholson, while gruff Cockney geezer Monty Modlyn went out and about with his 'roving microphone' – yellowing newspaper cuttings recall Modlyn's chance encounter with Ugandan dictator Idi Amin, whom he persuaded to play the accordion! No comment.

Foil to what Henry Porter, writing in the *Guardian*, called all this 'unedited emotion . . . whimsy, failed whackiness, dreary relevance, irritability, buffoonery [and] egotism . . .' was Richard Baker, whose slightly stiff, newsreaderly style actually worked rather well. Though critical pens were always ready to have a stab, the listeners continued to love it. It became the corollary to the tougher *Today* of the mid-seventies onwards and could be, as Porter fairly acknowledges in his article celebrating the show's first quarter century, also a place for 'argument and surprising wit'.

It was Robinson's waspish reflection on older people's sex lives in 1984 that caused the biggest furore, and the beginning of the end for his role on *Start the Week*. He made a slighting joke about disabled people's sex lives ('you can hear the wheel-chairs banging together all night in some parts of the country') that deeply offended the even-handed Radio 4 audience who showered the network with complaints. Finally, two years later, the end came, but Kenneth wasn't one to go quietly; he voiced his protest on air in one last scandalous outburst: 'I'm not going. I'm not going,' he shouted, furiously, to two million listeners. 'They've given me three days' notice after so many years. It's a bloody disgrace.' But go Kenneth Robinson did.

More change was on the way for *STW*. 'The programme needs *refreshing*' is the regular cry as long-running shows get stuck in a rut: 'We've got to do something a little bit different; we've got to change it.' Professor Laurie Taylor, has been observing Radio 4 at work for decades both as contributor and critic, and has heard often enough such comments, sometimes about his own programmes.

But you can have creativity *and* surprise within a very established format. I mean the idea of having rather distinct Radio 4 boundaries – this is what Radio 4 does; this is what Radio 4 should sound like – provides an extraordinarily good opportunity to experiment. There's a sonnet by Wordsworth:

> Nuns fret not at their convent's narrow room
> And hermits are contented with their cells;
> And students with their pensive citadels . . .

He's talking about the limitations of the sonnet-form *in* a sonnet. He's saying that it's rather a good idea to be confined within certain parameters because when you're within those parameters the opportunities for experimentation are quite strong.

And this is just what now begins to happen on *Start the Week*. The cast subtly changes; the format moves on. After seventeen years in the seat, out goes Richard Baker and in comes Russell Harty. Russell was at the height of his television career – he'd hosted arts programmes and chat-shows on ITV and BBC and came trailing stardust and, above all, humour; he was witty and camp and a little outrageous. Melvyn Bragg, an old friend and colleague (with whom he managed to clash on *STW*) admired the way Russell dared to ask obvious questions, often cheekily, while Rosemary Hart recalls with affection Russell's years as a Radio 3 talks producer, working alongside her in the 1960s. Across the corridor in the *Midweek* office, Libby Purves much later struck up a warm friendship with him, as guest interviewer on her show:

> Russell was a joy. I loved working with Russell. He was like a three-year-old you can't be cross with if he asked a rude question like 'Why has that lady got big bazoomers?' He had an utter innocence about him – he was the most *generous* of broadcasters. After my first solo *Midweek*, he rang up the studio just to say 'Well done.' He was lovely.

There's a great deal of sadness in the reflections about Harty;

his sudden death from hepatitis in 1988 came as a huge shock. I remember, as a listener, how unfair it seemed that a man who'd turned the old *Start the Week* into such a joyous and funny programme could be taken so fast and so brutally. 'Neither he nor anyone else knew how serious it was,' remembers Melvyn Bragg.

> Russell rang up and he said, 'They want somebody to take over on *Start the Week* for two or three weeks. The trouble is they might get Michael Parkinson or Esther or . . . and they're *good*!' There was a bit of a silence. 'And I'm backing you. I think you should be given a chance!'

In fact, as is normal in such circumstances, several voices were tried out. Russell's were sizeable boots to fill and, despite the endless press carping, the programme was a big and established gig, so Noel Edmunds, Sue Lawley and Kate Adie were also given guest presenter opportunities alongside Bragg. 'I was very nervous about radio; I don't know why,' Melvyn now says. He'd done some radio early in his career, but as producer rather than presenter. Television had long become his medium:

> On television I was always the producer and presenter so I was in charge of the whole operation. On radio, maybe because it was so important to me in my childhood, when I was sitting in front of a microphone I was thinking, 'Crikey, *The Brains Trust*, Gilbert Harding, *Take it From Here*, Jimmy Edwards . . . Oh God!' and I really would go into little panics. And on those early *Start the Week*s, while Russell battled with this illness, I was talking to him down the mic. I was saying, 'I wish you'd come back; it's quite hard work this!' But actually what happened was I got used to it.

It was Melvyn Bragg who eventually got the nod for the permanent vacancy: 'And I just loved it. I thought, "Yeah! Whether I can do it well or do it badly is not the point, at least I can do it. I know how to do it."' Once again, it was time for one of Laurie Taylor's tonal changes, as Bragg remembers:

I met this producer Marina Salandy-Brown and neither she nor I wanted to go on doing the same *Start the Week*. I remember we had lunch together – and I said, 'Well, if I'm going to go on I want to do this sort of stuff.' And she said, 'So do I' – or she said it first and I agreed – doesn't matter. And then we just conscientiously, steadily put that into operation and changed the programme.

Melvyn Bragg joined the nine o'clock Radio 4 line-up in 1988 and has been there, week in, season out ever since, eliciting ideas and opinions and occasionally rubbing people up the wrong way – his spats with Kathy Lette (critical observations about her book were characterised in the press as evidence of a supposed mid-life crisis), Michael Dobbs and Bill Cash all made headlines. Under Melvyn and Marina, the programme subtly shifted its cast and the tenor of its chat: 'like eavesdropping on a conversation in some minimalist bar in London' sniped one press description; Bragg, being successful and clever, was always the butt of London's competitive media chatterers. Thus *Start the Week*, despite having substantially changed its spots, remains a public forum that in some way *matters*; that, still, under two successor hosts, Jeremy Paxman and Andrew Marr, people continue to *want* to appear on – and not just to plug a publication. In many ways, according Melvyn Bragg, it reflects the Radio 4 audience back to itself.

I think Radio 4's a great educator and I don't mean just *In Our Time* or in the *Today* programme, but it's the comedy and the quiz shows particularly. I'm sorry if this is pompous, but there is a sort of subtext that this is where *Englishness* is, it rests here. I think the only channel people would march for in the whole BBC is Radio 4. People would actually turn out on the streets for Radio 4 because it matters to them and, in a peculiar way, they have an ownership of it. They feel 'Yeah, that's us and we can have an influence.'

Likewise, for Libby Purves, chair of Wednesday's nine o'clock conversation, *Midweek*, this form of 'entertaining education' that Radio 4 provides is what makes the network so compelling – from dawn to closedown.

You'll switch on the radio and there will be somebody telling you something in a not-showing-off way and a humble, you-might-be-interested-in-this way. Like how there are these sea-plants up near Birmingham in the middle of the motorway. In the winter [with] the salt spray thrown up by the lorries and the buffeting winds, they think, these poor little plants, that they're on the foreshore. Well I heard about that on some slightly anorakish nature programme on Radio 4 and it kept me very happy all day.

Middling matters

It's stories, personal anecdotes, strange journeys undertaken, unusual professions pursued – life lived in all its minor eccentricities – that have been the substance (some would jibe the *lack* of substance) of *Midweek*, more or less unchanged over the years. 'Nutters' they may not be exactly, yet even now, the guests on the programme tend to have human, rather than intellectual, tales to tell. 'And though I have operated,' adds Purves, 'a bit more at the perhaps showbizzy end of it, even there, there are moments that you're just pleased to have been able to share, to pass on. But yes, it's a bit party-ish, *Midweek*. It's four people stuck in a lift who might normally never have met – or wished to meet again in the case of Joan Rivers [and Darcus Howe].'

If *Start the Week* hardened up under Melvyn, then Libby's Wednesday equivalent has at least become 'drier' over the decades – in the sense that the regular 'birthday guest' (shorn when the programme was shortened at the end of the 1990s) was always historically serenaded with champagne, but the breakfast booze disappeared as ritual drinking ebbed more generally from the BBC working day. It may in part also have had something to do with a hilarious American TV documentary about Radio 4 filmed around this time that portrayed the network as fuelled by alcohol, in which (as I recall) the *Midweek* champagne featured prominently.

Libby has been in the chair since 1983, having previously

done a stint on the show (then hosted by Henry Kelly) as guest interviewer: 'I took it up because it fitted in very well with living in Suffolk and having small children who I could either bring up in carrycots or just leave for twenty-four hours.' In those days, besides the 'birthday guest', Nigel Forde's weekly 'instant poem' was a regular feature (see page 76). 'She's quite a big lady, so she's got a lot of presence' says Nigel, who later became a Radio 4 presenter himself.

> I learned a lot about interviewing from the way she interviewed. Most of all that actually the only way to interview people is to *listen*: you ask the first question and listen, and lead it cleverly on to the next point – you serve, they reply and you serve back again. I learned that from Libby.

Most weeks, the show doesn't aim for the sort of sharp exchanges that, with the exception of *Desert Island Discs*, characterise the other nine o'clockers, and 'anodyne', 'amiable' and 'chummy' are among the kinder epithets applied to *Midweek* over the years. In fact, Purves is quite open about it:

> *Midweek* has sort of grown up to be the way it is because I don't mind who they bring on, what's mixed with what. So somebody is deaf and lip-reads? Fine. So somebody's fourteen years old? Fine. So somebody hasn't got English as a first language? Fine. So somebody's well known to be 'tricky'? Fine, I'll give it a go. And also I do feel in a way that people sometimes listen in a spirit of 'get out of that one!' You know, they don't necessarily want it to be all beautiful and smooth like *Woman's Hour*. People are very well behaved on the whole, but I don't mind if things begin to go a bit off-beam.

And how! There have been a few rows on *Midweek* over the years, for many of the same reasons that they occur on its Monday morning sister programme, but the bitchery-factor tends to be lower, perhaps because the guest-list is more wide-ranging. Not so, though, on the edition of October the 19th

Instant stanzas – Midweek's *odd odes*

> A Green-room, at the best of times,
> Is a strange sort of place to be:
> It has a perplexing, no-man's-landish
> Ambiguity.
> Especially at eight thirty-two
> In the bowels of the BBC.

One of *Midweek*'s most enjoyable and loved features in its 'middle-period' were the 'instant poems' dreamed up within the 53 minutes between Libby Purves's welcome and the closing stages of the transmission, during which the odd ode would be recited. The man responsible for all *Midweek*'s verse was a clever young actor who lived in York, and who subsequently made a name for himself as presenter of the Radio 4 literary programme *Bookshelf*. His name: Nigel Forde. 'Victor Lewis-Smith was producing *Midweek*, and he knew I wrote poetry from time to time, so he got me on the programme to write a spoof Betjeman poem about a book somebody had written about "young fogeys".'

It was called 'Sir John Laments his Influence' and began

> Far beyond the brackish suburbs
> Gothic mansions stand alone,
> Where Young Fogeys chide and chunter;
> Not quite Aesthete, not quite Sloane.

This is neat Betjemanesque burlesque, wrought by a man who knows and loves the original. Lewis-Smith was delighted. 'When I'd

2005. 'A furious row' reported BBC News, 'between US comic Joan Rivers and broadcaster Darcus Howe erupted over the issue of race on Radio 4's *Midweek* programme.' The *Daily Telegraph* called it 'the funniest thing broadcast on the radio since *Round the Horne*' and it made headlines throughout the world.

written it, and he liked it, he said, "Perhaps we should do something at the end as well."' Nigel pondered a moment and then said, 'I might be able to do one during the show about what's going on. If you don't mind it failing miserably!'

So 'week after week, Nigel arrived, quiet and dark and smiling,' recalls Libby Purves in her Foreword to a collected edition of *Midweek* verse, 'with a neatly typed poem on a set theme to read at the beginning, and a scruffy little black notebook in which to write his "instant poem" on the week's guests.' Nigel's not a histrionic performer; he just goes somewhere quiet, ponders over a cigarette, and sorts things out. However, that first instant poem was inevitably a bit of a challenge for him, and didn't turn out quite as he'd anticipated:

> What I didn't expect was Anthony Burgess! Who was probably at the time one of the greatest intellects in the country. I think he'd just done a film and a book about St Paul [*The Kingdom of the Wicked*], but of course he talked about all sorts of other things as well, including music . . .

> Anthony Burgess's learning
> And Klangfarbenmelodie
> Can stretch from St Paul to Napoleon via
> Steatopygous Enderby.
> But have you heard Burgess's music?
> Or Bruckner's poetry?
> They're going to be done at the Proms this year
> With the Shakespeare Mass in C . . .
>
> ☞

The veteran American stand-up claimed that she had been called a racist by fellow guest, the Trinidadian-born writer and broadcaster Darcus Howe. Howe had begun to respond to a remark by Rivers, saying, 'Since black offends Joan . . .' when: 'Wait! Just stop right now,' interjected Rivers, 'black does not offend me. How dare you, how dare you say that. Black offends

It was quite terrifying sitting next to him [on] my first outing. And he was very complimentary, so that gave me a buzz, and it seemed to be OK, and people chuckled. And I was invited back, and I was invited back . . .

'He described his domestic poems once as "Giles cartoons in verse",' Libby continues in her Foreword, 'and there is something of vintage Giles about them: a sort of broad comedy founded on understanding, with a good eye for the small frustrations of life.'

Wish You Were Here

Oh, an English beach on a summer's day
Is a glorious place to be;
Where lovers lie glued – and practically nude –
And grandfathers chain-drink tea,
And maiden ladies surrender themselves
To the rough, male kiss of the sea.

I was intrigued to know whether inspiration had ever deserted Nigel on air. After all, what he was doing was like the ultimate in Christmas party pencil-and-paper games, played against the clock and with two million people waiting for you to fall over. Oh yes, and all the while he had to make it funny and sly and ironic at the same time.

me? You know nothing about me, you sat down here. How dare you!' The row intensified, with insults flying and both sides up for a real fight. In the midst of the battle, Libby Purves sought valiantly to maintain a sense of balance and fairness, while still keeping the programme on the air.

'Well,' I thought, 'let's let them go at it for a bit and then I will sort of shut them up.' I very much felt 'I am not their nanny. These are grown-up people; they're in a radio studio; they've got as much right to be angry or upset as anybody has. You know, let's clear the air here.'

Actually it's a bit like tightrope walking or juggling; I mean people listen hoping you're going to fall. And I did once. There was a whisky expert on who collected miniatures, and already I wasn't feeling particularly well that morning, and he produced all these whiskies which we had to taste, and I just didn't get through the poem, I'm afraid.

On one occasion Robert Maxwell, the subsequently disgraced owner of Mirror Group newspapers, was a guest alongside Nigel in the *Midweek* studio, and that morning a deal of suggestive writing went into the verse.

Mostly, I was complimentary – it's not my job to be rude to people. But occasionally when you've got people like Maxwell, or people that are hate figures for a lot of people, or at least slightly disturbing, then, it's like being an interviewer: you've got to ask the right questions; so you have to make the right comments. I was slightly sly about Michael Heseltine but he took it all in good part! But it takes quite a bit to be witty at nine in the morning I've discovered!

Extracts taken from *Fluffy Dice and other* Midweek *verse* by Nigel Forde.

Another guest on the show was a woman whom Libby was about to interview about photographing plants, so she tried to bring her into the conversation, which led in turn to a brand new coinage for the English language: 'I've since heard it's become the saying when somebody's having a hissy-fit backstage: "Shall we talk about plant photography, now?" So another little contribution from Radio 4 to the wider world!'

Backstage, too, there have been rows. The mordant television critic Victor Lewis-Smith, who also made a name for himself in radio comedy, was a maverick and sometimes brilliant producer on the morning conversation programmes; he it was who

famously booked the gruff Cockney comedian-actor Arthur
Mullard to deputise for Libby on *Midweek* for one edition. The
result: another legendary edition that left the audience in howls
of not-quite-intended laughter as Mullard squared up to the
philosopher Professor A.J. Ayer for an interview. Libby says
she's very fond of Lewis-Smith, though he has savaged her
mercilessly on occasion in the press, and their differences on one
occasion became physical:

> I did throw a chair at him, once. It was a very small chair and it
> didn't hit him. A small, harmless chair. But you see there's so little
> of that in Radio 4. There really is very little furniture-throwing
> and plate-smashing. I think there should be more!

Plum-picking

It was just the sort of incident that, if caught on microphone, the
Pick of the Week programme would have featured in its heyday.
Indeed *Midweek* has always been a regular source of human
stories and eccentrics for Radio 4's broadcasting digest (the
Arthur Mullard incident I seem to remember was one);
Margaret Howard, for many years its dominant presence, was
very partial to a bit of eccentric radio. Of course, it's never been
broadcast at nine in the morning, and so is only slipped in here
for convenience, but it's one of those shows that's been part of
the Radio 4 landscape for so long that I can hardly leave it out.

Back in the earliest days of the network, *Pick of the Week* was
voiced by a silky-toned presenter who cropped up all over the
airwaves then, the beautifully enunciating John Ellison, whose
job it was simply to read the script. The picking and the writing
was done by a former BBC comedy script editor Gale Pedrick.
When Pedrick died, the programme's future was questioned:
Tony Whitby asked one of his senior managers to report,
though a Radio Review Board minute in April 1970 clearly
shows he himself was keen on its role as a shop-window for
radio. Its uncomplicated ingredients – chunks of programmes

that make you laugh, make you cry or make you think – have always been the show's selling point. It was also pretty dependable: most of the items on 'Pickers' (as we knew it) would be good, sometimes brilliant. It was in many ways not just a shop-window for Radio 4, but for the BBC as a whole: TV producers, who might otherwise have been just a bit sniffy, would almost gasp with delight down the phone when informed that their show was being *Pick*ed.

I think it's true to say that today's version has neither the status nor the allure it acquired under Margaret Howard. Margaret had been a hard news journalist, cutting her broadcasting teeth on William Hardcastle's *World at One* (see Chapter Six). As a presenter, she had a beautifully modulated voice with a hint of a vocal smile – 'a tone of closet omnipotence' one journalist called it.

Technology has today completely transformed the way the show is made, but for me *POTW* will always conjure an image of Margaret carefully noting cues and details on a pad, one sheet for her, a carbon copy for the producer. Back in the 1980s, programmes would be fetched from the library on big ten-inch reels of tape and listened to intently in the office. Then, on a Wednesday, the reckoning would come – a mysterious process half of which was inaudible as it was going on in Margaret's mind. The sheets of cues would be separated out from the notepad and sorted into an order from which Margaret could assemble her script. 'Silk purses, silk purses!' she'd say in response to compliments, or perhaps, with a wry grin, 'Just *Pick of the* Cheap' when she'd been thwarted by some ghastly budget-busting copyright fee.

Although sometimes the connections between items were a little forced, the discipline and sheer journalistic sense that Margaret brought to the programme meant that it was almost always a good entertaining listen, something that today's largely producer-selected version doesn't always guarantee. For me, personally, *Pick of the Week* taught me how to appreciate the lure of the silly and the trivial, the power of popular television, as well as what made great theatrical performances truly remarkable; in fact, quite simply how to *listen*.

Meetings of minds

When the eighth controller, James Boyle, undertook his root-and-branch reshaping of Radio 4 in 1998, *Pick of the Week* lost its repeat and moved to a (less prominent) Sunday evening slot. Much more visibly, Melvyn Bragg left the *Start the Week* chair that he'd occupied for a decade, to be replaced by Jeremy Paxman. 'I'd had ten great years on *Start the Week*,' he told me, 'and I wasn't tired of it, but I got more and more interested in doing things at greater length.' There was also a little issue of editorial policy. Bragg had been made a life peer by Tony Blair in 1998 and took the Labour whip. It was felt that his impartiality on a programme that dealt with matters of the contemporary agenda might be compromised: 'Privately I disagreed, but I could see that they had a point.'

However, the result was the making of Melvyn's Radio 4 career. He was now offered his own original programme, a show that would allow him to deal with longer subjects and in depths unimagined by the first dreamers-up of these nine o'clock confections thirty years earlier. *In Our Time* would be a programme of ideas, uncompromising, tough and serious, with Melvyn as its everyman-guide. Some scoffed: it looked like schedule-suicide – wrongly it turned out.

> People took to it right away. Its appeal is that it's a very simple place to go, in the sense that only one thing happens on that programme – three academics talk about a subject to which they've devoted their professional lives. That's the deal – there isn't another deal. And even if people like me sometimes aren't able to follow the argument . . . speed of light, er, just a second! (and that's easy compared with some of the things we've gone into) . . . and it's fingernail time, I think people will still credit it with a place they can go to be nourished.

So much so that, with the advent of the downloadable-file version of the programme (or 'podcast'), *In Our Time* rocketed in the online charts, with tens of thousands of people copying the show to their MP3 players.

Stopping the rot

Melvyn Bragg's Thursday morning cerebral callisthenics mark the intellectual summit of the nine o'clockers in today's Radio 4. Once, however, that honour went to the show that was, in one sense at least, the week's literal conversation-stopper. *Stop the Week* was a conversation geyser, an *un*stoppable gusher that each week only faded slowly as the tinky-tonky closing sig tune floated in over the top.

The *Stop the Week*ers were like a bunch of regulars in a pub, meeting to chew the fat over a pint every Saturday night after the six o'clock news. Not that the host, affable, genial Robert Robinson, was the sort of person who'd gather his chums in the public bar. The *Stop the Week* repertory company (rudely dubbed, you'll remember, the 'wankers') would, one felt, meet in much more salubrious surroundings – Soho's Colony Club perhaps, or, latterly, the Groucho. 'It *was* a club conversation,' says Laurie Taylor, 'and it was in a way, to an extent, an overheard conversation; yes, it was a club.'

And their tipple? Champagne – bottles of the stuff, all round. Sue MacGregor, who once deputised for Robert Robinson on the show ('I was absolutely hopeless: I didn't have that sort of wry gravitas you have to have'), recalls it was 'certainly fuelled by booze: there were bottles of pop opened before it [but] I *never* drank when I was broadcasting – I would be under the table in a minute'. Others weren't so abstemious; it was 'only "BBC" champagne' recalls Laurie Taylor,

> but a tradition had developed that we were allowed to have champagne. Goodness knows how on earth it had ever been negotiated, but I can imagine some producer saying, 'We want effervescent conversation, so therefore we must have effervescent . . .' whatever. If there was one bottle left over it could be taken home – but there was very, very rarely one bottle left over.

There was something, too, of the style of lunches at the Algonquin, with regulars at the round table alongside Taylor – Dr Michael O'Donnell, Dr Edward (lateral thinking) de Bono, or Milton Shulman (drama critic of the London *Evening Standard* newspaper) – while the other chair was filled by various 'visiting' regulars like Professor Anthony Clare (later host of the hugely successful *In the Psychiatrist's Chair*), the jazz critic and broadcaster Benny Green, and journalist (and rare female regular) Ann Leslie. And if the conversation had some of the wit of Dorothy Parker, it also had some of the sharp cattiness of the *New Yorker* set. Professor Laurie Taylor 'of York University' (as he was then) remembers just how bitchy the men could be:

> It was male. Very, very male. I mean we were horrible . . . We played 'hunt the guests', really. So if a new guest came on who might be suddenly witty and clever, we had to put them down. Sometimes consciously, sometimes not quite so consciously. I remember we had another new woman on, from advertising – extremely well dressed, power suit, shoulders and everything. Bob walked across as he always did and said: 'Robert Robinson, pleased to meet you', and shook her hand (he was always very formal; very good at making guests feel at ease). Anyway, he said, 'What do you do?' 'Oh,' She said, 'Um, well.' She said, 'Um, I organise events.' And Bob said, 'Oh, I thought that was God's job!' Ach!

Stop the Week was heralded by a signature tune performed by the band Instant Sunshine, happy amateurs Miles Kington, Dr Alan Maryon Davis, Peter Christie and David Barlow, who for many years also contributed the midway musical interlude (later featuring artists such as Fascinating Aida and Peter Skellern). The conversation, for all the erudition of the gathered company of media and academic types, tended to the quotidian, the demotic and the downright ordinary – though, as Laurie recalls, often in pursuit of a higher meaning.

> I mean one week it could be about cutting your nails in the bath. And people'd say, 'Well how banal to talk about that' – but

Robert Robinson and [producer] Michael Ember's philosophy was that very, very small matters could give rise to rather energetic, interesting conversations. You know, you start off with toenails in the bath and see where it takes you.

If the on-air architect of these weekly gab-fests was Bob Robinson, the power behind the microphone was the show's brilliant émigré Hungarian producer, Michael Ember. Ember's insistent phone call was a weekly ritual, usually catching Laurie in the middle of a sociology seminar:

So then I'd break off from Max Weber and the protestant ethic; and he'd say, 'So what is interesting this week?' I'd say, 'Well, I couldn't help noticing the decline of the Pakamac. Now Pakamac's gone out of business, no one's wearing Pakamacs any more.' I could see these students staring back at me, because a minute before we'd been discussing western capitalism and the protestant ethic – and now the decline of the Pakamac. I'd say, 'I think that's really interesting.' And he'd say: 'No, it's not *really* interesting, Laurie. It's *fairly* interesting.' And then of course eventually the programme would come on and we would manage to somehow spend fifteen minutes talking about the Pakamac.

In his *Memoirs*, Robert Robinson captures brilliantly that sense of the everyday-made-universal:

You had to stare hard until you recognised the subjects . . . We were in the pub once and Ann Leslie's voice rang round the saloon bar proudly announcing there wasn't an ironed sheet in the whole of Kentish Town, and a man drinking Foster's with a lump of ice-cream in it said wasn't Kentish Town where they spread the sheets out on the hedgerows? Milton Shulman said No, he must be thinking of Eaton Square where the peeresses pounding the laundry with stones were a colourful sight, and Laurie Taylor said sheets must always be ironed but the iron must never singe the silk. I began a short address on the subject of the ironing board as symbol of our fallen state and only then recognised laundry as one of the great topics.

Robert Robinson: un bourgeois gentilhomme

Robert Robinson is, in many people's minds, the epitome of Radio 4. For thousands of *Brain of Britain* listeners on the Indian sub-continent, I'm told, he's a hero, and for nearly all forty years of the network's existence, he's been dropping his witty and acerbic *mots* into the ears of middle England, from *Today* when he was recruited to offer a dash of piquancy to the gentler style of John Timpson, to his continuing incarnation at the start of his ninth decade, as the amiable chair of *Brain of Britain* ('a proper grown-up quiz', says Richard Edis, still producing the show in his retirement).

Brian *of Britain*, as Bob (and Richard) always calls it, has been Robinson's since he succeeded Franklin Engelmann after the 1972 series, during which Engelmann died. Although the programme stayed much the same, the tone shifted: where Engelmann was slightly stiff and schoolmasterly, Bob Robinson always has a conspiratorial touch with his contestants, cheering on the no-hopers, exacting precision from brainboxes and always in league with 'Mycroft', his silent adviser and adjudicator on the quiz, until his death in 2002, Ian Gillies. 'Bob is probably the last of the great gentleman-broadcasters now that Raymond Baxter's gone,' observes Edis:

> He speaks properly, dare I say that? It's accentless. Although occasionally you can hear the south London grammar school, he's a Scouser, he's a Liverpudlian: his dad worked for Lord Lever.

Notice, here, the frame of reference, as it unlocks exactly the essential appeal of *Stop the Rot* (as the show was nicknamed). Aspects of class, class behaviour and the British obsession with class were central to the debate: the regulars were a metropolitan band of middle-class intellectuals, making slightly nudge-nudge comments about other social strata. Yet, embedded within the quotation are exactly the seeds of *Stop the Week*'s demise. The implicit snobbery, the endlessly self-referencing London scene

From the other side of the *Stop the Week* table, sociologist and long-time friend Laurie Taylor compiled this thumbnail sketch:

> Robert Robinson is a very intelligent man who had a very wry sense of the media, who found the media still slightly absurd. He was President of the Johnson Society, and he was very delighted to be associated with Johnson as he had a good sort of rumbustious delight in language and in the power of language. But as a lower middle-class person, he had a very, very, very good eye for pretensions.

You can sense that love of language and unquenchable articulacy in this description, from Robert Robinson's *Memoirs*, of the relish he felt on his first early-morning journey to the *Today* studio, in July 1971.

> As I drove out into the dark roads that lay between Chelsea and Portland Place round about ten to five that first morning I felt a bit peculiar. People were still in bed, and they'd be deep in their own domestic otherness when I pulled the cosies off the microphones and started doing it to them. I'd be sneaking in between the lavatory paper and the shaving foam and pushing my mouth up against the ear of strangers.

'I think Bob has a voice that is instantly recognisable,' says Richard Edis, 'and if you look at something he's written, he has one of those prose styles, in that when you read something that he's written you

☞

and the waspish in-jokes at others' expense in the end became unsustainable.

Rituals have a habit of becoming all rite and no substance, and in the series' later years there was undoubtedly a sense of the routine, of too many forced connections between, as it were, Pakamac and politics. By 1992, even with the attendant bubbly, the conversation had gone a bit, well, flat. The programme's run had embraced two major conflicts for Britain, in the Falklands

can absolutely hear his voice in your head.' I think it's a sort of lofty demoticism – a voice that knows quality but has lived ordinary, as Sir John Betjeman did in a slightly earlier age. However, some at the BBC found his style in the early days on *Today* 'so elaborate as to suggest that he was trying to display his ability', while 'mannered' was a word used by others.

In many ways, the Robinson voice is characteristically that of the educated middle classes who make up quite a substantial chunk of Radio 4 listeners. 'Middle-class was to him *not* a term of abuse,' agrees Laurie Taylor, 'he was also very proud of the idea of being middle-class. And Radio 4 listeners . . . he was a spokesperson for them. In a way he ratified their concerns. He legitimised some of their grievances or their irritations or their *petty* irritations.'

Robinson wrote grouchily in his *Memoirs*, remembering an early-morning irritation:

> I sat in the *Today* studio listening to a fatheaded MP assuring me from unfathomable wells of sincerity that it was every citizen's duty to round up stray dogs – 'But how,' I cried wildly, 'how do we distinguish the stray from the unstray? Do we lasso them? Is it done with butterfly nets?'

and the Gulf, and Mrs Thatcher had been gone from Number 10 over eighteen months. Radio 4's sound had evolved *around Stop the Week*; feminism had matured and the club-luminaries began to sound like club-bores.

And so, on Saturday July the 25th, for the last time on Radio 4, the *Punch*-cartoon sound of men in armchairs animatedly talking over one another burbled into oblivion as the theme music rose to quench the chat: 'It was a way of saying this lot are going to go on afterwards for hours!' remarks Taylor. And the continuity announcer closed the show with the time-honoured formula 'Stopping the Week with Robert Robinson were . . .' 'a little group of people who went out to the pub afterwards and drank an enormous amount of whisky and continued the conversations', in Laurie's description.

Today I suppose it's *Grumpy Old Men* on the telly that ventilates some of that spleen on behalf of the audience, but Bob Robinson's middle-classness is of an older, slightly more hard-won variety. Richard Edis is full of admiration:

> Bob is not politically correct, because he's white, male, middle-class, well educated, Oxford, and he speaks properly in proper sentences. All the subordinate clauses are in the right order, all the commas are in the right place; and certainly the reason he was such a hit on the Indian subcontinent was because they learned how to speak English properly.

And Laurie Taylor recalls a *Stop the Week* recording that must have been made some twenty or so years ago now, when a speaker on the show was 'slightly more radical' than usual . . .

> And the new guest, the new, radical, thrusting guest, said: 'Bob, I've got to say something to you. That's very, very middle-class, what you've just said!' And Bob said, 'Oh, is it? Oh, good!' And I thought that epitomised him, you know.

Which is what in fact, they did; though not at the pub. The last edition was bidden farewell with a party held, more suitably, at the Garrick Club.

CHAPTER FOUR

10.00 am: Progress and protest: Woman's Hour *and change*

Listening to the daily flow of Radio 4 today, I'm struck by a sense of metronomic regularity and smoothness. Just as the hands on a grandfather clock imperceptibly creep forward infinitesimally at each pendulum-swing, each clunk of the cog, so the news stories of the day creep forward through the regular tick-tock of the hourly news bulletins on the network. Once *Today* has launched us forth towards the beginning of the morning proper, the hourly two-minute summaries inch the stories forward – a reaction here, a rebuttal there – through to the next big staging post, *The World at One*. Things were rather different, however, before controller James Boyle's 1998 root-and-branch schedule change, which brought in the regular hourly bulletins. Back in 1967, there was a positive desert, in fact, of four hours between the 9.00 am bulletin and *The World at One*, and a gap of four more until the 6.00 pm *News and Radio Newsreel*. On the other hand, though, there just wasn't so much news then to hear about; not because it didn't happen, of course, but because it didn't have a chance to be reported. It was, in that pre-digital, virtually pre-satellite era, a slower world.

This chapter, then, is about transitions, and, inevitably, it's also about change – and there are few bigger Radio 4 changes that still rankle (at least amongst the production team) more than a decade and a half after they happened than the move in 1991 of *Woman's Hour* from its long-held spot at the top of the afternoon to a mid-morning slot. Of which more anon.

But long, long ago when Radio 4 was born, and long before two minutes past ten meant Jenni Murray's warm greeting, there was no marker worth speaking of that the hour had ticked by – because at that particular moment, listeners would have been bang in the middle of *Music and Movement* with Rachel Percival (or was that *Movement and Music* with James Dodding?), or any one of a myriad fairly joyless Schools programmes that clogged up the morning (and afternoon) of the network. And having Schools camped fairly and squarely across radio's primetime was clearly an irritation to Tony Whitby and a millstone for the network. Memo after memo reveals his focus on listener numbers and his desire to increase them:

> We have lost our Sunday evening audiences. We used to average 0.9% between 1900–2200. We now get 0.3% . . . Clearly our current music policy is not paying off . . .

He was full of plans to tweak timings and placings, but there was little that could be done about these great expanses of weekdays, except in school holidays when he could build a proper grown-up schedule. A revealing and surprisingly outspoken memo from Whitby's deputy and chief scheduler, Clare Lawson-Dick from September 1973 underlines the growing frustration. 'Schools have actually managed,' she writes, 'to increase their time by eight hours . . .' And, it seems, they weren't using their allotted space wisely, requiring endless fillers: 'Schools have never fully occupied the times but operate within them in a way which is most wasteful of air time for the general listener . . . These problems would, of course, be solved by an Educational Broadcasting wavelength . . .' In a telling last plea, Lawson-Dick, speaking no doubt with Whitby's full authority, adds 'the time the Radio 4 Planners would most like to regain for the general listener is 0905–1015, where we have recently gained audiences . . . during Schools holidays.' Commercial radio would be a reality by October 1973 and for the moment all Tony Whitby had to fight it with in radio's primetime was *Music and Movement*.

So, although the modern Radio 4 morning had broken at 9.00 am with shows like *Start the Week*, the coffee-time-to-lunch shape that we know today was a long way off yet. It wouldn't begin to be a possibility until Schools broadcasts were removed from the mainstream output (and placed initially on the FM

'A thing most wonderful': Religion on Radio 4

There can be few places, beyond the evangelical TV channels that pump out messages of faith across America, that have the audience that God has daily on Radio 4. This is not to be disrespectful you understand, but in our largely secular Britain the place that religion holds – and indeed holds on to tenaciously – in the primetime listening of perhaps the most influential 10 per cent of people in the UK, is remarkable.

Thus every weekday and Saturday, amid turbulent reports from Westminster and West Africa, three minutes of thoughtful reflection on a religious theme take centre-stage on Radio 4, a delicate wooden ship gingerly picking its path between mighty ice-floes. And in many ways *Thought for the Day*, for this is what I refer to, is an anomaly. Often decried by media journalists who would do away with Lionel Blue, Angela Tilby, Christina Odone, Elaine Storkey, Indarjit Singh, Jonathan Sacks, Tom Butler, Akhandadhi Das and the others, *Thought for the Day* hangs in there, a remnant from an age when we were far more religious – or at least when the BBC liked to think we were. So *Thought for the Day* with its often deeply resonant message reaches out to the audience, short enough for all but the determinedly anti-religious to stomach (or at least to boil a noisy kettle for the duration), long enough to keep the faithful happy until *The Daily Service* rolls along at ten o'clock.

option from September the 17th 1973). Even then, *Woman's Hour* would remain an after-lunch pleasure until the great battle that resulted in the changes of September 1991.

Afternoon delight

The show was in 1967 a Light Programme fixture, and very content where it had been since its inception in 1946. Already a venerable twenty-one-year-old, *Woman's Hour* could be rather

The Daily Service . . . I mentioned anomalies just now, but *The Daily Service*, which is eighty years old on January the 2nd 2008, is far more than an anomaly, it's an antiquity. From time to time the Radio 4 demolition team have come in, had a look, and then gone away again. It's had its face lifted – most famously when those twenty-eight men and women of the BBC Singers, who used to turn up religiously three mornings a week to intone hymns like 'It is a thing most wonderful' (number 81 in the BBC Hymn Book), were dropped from the service.

And, of course, it's moved around a bit. Back in 1967, the service appeared at 10.15; today it's a quarter to ten, and when Michael Green was in charge it appeared at the top of the hour. Listening to the service now, although it no longer has the Singers' warble (I'm afraid they always set my teeth on edge, reminding me a little of that famous 1960s Mastersingers record of the Highway Code intoned as Anglican plainchant), it's amazing how unchanged it is from the earliest days: hymn, psalm, reading and prayer. Perhaps it's even more surprising, given that in 1992, a critical report into the BBC's activities described *The Daily Service* as 'anachronistic', and recommended that the corporation open its doors to new religious movements and to 'multi-faith Britain' and non-Christian festivals.

Leafing through yellowing copies of *Radio Times* for summer 1967, I'm struck overwhelmingly by how *Christian* the whole of Radio 4 was forty years ago. A relic of Lord Reith's own principled position on

☞

staid, with a motley and rather general-magaziney menu. The presenter was Marjorie Anderson, by this time a legendary figure amongst the BBC's radio stars. Hers was a delicious (if distinctly posh) on-air voice; a warm microphone style has characterised all three – yes, only *three* – presenters *Woman's Hour* has had in forty years. Jenni Murray was at a programme party (she was then hosting the regular Bristol edition) when she met for the first time the woman whose words she'd hung on as a very young listener:

ethics and observance (the original Broadcasting House boasted a religious programmes studio that was got up like a small chapel), the Saturday schedule had religious observance at *Ten to Seven*; *Outlook* ('a Christian angle on the news') at 7.50; *The Daily Service* at 10.15; *Choral Evensong* at four in the afternoon; and finally twenty minutes of *Lighten Our Darkness* before bedtime.

Then again, I suppose only on Radio 4 could a regular religious spot actually become a best-selling hit, although when you're broadcasting to several million people, there's always the chance that you'll strike lucky. Back in 1970, in the early days of Tony Whitby's new schedule, the star of *Ten to Eight* (not yet actually part of *Today*) was the actor Bernard Miles. Miles made a second career from his jovial renderings of the Gospels, and the minutes of Radio Review Board capture the spirit of his success: a commercial book of them was about to be published, 'and Decca was issuing a record. There was no doubt at all that the readings made a big impact,' said the Head of Religious Broadcasting (Radio), 'whether pleasing or infuriating.'

For all Bernard Miles's popularising on weekdays, Sundays were

I remember just going, 'Oh my goodness! That is Marjorie Anderson!' and started sidling over and saying, 'Hello, I'm such a fan of yours', you know. And she said, 'Oh, you silly girl! You do exactly the same now. What are you making all the fuss about!' Quite right!

Alongside Anderson, another veteran of *Woman's Hour*'s first decade was Monica Sims. She'd produced it in the 1950s, returned as editor in the early sixties, and stayed pretty well until the birth of the new networks. Didn't it feel, I wondered, a bit of an anomaly while it was on Radio 2, the channel, after all, of *Music While You Work* and Jack Jackson's *Record Rendezvous*?

It was the only speech programme surrounded by music, and we really felt pioneers. We felt we are reaching the part of the audience that the others don't reach because they wouldn't

devoutly devotional: a typical 1967 example offered a reading from Benjamin Jowett's celebrated Sermons, plus *The Chapel in the Valley* ('hymns and sacred music introduced by Sandy Macpherson'). Next came a break from prayer for *The Archers* (where at the time they were rather more preoccupied with contemporary issues like Jennifer's illegitimate baby – see Chapter Nine), but we were back in the pew at 10.30 for forty-five minutes' worth of *Morning Service* (still, of course, a Radio 4 fixture, though now squeezed in after the 8.00 am news). This particular evening there was a religious special too, in *Let's Ask the Archbishop*, Michael Ramsay was quizzed by sixth-formers from Shrewsbury. At close of day, of course, there was another long-running devotional fixture: the *Epilogue*. None of it was much fun: formal, dull and still shrouded in the gloomily serious wraith of Reith.

Yet as Tony Whitby began to roll out the second phase of his new-look network with the *Sunday* programme, presented by Paul Barnes, the Tony Hancock-like feeling of gloom about the first day of the week began to lift, and a new age in religious broadcasting began.

normally listen to a serious speech programme that dealt with really quite weighty subjects sometimes.

Like folk music from Hungary, the Bishop of Ripon discussing his new book about the Vatican with Mary Stocks, aspects of 'the modern young', or 'Knocking About – Anne Suter confesses she's a blunderer'. Not a particularly Radio 2-sounding line-up, actually. But here's a thing. When these items were broadcast during summer 1967, *Woman's Hour* had actually temporarily migrated. While Schools were on their long summer break, the show had taken itself off to the Home Service, where, in its habitual 2.00 pm slot, it would stay until classrooms were filled once more. It was, if further proof were needed, clear evidence of the identity problems that the networks were facing at the time and which wouldn't be addressed, as we saw in Interlude 2, until the advent of *Broadcasting in the Seventies*.

There were too in the programme menus of four decades ago

an awful lot of men, with little trace of what was still then called 'women's lib'; and, with every item billed in *Radio Times* weeks ahead, there was little opportunity either to respond to events. A stiff post-war formality reigned. Before she took over from Marjorie Anderson in 1972, Sue MacGregor had been working as a current affairs reporter on *The World at One* under William Hardcastle.

> I think up to the point that I joined, the presenter of *Woman's Hour* always used the questions as they were written down for her by a producer. And this was *anathema* to anyone who'd come from news. It used to be heavily rehearsed – and that meant that the editor listened to the rehearsal in her office at 11.00 am and then sent down, probably on flimsy memo sheets, her instructions.

Jenni Murray, for all her young-fan enthusiasm for the Marjorie Anderson era, recognises that the programme was much less journalistic before Sue took over.

> There was never a sense in the early days that the presenter was anything other than someone who read scripts, and actually read the questions that she was given as well. You know the producers really did control things and so it was much more formal.

Perhaps most surprising of all to me is the number of men involved in making the show: for instance, Vivian Ogilvie (a well known – male – broadcaster of the day) is the commentator on youth culture, Stuart Burge is John Arden's interviewer about his new plays, while it's Barry Chambers who's been gathering interviews for an item on juvenile delinquency. 'There were quite a few chaps who reported regularly for *Woman's Hour*,' recalls Sue MacGregor, 'and there was always a male producer.' Of course, I'm being selective here, and there are many items about and by women (probably at least 60 per cent). New professional roles for women are featured, and prominently, but this is not yet the programme fully reflecting the social and sexual revolution for women that had begun with the development of the contraceptive pill at the start of the decade.

In fact, what price this item from the week before the big network switch (with kids back at school and *Woman's Hour* now safely returned to the not-long-to-be Light Programme)?: '*Not Quite Lady-like?*: Donald Norfolk objects to a lingering prejudice against women taking part in sport or games . . .' Sue MacGregor, *Woman's Hour*'s presenter from 1972 to 1987 recalls:

> There was equal pay legislation [that] went through in the mid-70s, and the equal opportunities legislation. And women were very aware of their – with a capital 'R' – Rights. And there was also the Women's Liberation Movement that had come over from America. [So] I think it was quite a difficult balancing act for the editor to achieve. Because half her listeners were people who were utterly happy to be homebodies and the other half were perhaps younger women who were at home only because they had a young family and were longing to get back into jobs and to take on things that women weren't traditionally doing.

Family ties

Woman's Hour has, as long as I can recall, been a special place within Radio 4, not just for listeners, but for production teams as well. 'It's a very intimate sort of programme,' according to Jenni Murray, 'and you feel when you're broadcasting that you're broadcasting to a group of people who know where they're at and what they're looking for.'

> And they feel that they're belonging almost to a sort of club. It's a pretty big club these days and 40 per cent of them are men, which is great! So I think it creates a kind of intimacy and the presenter is part of that intimacy.

And Sue MacGregor agrees:

> You enter into their homes in a way that people don't on

Olive Shapley: a pioneering voice

Back in the early days of Radio 4, a woman called Olive Shapley was one of *Woman's Hour*'s regular presenters from 'the outer edge of the wheel' in Leeds: so here she is in 1967 presenting items from Yorkshire featuring Fanny Waterman (founder of the Leeds International Piano Competition) and – very contemporary – a Sikh wedding. Another item, likewise typically socially aware, is about 'the pleasures and difficulties of adopting a backward child'. This was not surprising perhaps, because Olive, although associated with *Woman's Hour* for twenty years, had another still richer professional life beyond the programme. It was a life, as producer rather than presenter, dedicated to celebrating and exploring how 'ordinary people' lived; and Shapley's is still, amongst the BBC's documentary makers, a legendary name.

Olive joined the BBC in 1934 with a degree from Oxford, having developed a strong social conscience and firmly left-wing views (she was a great friend of Barbara Castle), and went to work in Manchester with another of the corporation's documentary

television. It's a more companionable medium, radio, a more friendly medium than television.

That closeness, I think, was for a long while also character-istic of the teams that worked on the production of the show. Many in the 1970s, for example, had been with the programme for a number of years and had a fierce loyalty to the ideals it enshrined. Sue MacGregor calls it 'the era of the still formidable *Woman's Hour* career producer'. Jocelyn Ryder-Smith was one such, and Teresa McGonagle another; Pat McLoughlin, Pat Taylor and Anne Howells were legendary producers even in my day, and serious and dapper Wyn Knowles and the jollier Sandra Chalmers were among the great editors of that earlier generation. Later, that mantle was taken on above all by the brilliant Sally Feldman.

The other side of such close-knittedness and loyalty is a

pioneers, D.G. Bridson. Together they brought the voices of working men and women to the microphone in an era when announcers really did wear formal dress and so also, metaphorically, did the majority of voices on air. In doing so, they founded a documentary tradition that flourished in Manchester for nearly sixty years until the late 1990s. Programmes on the life of bargees and miners' wives and long-distance lorry drivers and below stairs in a big hotel (not to mention *Homeless People* about rough sleepers) flowed from Shapley's fertile mind.

But it was her association with radical theatre director and writer Joan Littlewood that in 1939 produced Olive's most famous work, *The Classic Soil*, an unashamedly partisan programme, scripted by Littlewood, about the harshness of working people's lives in Manchester since the days of Friedrich Engels. Tireless in her quest to reveal the realities of tough lives, Olive herself suffered greatly with depression and lost two husbands to illness in the course of her long life of nearly nine decades.

Olive Shapley died in 1999.

passionate solidarity in the face of adversity when change – or the threat of change – looms. The ping-ponging between the networks that *Woman's Hour* experienced in the summer of 1967 was something of a harbinger of the coming tectonic shifts. Additionally, *Home for the Day*, the 'best-of' digest of the week's programmes, was already a fixture on Radio 4 and was rebranded in Tony Whitby's revolutionary April schedule of 1970 as *Weekend Woman's Hour*. Now too the items, though still formally billed in *Radio Times* and rather worthy (family budgets in Belgium . . . divorce and maintenance . . . welfare for the blind . . .), are at least all by women and aimed at women. It would, however, take two more years of negotiations finally to bring the mother-ship to the network where, spiritually, it belonged.

By 1972, *Any Questions?* had long migrated from Radio 2 to Radio 4, and plans to move *Woman's Hour* were under way.

Yet the strength of feeling on the part of the production team about the impending shift is clearly expressed in this memo of August the 4th 1972 to the controller of Radios 1 and 2 from *Woman's Hour* editor, Wyn Knowles:

> While recognising the case for transfer, we feel that there is much to be said for our remaining on Radio 2. First of all, we know that our present audience is predominantly working class and that while many of these may switch over to Radio 4 in order to hear *Woman's Hour*, a sizeable number may not be in the habit of switching channels and will lose us . . .

But this skirmish was never going to be won – it was part of a much bigger game – and in 1973, *Woman's Hour* finally found its modern niche on Radio 4, though still of course in its habitual 2.00 pm spot (at the outset deliberately chosen to avoid times when housewives would be busy with chores). It was a defeat that rankled: 'We were all very upset when it went to Radio 4,' remembers Monica Sims – editor until 1967, though away from radio running children's television when the transfer eventually came. 'I think it says something for the resilience of the programme that it did continue to reach a lot of people who didn't listen to other speech programmes much.'

Wyn Knowles's other argument in her memo opposing the move – and possibly in the long run the more relevant one – was the risk of duplication and clashes for the show in its new berth: 'overlap,' she said, 'would be a big problem on Radio 4, whereas it is far less important at present'. Such clashes have been a perennial problem on Radio 4, with, in the worst cases (now largely banished by a clearing-house system), the same authors or films being featured on several programmes within the same week. At the heart of this issue is that, of course, no item, whatever its subject area or remit, is ruled out of court for *Woman's Hour*, and therefore on a network stacked high with specialist magazines – arts, science, medicine, money, language, history . . . you name it – clashes are inevitable. Despite the risks, however, Jenni Murray is positive that it's the programme's all-embracing remit that keeps it fizzing . . . and its long-serving presenters in clover:

> I honestly don't think in nineteen years I've had a single day when I've thought, 'Oh gosh this is boring! What am I doing here?' I love every morning; there are some items that I'm clearly more interested in than others: you know, I'm not a great knitter for instance and I detest sport of every description, even when women play it. But theatre, books, cookery, politics – where else do you get that range?

A slightly less glowing report of life on *Woman's Hour* comes from those who work on the programme far from its HQ in Broadcasting House. It's always been a feature of the programme to ensure that at least some of Radio 4's perennial astigmatism that causes London to bulk larger in broadcasters' minds than other corners of the UK is challenged by broadcasting one of the editions each week from a regional centre. So, as we've seen, Jenni Murray debuted on the programme from Bristol, and over the years there have been regular editions from Scotland, Wales and Northern Ireland. From Manchester in the early 1990s one of the voices anchoring the 'northern' edition was Helen Boaden, now amongst the corporation's most powerful executives as Director of News. Helen remembers how doing *Woman's Hour* beyond the warm embrace of Portland Place could be a rather lonely experience.

> You and the producer would wait for them to have their meeting down in London about what they thought of it. And then the phone would go and we'd Get The Feedback. That could be very daunting on occasion. I think now they use videophones and all that kind of stuff, but I think unless you've been on the outer edge of the wheel it's very hard to know how isolated you could feel, and slightly denigrated because of it.

Shocking stuff

Controversy and headline-making have been a regular plotline of the *Woman's Hour* story, not least on account of the extraordinary roster of first-women who have come through the bronze doors of Broadcasting House heading off to the *Woman's Hour* studio: from Eleanor Roosevelt and Nancy Astor to Lady Thatcher, Benazir Bhutto and Aung San Suu Kyi, not to mention in March 1999 one Monica Lewinsky. The buzz in Broadcasting House when Lewinsky was in the building I recall was electric – as it was the day when Hillary Clinton, and on another occasion Cherie Blair, sat in the guest chair on the show. Lewinsky was asked about the stains on the blue dress she'd worn during her intimate moments with Hillary's husband, with attendant headlines to match the next day. Likewise, when David Cameron and David Davis were in competition for the leadership of the Conservative Party, it was differing styles of underwear that each contender wore that not only captured the front pages and diary columns but provided an early indicator as to the men's respective fate in the ballot.

While most of the publicity *Woman's Hour* has garnered in its sixty years has been positive, just occasionally it's been caught out. In the early 1970s, when Sue MacGregor took over from Marjorie Anderson, she found a culture in place on the programme – still an afternoon fixture, remember – that was, shall we say, gastronomic . . .

> *Woman's Hour* had this famous lunch which was quite formal when I first joined, and the drinks trolley used to come rattling down the corridors in the basement of Broadcasting House. The editor-of-the-day would be given a key and in there would be bottles of gin and lots of bottles of wine.

And in those days, as we've already noted, drinking *before* a live transmission wasn't always entirely frowned upon. As Sue tells me:

I can remember one well-known woman writer used to get through several glasses of gin between one and two and perform wonderfully, live, immediately afterwards.

However, *Woman's Hour*, as did many other aspects of Radio 4, got its comeuppance in the mid-1980s, when the programme featured in the notorious American television documentary about Radio 4. 'Oh yes, they came and filmed *Woman's Hour*.' Sue MacGregor smiled wryly when reminded:

And we were all suckered into letting them . . . You can imagine what American producers made of a programme called *Woman's Hour* for starters, and then one that was quite cosy in its way then. And of course they edited it so that it sent the whole of Radio 4 up!

One controversial *Woman's Hour* moment, though, is little remembered, and yet perhaps illustrates the programme's very individual cohesion and team-strength, its growing desire to reflect contemporary issues and a burgeoning national climate of permissiveness. In November 1971, six years after the notorious television broadcast that made the theatre critic Kenneth Tynan a household name for having uttered the word 'fuck' uncensored and live, a huge row broke out at the use of the word 'fucking' on – of all programmes – *Woman's Hour*. 'Now even *Woman's Hour* has climbed on the BBC's permissive bandwagon,' reported Director of Programmes to Radio Review Board, quoting comments he'd received about the programme.

But how had the word come to be broadcast in the first place, without, it transpired, the controller knowing about it? Reading the documents now, it's a bit like witnessing a slow car crash; everything was done with the highest possible journalistic motives and with the very best of intentions; all of which, nonetheless, ended up as a wonderful cock-up.

The item discussed the use of bad language in certain underground newspapers that were then gaining popularity and notoriety. In the course of the discussion, an example of such language – the word 'fucking' – was quoted by one speaker. Immediately the customary debate ensued about whether The Word Could Go Out. Various heads and chiefs – and the whole *Woman's Hour* production team – were consulted: was the broadcasting of the word, in the circumstances, legitimate? They all agreed it was fine (well they would, wouldn't they?); and this was good enough for everyone, it seems – except for Douglas Muggeridge, controller Radio 2, on whose network the word was uttered and who had been informed only that the programme 'might be controversial'. 'Had he been consulted in advance,' Review Board reported, 'he would have ruled that the word be removed.' Muggeridge's opposite number at Radio 3, agreeing that such strong language should be 'referred up' to the controller as a matter of course, observed that 'in the cultural uncertainty in which broadcasters operated, they had to be extremely sensitive to the possibility of strong reaction by the audience'.

Like so many controversies that are inflamed by not always accurate press reports and righteous indignation in the comment columns, this row brewed slowly. It's clear from the minutes that the BBC at first felt the problem had been contained, and although, embarrassingly, senior managers in the corporation had been alerted to the matter only by newspaper reports, the number of phoned complaints, at twenty-four, seemed not to warrant a major enquiry.

It was only a week – and hundreds of letters and further comments – later that the internal inquest really sprang into life. Pages of the minutes are now filled with the debate, and, reading them, it's not hard to imagine the red faces and confusion occasioned by this unexpected lurch of 'old faithful' *Woman's Hour* into the controversial realm of Tynan's *Oh Calcutta!* (which had premiered in London a year previously). Managing Director of Radio Ian Trethowan now stressed that:

> there was no question of regarding *Woman's Hour* as permissive. In fact the programme had been critical of certain anarchic and destructive attitudes towards traditional Christian values which found expression in the underground press . . .

He was concerned that 'the press as a whole had presented a false and simplistic picture of a responsible programme going berserk'. He would set out on a mission to explain the situation at departmental meetings around Broadcasting House. Rather reassuringly, I think, in the age of Aquarius feathers seem not to have been further ruffled and this appears to have been an end of it.

Ah, such are the measures by which we judge an age, and *Woman's Hour* has always had to encompass radicalism and protest on the one hand – as the Women's Movement swelled to being a society-changing cultural shift – while, according to Jenni Murray, maintaining the same warmth of feeling towards those for whom home is where the heart is and who'd never ever dream of linking hands around a US airbase.

> I've been accused of running a feminist forum (not in a nice way: that was an insult) and of running a kind of aural WI. And that has been the two extremes of criticism of the programme as far back as 1946 when the programme started and it still happens now. I think that's because probably those of us who've done it are fairly typical women, and we have really radical interests and thoughts, but we also quite like to go home to the family, put the kids to bed and cook supper and maybe knit occasionally. What a lot of people seem to fail to recognise about women is that you can be the most radical feminist and still like looking after your kids.

An orderly succession

Jenni Murray joined Radio 4 from TV's *Newsnight* where she'd won her spurs as a formidable presenter in an era when the programme boasted not only Peter Snow but John Tusa and Olivia O'Leary amongst its talent line-up. However, the passage to *Woman's Hour* wasn't particularly straightforward and for a slightly surreal moment, both she and Sue MacGregor were presenting *Woman's Hour* as well as *Today*:

There was a curious period when I sort of filled in for Sue on the days that she wasn't on *Woman's Hour*, and I suppose at some point the then controller said, 'Look this is daft; why have we got the two main female voices on the station doing both programmes. Let's rationalise it.'

So in 1987, Sue MacGregor moved permanently to *Today* and Jenni took over her seat on *Woman's Hour*. There was a new arrangement at the top of the network too: David Hatch, who'd been running Radio 4 until 1986, suddenly found himself propelled unexpectedly upwards, a process that (in a strange concatenation of circumstances) was indirectly to change *Woman's Hour* for ever.

It started with one of those great BBC nights of the long knives, bloody removals of senior personnel that always make big headlines within the corporation but which rarely engage the listeners' attention for more than a second or two. The slaughter carried off the Managing Director of Radio, Richard Francis and his deputy, the Director of Programmes, Charles McLelland. Bearing the news was the Director General himself (likewise swept from power in another coup a year later) Alasdair Milne.

'I was sitting in the rugby club and I got a call from my secretary,' David Hatch told me. 'She said, "Alasdair wants to see you."' So at the appointed hour, Hatch duly knocked on the DG's door; Milne was in a hurry, and somewhat telegraphic with the news:

He said, 'We've had a Governors' meeting this morning, David. We've fired Dick Francis.' I said, 'Oh, fine.' 'And we've fired Charles McLelland.' I said, 'Oh, er . . .' 'And we want Brian Wenham to be the Managing Director of Radio.' 'Uh, OK.' 'And we'd like you to be the Director of Programmes, Radio.' 'Uh, I see.' 'With a seat on the Board.' He said, 'All right, boyo?' I said, 'Er, yeah . . .' I said, 'Could you just give me that again? Just slowly.' You know! I mean he'd said it, I promise you, in ninety seconds! And I remember phoning home and saying, 'There's been a bloodbath here . . .'

But in the life of a Radio 4 controller, the daily duties still go on:

> I was due to give the prizes at *Top of the Form* down at the 'Paris' [Light Entertainment studio], so I get in the car, and of course it's all over Radio 4 News. But I just go to *Top of the Form* and deliver the prizes. It was a very weird sort of day!

With the sudden updraught that sucked David Hatch into the deputy head of radio's seat inevitably came change at Radio 4. The new appointee was Michael Green and, like every new controller, he had a bagful of things he wanted to do, not least to *Woman's Hour*.

By 1990, three and a half years into Green's controllership, the programme had already achieved a much sharper journalistic edge than in the more genteel days of Marjorie Anderson. However, with a woman as Prime Minister who in many people's eyes was more resolute than most of the men in her cabinet, women's roles from the top of the British establishment down were undergoing radical reappraisal. To *Woman's Hour* too Jenni Murray, and her editor Sally Feldman, brought an edgier more engaged touch.

> Sue had taken it through the start of the Women's Movement and the really hard politics of that period and I really just took on her mantle, only – yes – I brought a lot of current affairs experience to it. There were some people who thought I might be too hard for the programme but I just loved it.

New faces, old wisdom

I shall always remember the first time I met Sally Feldman, one of the programme's most striking and original editors. We were standing in the queue for lunch and immediately she started to chat to me, bubbling over with conversation, engaged, recently arrived from the world of magazine publishing and bringing new zip to staid Radio 4. According to Jenni Murray she was:

> A really inspiring editor: always looked at things sideways, never went for the obvious, very funny, knew how to make things light as well as serious, had the most flamboyant clothing of anyone I've ever met and she still does! She was just great fun to work with, and I think was really instrumental in taking the programme through that period from the 80s into the 90s where we could have gone too far.

Another source of good advice was one of the programme's most respected and best-loved 'lifers': Pat McLoughlin, who looked after the *Woman's Hour* readings, the fifteen-minute serial that closes each day's programme. Today, it's a mini-drama, but while Pat was in charge it was a simple, elegant and unadorned reading. Pat was simply one of Radio 4's great figures, largely unsung outside the corridors of Broadcasting House, but who brought verve and a wonderful, funny energy to the place. You always knew when Pat was visiting a colleague from the explosions of laughter that would sail through the wall from a neighbouring office. Sue MacGregor says:

> She was very fierce with the actors, and I remember Janet Suzman, the South African actress (who's a friend of mine), when she was reading one of the Jane Austen novels, being told by Pat very fiercely, 'Janet, I can hear your South African vowels!' Now nobody had ever dared say that to Janet, but Pat McLoughlin did. And it was the only time I've ever heard Janet sounding utterly English. Actors all adored Pat actually, because she loved them.

Later, when Jenni had replaced Sue in the presenter's chair and many of the older producers had retired, it was Pat's wise counsel, born of long experience, that helped curb some of the programme's wilder instincts: 'We'd say, "Oh, let's do so-and-so," and Pat would say, "Tsk. Won't play well in Middle England!" A calm little voice would say, "Steady on, girls, grow up! Be sensible."' With Pat McLoughlin's untimely death from cancer at the age of 66 in 2000, one of the last links with an older, gentler shape of *Woman's Hour* was broken, but she, alongside Jenni Murray and editor Sally Feldman, had seen the programme through the biggest change in its lifetime, certainly as radical as its channel-hopping back in 1973, and in many ways more fundamental.

Moving the furniture

It was, when all's said and done, only a time-change. Doesn't really sound much when you put it like that. Just a little shift a few hours earlier – no big deal, surely? But, as the interviewees for this book have repeated many times, radio listeners have a very close relationship with the way the programmes unfold across the day, and dedicated Radio 4 listeners in particular not only know the daily broadcast schedule but actually *live* it. Take, for want of a better example, David Hatch's mother:

> She used to turn the radio on in the morning and turn it off when she went to bed; she called it 'chatterbox', and wherever she moved rooms, she'd take it with her – she listened to it *all day long*. And I tell you, there are loads of people who listen to Radio 4 probably eight, twelve hours a day. It's part of their life, they hear more of it than they hear of their husbands or their children so they think very highly of it.

'For lots of people, it's a companion like no other; I mean it is a friend,' agrees Helen Boaden, who was controller of Radio 4 from 2000 until 2004, following a period of intense turmoil in the network's schedules. She knew that her role was more of a consolidator than a revolutionary:

> You have to respect that; it doesn't mean to say you don't change things but you have to have deep respect for the emotional connection they have with it. Because if you don't they will feel that you're abusing them.

That's how the *Woman's Hour* team, not to mention their listeners, felt when Michael Green started to think about altering the placing of the daily show. Green, you'll remember, is a Radio 4 man through-and-through. Few senior BBC executives were as imbued with the culture of the network, and few if any knew better how, once roused, the faithful listener can turn noisily angry. Questions in the House, leaders in *The Times* or the *Telegraph* . . . change – or at least *sudden* change – is not something undertaken lightly at Radio 4. 'The essence of my policy is to evolve slowly,' Green reassured the press when he took over as a result of the coup that had promoted David Hatch in 1986, 'gradually refreshing some parts of the channel with a few surprises and experiments. The idea of radical change is simply not on for Radio 4.' Six months on, and again Green was offering reassurance: 'I've been lifting the stones, seeing what was underneath and putting most of them back.'

Yet in his ten-year tenure, Michael Green effected almost as many significant alterations ('moving the furniture' was his favourite metaphor) as any of the network's more showily radical controllers. 'I think, as a controller, what you have to understand,' comments Helen Boaden, 'is you're talking about an emotional connection here in a way that really and truly television as a medium doesn't have. Particular television programmes people love passionately, but about Radio 4, people feel possessive; it's actually the architecture of the whole schedule that they're protective about. So if you're going to change, a) you have to have a bloody good reason and b) you have to understand that you're treading on what they feel is emotionally precious to them.'

And so we come to the Radio 4 Hammock. This is not, unsurprisingly, a comfortable trapping of the controller's high office, for use on summer days on the roof of Broadcasting House. No, the 'hammock' is the official name for a statistical phenomenon, and a problem that every controller has had to try to do something about. The reason it's called a hammock is that it looks a bit like a drooping piece of cloth strung between two poles when illustrated on a graph. What it in fact represents is a drop-off in listening in the mid-morning (and mid-afternoon and mid-evening too – there are three hammocks altogether).

It is, also, very difficult to dent, significantly. Consider your own listening habits; maybe of course you're like David Hatch's mum and simply listen religiously to everything set before you, but most people have busy morning lives to live and must, perforce, abandon the delights even of Radio 4. Conversely, as preparations are laid for lunch (or in the late afternoon, for dinner) and the big news bulletins of 1.00 pm (and 6.00 pm) approach, that's the moment people start switching back on again. But if you could just, somehow, persuade listeners to linger just a little . . .

Well, there is one sure-fire trick, and that's to transplant, metaphorically speaking, one of the most flourishing and well-established plants in the back garden and place it in the middle of your problem area in the front. Which is precisely what Michael Green set out to do, beginning in 1990: 'The move of *Woman's Hour* is intriguing,' he said, as I reminded him of the uproar that greeted his plan to shift the show from the 2 pm slot it had occupied since 1946 to a morning placing, at 10.30 am.

> I remember one woman saying, 'Well, I couldn't possibly listen in the morning,' because that's when she exercised her horse. And the women who did the ironing at two o'clock in the afternoon . . . it's absolutely impossible. They're out shopping in the morning and they do their ironing listening to *Woman's Hour*. I remember saying facetiously at the time, 'Well, maybe perhaps they could do their ironing in the morning.' It unearthed a whole tidal wave of personal anecdote of that kind which is part very funny but also actually quite serious. You tamper with these things at your peril.

The early headlines screamed that the show was to be axed: 'After 44 years, time is up for *Woman's Hour*' said *The Times*. The *Guardian* more accurately reported it as being moved 'to fill the 10.30 am patch of wasteland between the *Today* programme and *The World at One*'. It took nearly a year of discussion and piloting before the shift actually took place, and much of it *à contre-coeur* on the part of the production team. At the sixtieth anniversary party in 2006, I'm told the complaints could still be

Disaster in Ditcham – the Citizens saga

Want to go to Ditcham Heath? Can't find it on the map? Well, it's not a mile away from Albert Square in Walford, or indeed too far from Waggoners Walk, NW. Then again, you may still find it tricky to get there, because look them up in the *London A to Z* and you'll not find them. They're all in that part of the index marked 'imaginary places', and all featured in BBC soap operas – but the one almost everyone's forgotten is Ditcham Heath, partly because it only lasted a couple of years, partly because it was a bit of a disaster.

It was autumn 1987, the world's stock markets had just crashed, and across southern England the sound of chainsaw on wood still filled the air after the Great Storm. To Michael Green, a year into his ten-year stint as controller of Radio 4, Ambridge and the rusticity of *The Archers* seemed to be just a little out of step with events when our screens were nightly filled with sharply dressed women with big hair, the red-braces of Thatcherite stock market traders and the antics of *Spitting Image* on the still radical five-year-old Channel 4. So, on the morning of Tuesday October the 27th, Radio 4 broadcast the very first episode of its new London soap opera, *Citizens*, set in and around a house in Limerick Road, Ditcham Heath, SW21.

Green had set as one of his ambitions the introduction of some fresh air into Radio 4: he's always had a taste for the tang of reality, and a new drama that would perhaps parachute in an extra couple of hundred thousand listeners to saggy mid-mornings on the graphs was always going to appeal. 'An interesting attempt' is how Michael now describes the ultimately unsuccessful urban soap: 'I felt there

heard. 'I still get people who say to me, "And why did they move *Woman's Hour* from the afternoon?"' reports Helen Boaden, 'And to this day the *Woman's Hour* people talk about the specious reasons [Michael Green] gave,' says Gillian Reynolds of the *Daily Telegraph*. 'They also have to admit that the programme *has* gained audience, has sustained the Radio 4 schedule, has grown in its own way and flourished. The move from the afternoon to the morning was a big move, and a bold one. But all

was room in this great radio drama thing that was largely single plays ... there ought to be an opportunity to develop another kind of serial.'

So five young people meet at Leicester University (symbolically dead in the centre of England) and then fetch up in Limerick Road in south London, sharing a house together; the storylines would involve Alexandra, the single-mother landlady of the house they share, as well as the backstory of the young people's families in Norwich, Birmingham, Liverpool and Kilmarnock. The composition of the house-share hopefuls smacked rather of a first primer in How to Construct a Successful Soap Opera, with medic Anita Sharma and her pharmacist boyfriend Jatinder, the Irish Brennan twins – Julia, a management trainee and unemployed Michael in search of a future – and finally trainee merchant banker Hugh, straight out of the yuppie mould. Odd how, ten years on, Amy Jenkins could assemble a bunch of youngsters in not altogether dissimilar circumstances in south London and create one of the biggest drama hits in recent television history, *This Life* ...

To get his urban baby on the road, the new controller rolled out several large red carpets (at least in Radio 4 terms), with a special train arriving at Euston station, the cast of *The Archers* greeting their new urban soap-cousins, and lots of TV coverage, oodles of warm white wine and assurances from the Head of Drama that Radio 4 was intent on capturing a younger audience. In the Radio 4 press office, Marion Greenwood was struggling with the supportive publicity: 'My memory of it was of this awful "let's put it together",

☞

things considered, he was probably right, although they'll never forgive him at *Woman's Hour*. Never, never, never, never, never!'

Green has now had almost ten years since he left BBC storms behind and, at least publicly, takes a pretty long view of his run-ins with loyal Radio 4 fans.

These are all seven-day wonders on the whole. The adage is, if you're going to change something or move something, for God's

focus-group thing: this is what you need in a soap. You always had the feeling with *Citizens* that it had been pushed together, that it wasn't real.'

Green's boss, the Managing Director of Radio, David Hatch, put it rather well, if ominously, when he declared that a new programme was like a cigar: 'If it's a failure, no amount of puffing will make it any good. If it's a success, everyone wants to try it.'

First responses were only cautiously positive and, unsurprisingly with all the trumpeting (there was even a 'making of *Citizens*' documentary on Radio 4), reviewers stayed watching the show like a hawk; even the title was dull, they complained (Marion Greenwood confirms that an early, rejected, name was 'Mind the Gap' after the warning announcement on the London Underground).

Six months in and the figures weren't looking good. David Hatch's cigar was beginning to taste a little sour. 'More cliffhangers, fizzier story lines, sharper characterization' would be injected, reported Paul Donovan in the *Sunday Times*, in an attempt to beef up the unsudsy mix. It all sounds so like TV's *Eldorado* only five years earlier. In the Radio 4 press office, Marion Greenwood was saying nothing, but thinking volumes. The problem lay with the serial's schedule: 'It needed to be every day, because you had to make that habit, had to get to know the characters,' – but Radio 4's complexity meant *Citizens* was only on twice a week – 'and unless you could give it that

sake let what replaces it be good – if it isn't you're in serious trouble. Because a) you're a fool in taking the thing off originally and b) you're a fool for having commissioned this rubbish that now replaces it. And that has happened.

Postscript

So *Woman's Hour* has managed to survive broadcasting fashions, fisticuffs and financial crises, charting and pioneering the destinies of women the world over. Jenni Murray sighs though at the fact

sort of outing then it's not going to work however good it was. Actually this wasn't terribly good, anyway.'

On its first anniversary, Paul Donovan was blowing out the candles with real venom: 'Time to make a Citizens arrest' is the headline over an article about the 'dreary and whining soap' . . . 'whose continued existence,' he writes, 'is no cause for celebration, only gloom. A quick killing would be more merciful.'

'I realised in hindsight that to schedule something twice a week wasn't enough,' Michael Green tells me with a rueful smile, 'and as we all agreed in the end, the storyline wasn't absorbing enough; those characters were not characters that people felt sufficiently close to.' *Citizens* folded on July the 25th 1991.

However, with the wisdom of a man who knows the incremental way in which broadcasting evolves, he emphasises that each step back offers the chance for a bigger leap forward:

> It created the opportunity to start to do more series and serials, to demolish one or two of the bricks of the edifice, and that allowed you to try other experiments. *Citizens* was an attempt to say something a bit more contemporary about British life, but I would argue that it has allowed *The Archers* to come of age in some ways. And radio drama suddenly became slightly more open and contemporary. So all was not lost, even in things that didn't quite work at the time.

that, despite years of crusading journalism on women's rights, it still takes something big – war in Afghanistan, for example – for some issues concerning women to be taken up more widely.

We had been doing reports on the impact of the Taliban on women's rights in Afghanistan for three or four years before anybody else even noticed it was happening. It was really only when the Government decided that they would go in and do something that those questions even began to be raised in any other news media. Which is great for *Woman's Hour*; but it's also very sad that those parts of the media don't acknowledge women's stories in the way that they should.

It was, however, a moment of sheer personal indulgence (and huge professional pride) that Jenni came up with at the end of our conversation when I asked her the impossible – to pick a favourite from the myriad items she'd hosted or listened to. Instantly she responded: 'Joan Baez'. Inevitably, perhaps, it was a story that had deep personal roots in Jenni's own youth, and featured the musical legend who was passing through London: 'I was a huge fan of Joan Baez during my teenage years,' she explained, 'and I was terrified that she was going to be horrible; and she was charming, she was witty.' In the course of the interview, Jenni asked Baez whether she still remembered a song she'd sung to Martin Luther King during the civil rights marches when he was too emotional to sleep.

It was a very unknown sort of lullaby-spiritual, and she just sat back from the microphone – she knew exactly how to deal with it – and, unaccompanied, out came that voice. The hair stood up on the back of my neck and I looked out to the control room where all the producers and technical people were and I could tell the hair was standing up on the back of their necks. It was the most beautiful sound I've ever heard.

The great Long Wave protest

Maybe it goes back to Aldermaston, certainly Greenham Common played its part, and the anti-roads protests of the 1990s; whatever the root cause, Radio 4 listeners never let a change to their network go by without loud shouting, and sometimes even a demonstration. In one sense it seems daft, a bunch of people gathering together to march the streets of London carrying banners about changes to a radio station? Madness! Yet Michael Green's tenure of controllership was marked not only by the howls of indignation that attended his shift of *Woman's Hour* to the morning, but by the great Long Wave protest.

'Governments – political parties – have learned long ago that you really have to take it very easy with anything that could be seen as threatening middle-class interests,' observes sociologist Professor Laurie Taylor. 'And indeed, when you suddenly see that the movement of *one programme* on Radio 4 is enough to produce a *march* of concerned citizens up and down Upper Regent Street, you suddenly think, just a minute!'

The story of the Long Wave protest is one which has seeds buried throughout this book, but its overt origins lie somewhere deep in the encounter Michael Green described in Chapter Two with the then Deputy Director General, John Birt, on the morning of the Great Storm of 1987. Birt, you'll remember, was annoyed, according to Green, that Radio 4 had returned to normal programming after the end of *Today*. Five years and one major international conflict in the Middle East later, the advocacy for a 'rolling news' service had become a loud chorus. 'Scud FM', the nickname given to the successful programme of continuous current affairs broadcast during the 1991 Gulf War (see Chapter Six), had done much to demonstrate a real appetite for some sort of radio 'wire service' catching events and commenting on them as they happened.

Birt was dead right: he'd seen the signs and read them accurately – news was the big new opportunity for the corporation, something after all that the BBC did supremely well. Although there was no way of knowing at the beginning of the 1990s that there would be such a thing as 'bbc.co.uk' which billions of people would choose as a source of news and information from the BBC every year, Birt knew he was on to something big. Technology had advanced and information about events was deluging the BBC Newsroom from every quarter of the globe by satellite feed and better quality phone lines twenty-four hours a day. John Birt's ambition was now a practical reality, and in July 1992, the BBC announced a plan to launch a rolling news service using the frequencies at Radio 4's disposal.

Ironically, however, the technology wasn't quite good *enough*; and therein lies the heart of the great Radio 4 Long Wave march. With the benefit of hindsight and fifteen more years of accelerated technological advance, it now seems frankly laughable that things got to such a pitch in October 1992 – but, remember, the internet was still very clunky and was barely talked about; CDs were only nine years old as a commercial reality; and the technology for national digital TV and radio was still a laboratory dream. So, in order to create some sort of news service, the BBC and Radio 4 had to use what they had.

And what they had was FM – good old VHF – which had developed very slowly during the 1960s, but was now firmly established and delivering a decent stereo signal widely but imperfectly across the UK. And they had Long Wave – old, very wartime technology, unused in large parts of the world, though still widely employed in the UK and mainland Europe. There its rangy, bouncy signals ensured that listeners could still just about hear something a thousand miles from the transmitter; I remember as a kid tuning in for fun, night after night, to France Inter broadcasting from Paris and perfectly listenable to on Long Wave. Expatriate Brits also, now just beginning to find retirement homes in the south of France and Spain, could stay in touch with home via Long Wave, even if it meant from time to time that the programme sounded as if it was broadcast from 40,000 leagues under the Atlantic.

There was another problem too. The FM signal got very patchy in outlying parts like the Highlands and Islands, but also in some inland parts of England as well. In parts of hilly Bristol, even residential streets could barely get a signal. So if news was going to occupy Long Wave, all these good Radio 4 enthusiasts would lose their programme – entirely. *Now* does it seem more worth marching for? 'Some of us in Broadcasting House, who were old lags if you like, felt in our bones that that was going to be a big problem, but none of us imagined that the listenership would pick up the baton,' says Michael Green who, as controller, had the most furrowed brow:

> People just cannot believe that a bunch of people can have got placards and walked on Broadcasting House about *radio*! I mean, this wasn't the council tax riots or anything like that, this was part of radio – Long Wave, you know! I mean what's Long Wave, what is this thing? Listener-power had suddenly surfaced, though whether they would have marched for anything *other* than Radio 4 I'm not sure – it's an interesting question.

Leader of the protest was a young teacher from Winchester, Nick MacKinnon. MacKinnon knew all about bad FM reception because he regularly took his holidays in the Scottish Highlands: he told the *Sunday Times*, 'The BBC are quite deluded about this. They claim 96 per cent of the country can get Radio 4 FM at present, but it's one thing for a BBC engineer to get FM on his equipment, even in the Highlands and Islands, quite another for people to get it on their old tranny.' The *Feedback* programme was inundated with letters of protest; there were thousands of pledges of support for MacKinnon's campaign; but there was little that could be done, it seemed. The decision had been taken by the BBC's Board of Governors, with enthusiastic support from the BBC's Director General John Birt and Marmaduke Hussey, the Chairman – but against the wishes of the controller – and was final.

In the BBC's press office, Marion Greenwood was in charge of trying to defend a policy which many at the network disagreed with: 'At the time it was difficult, because we felt that Radio 4 was being done to by the rest of the BBC, that it wasn't Michael's decision,' she says with a wry smile, 'it was a decision of the Governors and he just had to make the best of it.'

Alongside Nick MacKinnon's Campaign to Save Radio 4 Long Wave, a European committee was established – small, but vocal – and it was even reported that Prince Charles had written to the BBC Chairman, seeking more details of the plan. Here we have a little sign of the big lever that Radio 4 protest always has up its collective sleeve. Many influential people listen to the network; many influential people appear on the network; and it doesn't take much conversation in the tearooms and bars of Westminster, fuelled by a suitably placed editorial or front-page splash, to get 'questions asked'. In the face of the mass protests, high-level concerns, and with only a week to go before the Campaign was to mass its supporters in a march on Broadcasting House, the BBC Governors announced they were postponing a final decision. The date of the move would be delayed 'until [the Governors] are satisfied that transmission arrangements meet listeners' needs throughout the UK'. It was a victory – of sorts.

But the protestors were suspicious. Might this delaying tactic only be just that, and their triumph merely Pyrrhic? After a winter of growing discontent at the BBC's explanatory meetings, where news mandarins were repeatedly heckled, more direct action was again mooted – and on Saturday April the 3rd 1993, the massed Long Wave protestors, now led by Rachel Mawhood, rallied at Hyde Park Corner in London to begin their march. The *Independent* reported:

> Calling out their slogans in received pronunciation, the nicely dressed multitude assembled . . . from many corners of the nation . . . Quite a few of the men wore beards, anoraks, polo-neck sweaters, cream corduroy trousers and aggrieved frowns. Many of the women might have been heading for a gymkhana . . .

Outside Broadcasting House, the chant was 'What do we want? Long Wave! How do we ask? Pleease!' Radio 4 press guru Marion Greenwood was watching from her window:

> There were only about 200 of them – it was a very small demonstration – but it was interesting, because I don't know whether you'd say it was the first middle-class protest after things like Aldermaston but perhaps it paved the way for the Countryside Alliance – who knows? It said that it was all right to go and demonstrate and do it in a way that was very polite and very English and very middle class. They made a joke of that; and they knew exactly what they were doing. So in a sense they were laughing at themselves before anybody else could laugh at them, but nevertheless making a valid point.

In the end, the Governors were forced to reconsider and, six months on, a different, younger and less defensively armoured service was announced as the sacrifice to news: the fledgling Radio 5, less than three years old, would become a continuous news and sport network, and serve UK listeners in a different way. In the long run it was a remarkably satisfactory outcome, both for Radio 4 listeners – who continued in that pre-digital age to be able to tune into beloved Long Wave – and for Radio 4 as a network, which now had a vigorous and, it soon became apparent, successful challenger to its news crown. The competition has been invigorating. 'If you start taking all of this stuff personally, and you allow your skin to get seared too easily, then this job does become difficult,' comments the current holder of the wand of office at Radio 4, Mark Damazer. He's already, as we've seen, had his own taste of protest, when he scrapped the UK Theme, and he takes the press and listener attacks with the sort of resigned calm that you acquire as a long-serving newsman.

> In a way, I prefer it that people get hyperventilated about it, though it doesn't feel like that each individual moment when they're hyperventilating. Whether it's about something big like the UK Theme, or whether it's something smaller like a few

comedies at half past six which haven't gone right, or the trails and promotion strategy, or whatever else it is, the extent that people still get exercised about it is a reflection of Radio 4's national significance in defining and reflecting a certain kind of Britishness – which no other radio station does.

CHAPTER 5
11.00 am: A matter of factual

On March the 9th 1970, Tony Whitby, only a month ahead of introducing the most radical schedule change yet to a BBC network, wrote a memo to his Director of Programmes, Gerry Mansell. The subject was 'an imaginative account of life for the ordinary man in Britain over the past two millennia'. As usual, he strikes a note of circumspection, yet the memo nonetheless bubbles with enthusiasm: 'I find it a very exciting idea which could, if it goes well, attract a wide audience . . .' The subject was a 'major Michael Mason project'. It was one of the great documentary undertakings of the new Radio 4, and a monumental series that is still remembered by listeners and programme-makers with a combination of fondness and respect. It was called *The Long March of Everyman* and, in producer Michael Mason's reasoned proposal to Whitby, it sets out its stall with clarity: 'A History of the British People' no less, 'on a large scale, aiming at popular appeal through high quality, designed not only for its own ends but also as a striking advertisement for audio generally.'

The Long March of Everyman was a huge project – 26 episodes, each forty-five minutes long, made in stereo and calling upon resources rare since television (with programmes like Kenneth Clark's *Civilisation*, broadcast the previous year) became the chief provider of sweeping, cinematic documentary. The opening programme wings its way over the British Isles like a bird, looking down loftily over the kingdom and pondering the millennia of lives lived and lost, of deeply stacked strata of history, piled up across the land. It's a majestic beginning, and not a bad place to start a consideration of what today is known blandly and unexcitingly as 'factual' radio. As opposed, that is,

Featuring

The ward was full to bursting, a respectful silence, a sandy-haired doctor moving purposefully amongst the patients: 'Gunshot wound to the forehead.' We were in a hospital ward in Mogadishu, Somalia, and amazingly the patient with the perforated skull was still alive and conscious. The doctor by my side is Frank Ryding, International Red Cross emissary, calmly dispensing clinical advice to his local colleagues in this war-ravaged city. The patient, he says, will do well, in spite of his horrific injuries, so long as the wound is kept clean.

Except that I was never there – my experience of the hospital in the Somalian capital was precisely that of the Radio 4 listener: through my ears and my imagination. The difference was, of course, that Frank Ryding's remarkable recordings had arrived in a battered airmail package together with a note saying 'I don't know if you can make anything of all this rubbish.' Across thirty years of making features for the network such has often been the story. When *World at One* presenter Nick Clarke travelled, following surgery for cancer, to his first session of chemotherapy he chose to share his inner despair – a moment of unutterable intimacy with his wife Barbara and a Radio 4 microphone which he held himself.

The vicarious experience of plugging into both the moments of drama, anguish and the day-to-day has given the richest of satisfaction to me as a documentary producer. Next, of course, comes the tale-maker's task of unearthing within that raw material a narrative that will keep us all hooked for half an hour or more. Thus

to 'fiction' (drama) and other known genres like news and current affairs, arts, religion and comedy. At the heart of this chapter, therefore, is the substance of today's late-morning mix – from the documentaries of weekdays at 11.00 am through to the consumer concerns of *You and Yours*, since October the 5th 1970 the antipasto to the lunchtime main course of *The World at One*.

I can remember even now, fifteen years on, my sense of real exultation as, for the first time, I heard what I knew I would make the denouement of the Somali story – the joy of the international doctor standing on the quayside at Mogadishu as five tons of life-saving medication for those bullet-wound victims were eventually, days late, brought ashore.

Similarly indelible to me was the story of an ordinary Lancashire couple, Linda and Keith Morley. Love and loss were played out among the fallen leaves and spring flowers of Taylor Park in St Helens when Keith, still a young man, tragically died. *The Park* was the simplest of tales, yet it moved many listeners; and, at its most powerful, that's what the Radio 4 feature can do – reach out through the loudspeaker and say, 'Listen; you *know* what I'm going through.' Illness is frequently, sadly, good copy for broadcasters, but most of the moments I remember best have been fun – and indeed (sometimes blackly) funny. How can I forget finding myself nearly twenty-five years ago at the University of Texas in close proximity to an urn full of ashes. Regrettably, I can't today remember the deceased's name, but I do know that her remains now lay, undisturbed, in their last resting place which was a grey filing cabinet in Austin – preserved because they were the working research materials the writer Jessica Mitford used when preparing her famous 1963 book on the US funeral business, *The American Way of Death*.

But there was more: with a final flourish, the curator yanked open another drawer and fished out from a tangle of smelly odds and ends, a sporran. A sporran! And why? Only because it had once

☞

The master Mason

Michael Mason is – was – one of the great modern documentarists of radio, alongside people like Piers Plowright who made features for the network a little later, and, in my era, Alastair Wilson and Peter Everett. From an earlier generation, Charles Parker, who had created the innovative poetic form known as 'radio ballad', starting with *The Ballad of John Axon*

pendulously adorned the waist of the novelist Compton (*Whisky Galore*) Mackenzie. Surreal it all certainly was.

On another trip to America, the discoveries were more impressive: the daughter of the cartoonist, satirist and urbane poet Ogden Nash was fishing around in a stock cupboard for some things she wanted to show my presenter Russell Davies and me. She emerged with shoebox upon battered shoebox containing an uncatalogued treasure of hundreds of sketches, drafts, bills and letters, often adorned with doodles, odd couplets and early versions of forgotten ad campaigns from his time as a copywriter, long before he became a legendary member of the *New Yorker* magazine coterie. At that moment, I felt just a frisson of Howard Carter's excitement when he first set eyes on King Tut.

However, it was a more humdrum, British story that really captured my imagination, one that perhaps sums up my thirty years in feature-making for Radio 4. I'd travelled to Australia in pursuit of Joseph Lingard, a man from Chapel Milton near Glossop in Derbyshire

in 1957, had by 1970 completed his greatest work. The ballad form – documentary testimony gathered by Parker, edited and romanced with specially composed folk-style accompaniment by Ewan MacColl and Peggy Seeger – was a monument of its time. *Singing the Fishing*, *The Big Hewer* and others followed, but Parker had by the end of the decade fallen foul of BBC management who were demanding more output even from their poet-programme-makers. So Parker's is essentially a name from the glory days of the Home Service and the Third Programme, not Radio 4. There are many other makers of distinction too, whom we'll meet along the way in this chapter, but Michael Mason's is the first name we encounter, not least because *The Long March of Everyman* made such an impact.

It's perhaps helpful here to give you a little hint about the ways documentary and feature programmes are made. Unlike, say, *Just a Minute*, or *I'm Sorry I Haven't a Clue*, or news and conversation programmes such as *Today* or *Midweek*, features are frequently associated as much with the name and work of

who, 200 years ago, had been accused of stealing an ordinary little door-latch, worth sixpence-ha'penny. Melvyn Bragg and I were working on a series called *Voices of the Powerless*, and we'd discovered Lingard's written account of his transportation in a dusty, unread Victorian volume in Derby municipal library. Lingard's individual story remained, 160 years after he wrote it, very moving and in its simple honest way had the power to bring into sharp focus the fate of the thousands of powerless men and women taken to Australia and elsewhere for their often insignificant misdemeanours.

And thus it was that I found myself in the chill of the Tasmanian winter, amid the world's experts in Transportation studies, surrounded by rainforest, and in sight of the penal settlement of Sarah Island. It seemed an enormous distance to travel in pursuit of a fragment of a single human life, yet it characterised what all of us who make features for Radio 4 seek to champion, and that is the illumination of a corner of our present, past, or perhaps future world, through spinning riveting stories, told with passion.

the *producer* as with the presenter. So we often speak of *Michael Mason*'s *Long March* or *Piers Plowright*'s Prix Italia-winning feature about death *Setting Sail* rather than using the name of any presenter, host or reporter.

Of course, big names – and lesser ones too – are often intimately associated with these programmes, but the essence of a feature is as much *how* it's made as what its subject is; and the 'how' is very much the producer's preserve. Radio features are also often closer to the *film*-maker's art than to other sorts of radio: 'a very special radio form' is how controller Michael Green describes them. Responsible for commissioning some of the finest across the four decades of Radio 4, Green considers that, though relatively costly in time and sheer cash, features are 'the real adornments' on the network.

You can never take that stuff for granted when it comes out of the airwaves and hits you between the eyes – you know 'My God that really was very special'; using *sound*, creating a sense of place and

so forth. The real creativity that goes on in feature or documentary making, that realm of the imagination, that I think
people really value; without which I think Radio 4 is infinitely the
poorer.

'To be enduringly popular you must appeal at depth – the
great commonplaces.' So writes Michael Mason in his outline –
as yet untitled – for *The Long March of Everyman* in the spring
of 1970. 'We take the history of the British people "who have
never spoken yet", and present that, with full scholarly integrity,
as a great popular epic of everyday life.' *Everyman*, then, was
not history in the tradition of kings, queens, conquests and
cardinals, but the experience of the ordinary man and woman
on the old Roman road, caught as in some anachronistic
snapshot labouring in the fields or feasting in the Great Hall; a
sort of Lutterell Psalter on radio. To achieve this, Mason didn't
use actors to speak the words of medieval merchant or
renaissance reeve, but their modern counterparts. So a baker's
words from the fourteenth century would be spoken, albeit a bit
woodenly sometimes, by a baker from the late twentieth
century. The other prong of Mason's idea is an ambitious
production style; stereo radio, remember, was still in its relative
infancy on Radio 4. 'Good straight documentary not enough
here', he notes, '"spectacular" approach needed: audio as a total
music for the mind and the imagination.'

Michael Mason's controller, Tony Whitby, immediately saw
the potential in *Everyman*: 'I propose', he wrote, 'commissioning a series of twenty or twenty-six episodes of 40-minutes each
to be repeated twice.' But he pointed out that 'the project needs
a full-time team of three producers and there are consequent
organisational problems . . .' One of those producers, interestingly, was to be Charles Parker, who was charged with
gathering the 'voices of the people' speaking the antique words
of their occupational forebears.

'Green Land, Red Bricks' was the title of the first, overview,
programme, and from there Mason and his co-producer Daniel
Snowman trekked through the centuries from the earliest
Britons, the Celts ('A Sigh on the Harp'), through the

Renaissance ('Madrigal for Mixed Voices') to the world of pre-industrial Britain ('Arcadia?'), finally ending up, in episode 26, with a view of the country in the late twentieth century ('Between Two Worlds').

Listening to *The Long March of Everyman* today, you're still struck by its breadth of vision. Inevitably, it sounds a little dated here and there – the awe-struck narration for example, though the 'voices of the people' which I'd remembered as awkward, now sound rather authentic. Reviewing the first episode Review Board were unanimous in their praise: the idea of providing a bird's eye view had been 'an inspiration', commented Director of Programmes, Gerard Mansell. He had been 'left waiting impatiently for the next 25 instalments'.

Two months later, with the Christmas schedules out of the way, the mandarins returned for another bite, and Tony Whitby, perhaps sensing a more critical mood, went on the charge. One of the basic aims of the series had been 'to provide an affirmation of faith in the future of radio', he declared, and to 'create something which would bear hearing more than just once or twice, and would indeed be worth going back to again and again'. His adversary across the Council Chamber was the highly analytical Head of Drama, Martin Esslin, who complained that the whole concept was 'anti-radio and self-defeating'; it was 'a horrible hybrid'. Far from thinking it horrible, parried the controller, he found it beautiful and compulsive listening. Others drew up their chargers on either side, and in the end the majority view was favourable.

And history, as we now know, would award the palm in that particular skirmish to Whitby and Mason. 'I was given ears by Michael Mason.' The speaker is Alastair Wilson, one of the greatest of Radio 4's feature-makers of the past quarter century, who first encountered Mason as a studio manager. 'My inspiration was totally Michael Mason, a man who could take personal testimony and intercut it with other things in such a way as to make an emotional effect. Inspirationally, Michael Mason was the man who transformed me from somebody who might have gone on to do radio drama into somebody who spent a quarter of a century doing factual programmes. I take my hat off to that man, he was brilliant!'

One of the unmistakable 'people's voices' on an early episode of *Everyman* is that – uncredited – of a young broadcaster who haled from Northampton and was rapidly making a name for himself as a maverick and original writer for radio; his name, Ray Gosling. A couple of years after he'd finished *Everyman*, Mason was to work more closely with Gosling, and Wilson was given the job of editing the piles of tapes they recorded together: 'Michael would arrive in these rather attractive large rooms on the fifth floor of Broadcasting House in which there were great green tape machines that looked as if you could open the front of them and cook turkeys in them.'

> And Michael would bring in two hours of Ray Gosling, unscripted, and say, 'Dear boy! I . . . I . . . want to try and cut this to fourteen minutes . . .' and I would say, 'Oh fuck, how long will this take, Michael?' 'Well, days . . .' he would say, '. . . days.' If Michael Mason arrived, there was always a sort of spring in the step if there was a Gosling script.

Colonial voices

However, Gosling miniatures – at that time he specialised in brilliantly constructed and perfectly observed talks and features – were not the warp and weft of Michael Mason's documentary output. He, like another features luminary, John Powell, loved the grand sweep of experience, and when he'd finished chronicling the history of the British at home, Michael turned to the lives of colonial Brits in India.

On December the 9th 1971, Controller Tony Whitby had convened several senior editors and producers, including Mason, Charles Parker and Helen Fry who ran the Sound Archive Production Unit, for a meeting 'to examine the need for collecting material about current and recent history and the contemporary life-style'. Producers arrived bearing gifts, including from Parker the (for him) rather conventional idea of a programme about surviving children's games and playground chants ('working title: *The Singing Street*') and, more significantly, from Mason 'The British Raj' ('Likely programme outlets are', the minutes note, '(i) a stereo epic for Radio 3; (ii) 3 or 4 spin-off programmes for R4').

However, Whitby made sure that, four years later, it was *his* network that got the epic, in the form of *Plain Tales from the Raj*, the first of a lengthy sequence of mesmerising programmes that recorded – in a way never before captured – the intimate, funny, pathetic and often unedifying experiences of British colonial rule. One remarkable episode was by the comedian and writer Spike Milligan; in his north London flat, Alastair Wilson was listening:

> I sat down with a Vesta curry and although I was working in radio let the curry go cold, because I could not believe how he had conjured a sound world out of one man talking plus a few sound effects.

Spike Milligan's *Plain Tale* was an exceptional programme that still today resonates: sad, powerfully emotional – he breaks down at one point – slightly at odds with the world, honouring the positive aspects of the colonial experience as well as its wrongs, it had a huge public response because it was just so intimate; a greatly loved public figure being brutally honest. Yet the look-at-me nature of that one programme slightly distorted the huge impact of the whole series which, with its successor programmes – *Tales from the South China Seas* and *Last Tales from the South China Seas* – quietly recorded as no one had previously done the day-to-day experiences of ordinary men and women thrust into extraordinary and often terrifying worlds.

Michael Mason's production rate was enormous, partly thanks to his unconventional practice of using marked-up transcripts as a guide to his tape editor whom he'd then just leave to get on with it. Thus in the same autumn 1975 schedule that unveiled his *Plain Tales*, he was also making *Icarus with an Oilcan* on the early days of flying. Alastair Wilson was again the studio manager who painstakingly assembled the programme

Henry and Clare

There's something vaguely sinful about enjoying comedy in the middle of the morning, like sneaking a Viennese truffle while you're supposed to be hard at work. But when he re-engineered his network schedule to reflect more closely the tastes and habits of his listeners, controller James Boyle found that light mid-morning drama was just what people wanted over a cup of instant and a Hob-nob. It somehow just felt more *right* there than at the later time of 12.27 which had been a comedy and light drama slot for generations; so lunchtime long-runner *King Street Junior* transferred to the mid-morning for its tenth series. And that was naturally where listeners also found Radio 4's wondrous coffeetime hit series of the first decade of the new century, *Clare in the Community*.

In 2004, Harry Venning and co-writer David Ramsden took their *Guardian* strip cartoon about social workers and their clients and realised it as a comedy drama for Radio 4. It was an instant hit, catching the PC tone of our times, the new-speak of systems, targets, caring and concern, and contrasting modish laid-back attitudes towards gender and sexuality with the day-to-day anxieties that beset us all: like who borrowed that favourite DVD or why does the photocopier always jam just before you need to use it in a hurry?

from its ingredients. No multi-track, no digits, no computers at all in the BBC in those days; just long hours of perfectionist rehearsal and recording.

Now this took four days in a Broadcasting House studio, which was almost unheard of – only Michael Mason could get that kind of time in a studio. It was made in stereo, which again was rare in 1975, and he had First World War songs about air crashes and how the crank case goes through your brain; and he had that intercut with experiences of airmen talking about how you got oil on the windscreen and how it was difficult to see. And you got this sense that here was somebody capturing experience at first hand that was exceptional.

Sally Phillips is Clare 'a social worker with all the politically correct jargon but none of the practical solutions' as the show's blurb describes her. In fact, she's a bit of a monster, having read all the theory and yet never having let experience of reality touch her. With her nasal Jennifer Saunders-esque whine, Phillips' performance has the tone to a tee.

Like the best sit-coms, *Clare in the Community* is an ensemble piece, set, however, not in a useful physical environment (say, a tacky hotel, a country vicarage or a staff canteen), but in the much more fruitful *radio* surroundings of the fashionable zeitgeist. You don't have to see the place Clare, Megan and the others inhabit – Radio 4 listeners *live* it every day; or as the judges said of it when *Clare* walked off with a Sony award for comedy in 2005, 'a radio sit-com which pleasingly stresses the "com" rather than the "sit".' Sample, from a Christmas edition re New Year resolutions:

- This year, instead of the usual blitz on cigarettes, booze and chocolates, I've selected a goal which is both appropriate to my lifestyle and eminently achievable.
- Really? What are you giving up this year?
- Hope.

☞

Rough stuff

Working in a different part of the radio forest was a very different sort of feature-maker, a reporter whose subject was often himself, and who, unlike the tall, somewhat parsonical figure of Michael Mason, reeked of tobacco and a life lived to the full. Unsurprisingly perhaps, at Whitby's 1971 meeting to encourage ideas reflecting the contemporary world, he had come up with a project entitled simply 'The Lesbians'. His name was Tony van den Bergh, and in contrast to the subtle assemblages of Mason, Plowright, Wilson and others, van den Bergh's documentaries thrust the reporter centre-stage. A 'magical broadcaster' responded radio writer Gillian Reynolds when I

Now let us spool back twenty years to the heart of Mrs Thatcher's Britain when, on April the 17th 1985, Radio 4 broadcast the first episode of another landmark sit-com, though not in those days in a mid-morning slot. It was to run to 34 editions and spawned a highly successful TV version, produced (as so often in those days before BBC television wised up to radio's piloting potential) by ITV. It was entitled *After Henry* and was written by Simon Brett. Prunella Scales (warm and put-upon, rather than Sybil Fawlty-bossy) played the central character Sarah, a widow with woes. Indeed, you could almost imagine Sarah voicing the exact lines of the gag I've just quoted from *Clare* without stepping too far out of character. Her interlocutor in *After Henry*, though, would be the world-weary Benjamin Whitrow playing Russell, gay owner of Bygone Books who is Sarah's confidant.

There was a delicious chamber quality to Brett's writing in *After Henry*, with a simplicity of situation that allowed real comedy of character – ideal, in fact, for radio: unsurprising perhaps, since Simon Brett had been a BBC radio Light Entertainment producer for ten years (with *Hitchhiker* and *Week Ending* to his credit) and knew the medium inside out. Again, as with *Clare*, it's Sarah's

mentioned his name. 'In real life he was the most irritating man you could wish to meet who had this persistent habit of talking dirty. He was also very lovable in many ways, but as a broadcaster he brought an edge, an excitement.' The announcer Peter Donaldson also remembers van den Bergh affectionately as one of the stalwarts of the old days when 'everybody drank and everybody smoked'. 'He was a wonderful programme-maker, a little Beecham look-alike with a goatee beard – he said: "We may have been a load of drunks, but we made bloody good programmes!"'

Tony van den Bergh gave Radio 4 features about going through life's hell, with his own experiences as a guidebook. He charted his own bankruptcy, and the agony of his five hip replacement operations with only an epidural to reduce the pain. He was, as his obituary in the year 2000 put it, 'can-

situation (recently widowed – her husband Henry died in a car crash) not the locale that's important – and the characters, of course: Sarah's monstrous mother Eleanor and teenage daughter Clare are family and thus trouble, while outsider Russell is Sarah's confessor, muse and her oracle. And does she need help! Eleanor is imperious and impossible – Joan Sanderson reprising her famous cameo of guest 'Mrs Richards' in *Fawlty Towers* – and Clare, desperate for independence yet equally in need of maternal comfort and cuddles.

And so the tides of alliance play out: grandmother and granddaughter versus mum; daughter and mum in league to defeat granny; or, just occasionally, Eleanor and Sarah plotting to sort out Clare. The permutations are endless. There are of course very distant echoes of *Absolutely Fabulous* in the generational triangle and the outsider who shares the lives. Yet delicate, audience-less *After Henry* and raucous *Ab Fab* couldn't be more removed from one another, for always in the background was the pathos of the dead Henry – a very textured backdrop for comedy – that lent *After Henry* its sophisticated bittersweet quality.

Just right for coffeetime, in fact.

tankerous'. 'I see things too often in black and white, especially when my sense of injustice is involved. This can result in my saying things which I will deeply regret later in those grim hours of early morning,' he once admitted. And his taste for programme subjects rarely strayed from the sensational – for instance, *Who Killed Freddie Mills?* examined the case of the boxer turned gangster who was found shot in the head in 1965. 'Tony lived his life quite dangerously,' says Reynolds, 'and he brought that sense of danger to the microphone. Smoker, drinker, screwer – everything. To the edge of everything!'

A Ray of brilliance

If Tony van den Bergh, Reptonian ex-boxer, son of the founder
of Unilever, turned over the stones of the underworld with
gusto, Ray Gosling grew from the most ordinary of back-
grounds in Northampton to unpick in stylish radio poetry the
lives of the great and powerful, like architect Buckminster Fuller
and businesswoman and supplier of floral patterns to middle
England Laura Ashley. However, it's for his touching, textured,
delicately turned but often dartingly pointed observations of life
in ordinary Britain that he's equally loved and respected.

Described by *The Times* as 'one of radio's few genuine
originals', Ray has, it's said, made more than a thousand radio
appearances – but personally I shall always treasure a set of
simple descriptions of English seaside life out-of-season, called
A Promenade of Resorts, in which his image-maker's eye for the
telling detail ('the "Do Pop Inn" café') is as poetic and as
revealing as any photographer's. 'I can remember once he did a
programme about a Protestant church in a part of Catholic
France,' recalls Laurie Taylor, 'and not many people came to the
church.' That 1987 programme, *Waiting for Mrs Forbes*, won
the most prestigious award in the broadcasting canon, the Prix
Italia, for radio feature; it was produced by Alastair Wilson and
painted the sad, yet smiling life of the Reverend Kenneth
Forrester, vicar of Pau, chaplain in the diocese of Fulham and
Gibraltar, an Englishman marooned in a sea of French life,
desperately and quaintly keeping up the conventions in a foreign
field. Piers Plowright, the most eminent of recent Italia feature
winners calls it 'an absolute masterpiece', counting it amongst
his trio of finest features of all time. Reviewing it in *The Times*,
David Wade praised 'Gosling's own inimitable brand of narration – quirky, plaintive . . . but here also elegiac'.

It was Gosling's way with words too that first captured
Wilson's ear, when he was still a student.

This man Gosling made contact certainly with me by the sheer
power of the writing. I could tell it was scripted – there was

nothing ad-libbed – it was almost written as poetry and the thing it reminded me of was Dylan Thomas without the mannerisms. And I always thought if I ever joined the BBC, I would like to work with this man.

To meet Ray has always been to catch a whiff of the 1960s – he wrote an autobiography at a very tender age in 1962 – and perhaps that has something to do with why he fell from favour with Radio 4 when the shiny new schedules came into force in 1998. Yet saying goodbye to Ray was a big mistake, and only now is he creeping very slowly back on to the network. Unsurprisingly, when Wilson met Gosling face to face for the first time towards the end of the 1970s, there was already a tinge of the period about the man:

> Gosling turned up and leaned, like the teddy-boy mentally he was in a striped suit and a shirt with a huge collar, against the wall of my office, and metaphorically says, 'What you lookin' at, eh?' Just like the kind of guy who's threatening you with a razor in a bus queue. And I said, 'I'm thinking of doing a programme about Butlin's holiday camps, and I want to call it *Workers' Playtime.*' 'What d'you want to fuckin' do tha' for?' – and I said, 'I think Butlin's one of the few people who tried to make ordinary people's lives better.' At which point Gosling's demeanour totally changed and he sat down and he said, 'Yeah. Who else, then?'

It was the starting gun for a string of brilliant and iconoclastic features they made together that studded the Radio 4 of the late 1970s and 80s. Raised voices and frequent disagreements were all part of Gosling and Wilson's explosive creative process; watching from close hand was Helen Boaden, then a young reporter, who shared a corridor with Alastair in the BBC's Manchester headquarters in Oxford Road: 'And obviously smoking was totally forbidden, [but] Ray completely ignored this and threw a lighted cigarette or a match into the waste paper basket, and there was a fire!'

Ray's is a very particular radio voice, slightly whining but full of swoops and surprising, precise articulacy. 'People used to write in and say "his voice is irritating",' recalls Laurie Taylor, 'but, God, it was distinctive!' The critic Gillian Reynolds also sometimes found Gosling's vocal mannerisms annoying, 'but I loved the way Ray would inflect an idea':

> He'd start talking about [visionary architect] Buckminster Fuller or a community press or something and his ideas would start growing like one of those stop-frames of a plant growing that you see in films, and by the time you'd finished, the idea was reaching to the top of the ceiling and you were scrambling up it like Jack and the Beanstalk.

And it's with real sadness at Ray's current absence from Radio 4 that Reynolds adds, 'I miss him. I miss him!' 'I think he was the best,' concludes Laurie Taylor. 'I think Ray was the greatest in many ways. I mean he had a good social conscience, he was very concerned, and he knew *things*. He *knew things*.'

A keen wind from the north

Ray Gosling was an early swallow in what was to become a glorious summer of documentary whose zenith was reached in the 1980s and 90s: in some ways a return to the roots of the radio form that had developed at much the same time as the British film documentary movement in the 1930s and 40s, with the pioneering work of producers like Olive Shapley (see page 98).

So what sort of documentary fare was previously on offer to Radio 4 listeners, before *The Long March of Everyman* changed the landscape? Well, a glance at the 1967 schedules reveals a fair sprinkling of meticulously scripted dramatised documentaries on historical subjects and the odd piece of factual reportage, but of the sorts of feature production I've described so far in this chapter, not a glimmer or gleam. For example, the Third Programme boasted epics like *The Life and Death of Dr John Donne* produced by one of the legendary names of radio, Douglas Cleverdon, and performed by actors, with a literary script, lashings of sound effects and bags of specially commissioned music. Over on the Home, it was again as often as not historical *dramatised* documentary that was on offer, such as *Hearts of Oak* ('a musical account of social conditions in the British Navy 1650–1850') – yet another epic, by yet another famous producer Charles Chilton.

However, flip forward in the old bound editions of *Radio Times* a couple of years, and you're beginning to find the odd piece of journalistic documentary cropping up: here's Joseph Hone, a favourite Radio 4 writer-reporter of the time, with an enquiry into contemporary Egypt for a new series called *Radio 4 Reports* – Tony Whitby's touch on the Radio 4 schedule is clearly beginning to be felt – and earlier the same day, reporter Leslie Smith has a documentary series called *Parents and Children*.

However, it was only a full fifteen years later that Michael Green, mindful of the great tradition that Shapley and others had pioneered before and after the war, got his chance to place radio features in the spotlight. Green wanted to showcase not just the contemporary, but the fully-fledged *aural* feature that took full advantage of the radio medium and the high quality of stereo (and, later, digital) recording that was now technically straightforward to achieve.

> Radio had become, in my judgement, a neutral kind of medium, a bit colourless, very pastel. [So I was] trying to extend the palette if you like of radio, creating colour through sound and actuality – I mean we devised eventually a series called *Actuality* which was rooted in that: What is life like out there? [It was] part of a renaissance of radio, a rediscovery of what radio could do well.

'I was turning up at a doctor's surgery in Liverpool and recording whatever came through the doors,' recalls Alastair Wilson, who by now was based in Manchester and worked there on the series with colleague Peter Everett, 'which took an immense amount of negotiation and thankfully cooperation, from patients in a desperately poor area.' *Actuality*, and its successor *Soundtrack*, were remarkable, lengthy series of forty- or forty-five-minute documentaries that used montage (i.e. scriptless) production to tell their stories. Infinitely harder to achieve than the scripted programme, as there's clearly no reporter to explain or identify things, montage uses sound – from the hubbub and clatter of a prison exercise area, to the happy splash of a swimming pool, to the roar of the Belle Isle Working Men's club in Leeds on show night, subject of one of Everett's finest pieces.

Writing in high praise of the way *Actuality* and its Manchester production team used the medium to reveal worlds we know little or nothing of, David Wade in *The Times* admired the 'technical expertise [and] superb compilation and editing . . . presenting a clear, vivid and absorbing impression – of a holiday camp, a hospice, a jazzband – week after week.' The programme that had particularly attracted Wade's attention was an *Actuality* documentary by Everett and Helen Boaden about Grendon Psychiatric Prison. The two collaborated again on one of Everett's blockbuster series of programmes revealing, through first-hand testimony, aspects of contemporary Britain in *Twentieth Century Sex* ('or *Twentieth Century Fucks* as we used to call it', remembers Boaden).

> I roamed around the country on my own with my little tape-recorder interviewing the most extraordinary range of people. And it was fascinating for me, being a young person who thought at that time that all sex stopped when people reached about 35, to discover old people had loving and sexual relationships; and also just the social history of how people's mores flexed during wartime: really fascinating.

Plowright's passions

Working at the other end of England, and at a rather different end of the feature-making stylebook, were Piers Plowright and his fellow-producer John Theocharis. Although they almost exclusively made documentary output, their BBC home was in London, a little feature-making cell within Drama Department, which perhaps contributed to their more measured classical approach to subjects. 'And that little features unit was really left pretty well to itself,' Plowright observes, 'so it was a lovely place to work in.' Plowright is at his best as a miniaturist, taking a single person or situation and revealing depth and meaning and humanity, as in his feature about a well-spoken elderly woman window-cleaner, *Windows: Views from Outside*. There too he also made *Setting Sail*, a deeply moving feature on death ('luminous', said *The Times*) featuring contributions by widows, undertakers and gravediggers, as well as oars, possibly of Charon's boat as he bears the bodies of the dead across the River Styx. *Setting Sail* won the Prix Italia, as did two of Piers' other programmes, *One Big Kitchen Table* and, a particular favourite of mine, *Nobody Stays in this House Long*.

The house in question was a rather grand one in Kensington in London, originally staffed with servants, and though it is the central 'character' in the feature, the elderly couple who have lived there all their lives are the subject of the programme. They face the approaching prospect of a life much reduced in a bungalow, and bear the loss with dignity, yet love to recall the great days of balls and banquets of their youth. It's a gemlike little programme that speaks vast volumes about humanity.

Not so long ago, Piers Plowright accompanied me to another venerable place with a history, the fifth floor of Broadcasting House in London, where Alastair Wilson had carved out masterpieces for Michael Mason thirty years earlier. Now these rooms and their memories were about to be knocked into oblivion, to make way for the new Broadcasting House. 'You can peer through the glass and see mysterious things going on,' he said, facing a row of portholed doors:

There was a sense of both a laboratory and a kind of art-school about this floor, the fifth. And secrets. And there is a magic to me about it still. Although what is it? There's always been a debate about 'Is radio an art or a craft?' I think it *can* be an art, but more often it's just knitting away. And of course when you had tape it looked like knitting. I still treasure reels of tape spooling on to the floor in that wonderful mathematical way – some law of science is taking place as it spools off which you can never re-create with digital stuff.

Fanatical about features

It's a sobering fact for those of us who work in the form that there are probably not many more than three dozen feature-makers at work across the country for Radio 4 at any one moment. At about the same time Wilson and Everett were lighting up Manchester features, London could boast Alan Haydock, Nigel Acheson and Peter Hoare, Sharon Banoff, Jenny de Yong and Joy Hatwood, and then, as the 80s gave way to the 90s, there was a new breed of young adventurous producers: Alan Hall, Matt Thompson, Hamish Mykura, Tessa Watt and Elizabeth Burke.

Few who heard them can forget Tom Vernon's programmes about cycling through France in Jenny de Yong and Joy Hatwood's beautifully evocative documentary series *Fat Man on a Bicycle* and its several sequels. Then there was *Soundtrack* (described, with a touch of pretension, as 'films for radio'), edited by Sharon Banoff and Peter Everett, that continued where *Actuality* left off. Banoff's *Katie and her People* was a remarkable study of multiple personality, while her 1988 feature (*A Lone Voice*) charting the terminal illness suffered by journalist Glyn Worsnip was heartbreaking in its honesty, directness and anger. Fifteen years later, another terrifying story of illness, told first-person and without flinching (and with a more jovial tone) was playwright Nick Darke's feature, that I produced, about the stroke that left him unable to write, read or speak. 'Such moments,' wrote David Sexton in the *Sunday Telegraph*, 'caught by the producers of these documentaries, are beyond all but the greatest of dramas.'

Whether it's an event like Darke's devastating stroke or Plowright's Kensington couple facing a dim future, it's so often (though by no means exclusively) the way in which humdrum human reality is tested by crisis that speaks most loudly. Take

Matt Thompson's remarkable Radio 4 documentary *Touching the Elephant* from 1997, in which a bunch of birth-blind men and women were invited to experience touching an animal they'd only ever imagined in their mind's eye. A perfectly judged subject for radio, this ostensibly simple feature spoke with humour about the experiences of being visually handicapped, but also about the internal loops of the imagination: 'Phwoah! What a tummy!' says a ten-year-old, except that he's touching the beast's head; while another youngster got most of the details right but had imagined the elephant would be *furry*. 'An object lesson in not taking things for granted,' commented the *Independent on Sunday*.

It's to the network's enormous credit that it continues to invest in features by the lorryload – every day, week-in, week-out, there are single programmes and series, not always of international prize-standard, but there studding the schedule with their dazzling and diverse visions of the world – the lives of the port cities of North Africa, a small-town endurance test in Texas that goes violently wrong, the story of the British travel guide leading students through North Korea, the wealth of sounds made by an old house creaking under the strain of English weather, the essence of British park-life, and domestic lives as varied as the rat-catchers of Barnsley, pea-harvesters of Scotland and boy racers from Essex . . . not to mention a programme about silence itself.

Radio 4's features have also offered across four decades a chronicle of Britain's evolving social climate, with insights into the world of enclosed religious orders, life behind the Muslim veil, the growing openness about homosexuality – a remarkable pair of programmes by Nigel Acheson called *Mum, I've Got Something to Tell You* – and drug culture and its victims, often grouped today under the series banner *It's My Story*. One of the greatest of these pieces of social observation from a very individual standpoint is a single programme from the early 1990s about life on a Glasgow housing estate in Faifley. Listening today to *Jason and the Thunderbirds*, which won a much coveted international young feature-makers' award as well as the highest British accolade, a Sony Gold, for its producer Mairi Russell, it's still as devastating as when it first caused a minor sensation fifteen years ago. Jason and his mate Wee Maxie, his sisters and lovers weave their stories of tough life and love through forty minutes of filmic radio.

Jason is in some ways the prince of his dead-end estate, ruling the roost and leading a life of pleasure, supported by his many women friends and his streetwise mate Maxie, who has a wonderfully poetic turn of phrase:

> People call me Maxie. My name's a good name in Faifley 'cause everybody always thinks 'Wee Maxie! Och I know him! He's dodgy.' That's what they always say: 'He's dodgy!' because they know I know the score. See, if the world was in Faifley; see, if the world *was* Faifley, I would be really famous. I'm a small fish in a big pond but I'm the small fish that everybody knows. Wee Maxie knows the score. The score is *life*.

Jason and the Thunderbirds remains even now one of the most remarkable features broadcast by Radio 4 in the last quarter century: rarely have ordinary lives been chronicled in sound with such sharp observational honesty, humour and gritty relish, that are matched only by some of the films of Michael Winterbottom or Mike Leigh.

Grand designs

Jason was a chamber piece, an intimate study of contemporary life, but the large-scale Radio 4 documentary series is still alive and well, too. Brian Redhead's monumental series on the Bible, *The Good Book*, was one of the highlights of 1986 and five years earlier another religious epic, *Priestland's Progress* was the BBC's Religious Affairs correspondent Gerald Priestland's 'search for Christianity, now' as he put it. In arts, producer John Powell specialised in lavish drama documentary series on the lives of composers like Puccini and Tchaikovsky, as well as working with Sir John Gielgud on a luminous radio auto-biography. In the last few years, there have been just too many huge factual series to mention, but few arenas of history and the arts, science and contemporary life have escaped their gaze – Adam Hart-Davis on engineering, Ed Stourton on religion, Evan Davis on the history of universities, Tom Mangold on the oil business and Michael Portillo on revisionist history or Ian Hislop on the middle classes, they've all had their Radio 4 blockbuster moment in the recent past.

At the turn of the millennium, my own *Routes of English* with Melvyn Bragg ('one of the best experiences I've had in radio' he called it) had a remarkable impact that surprised us all, and eventually ran to as many episodes as Mason's *Long March of Everyman*. It was the living history of spoken English that came to life in the mouths of the speakers we interviewed, like Bragg's old school-chums from his Cumbrian hometown of Wigton, or the woman from Northumbria (with 'the real whang of a Geordie accent') whose tale of her medic daughter, who'd had to change the way she spoke, particularly appealed to Melvyn: 'When she's doing an operation,' the woman told Melvyn, 'she can't say, "hoy that ower here!" They won't know what she's talking about: hoy that ower here!'

If factual and personal series like *Routes* are part of today's regular fabric of Radio 4, in 1967 and to a degree still through Tony Whitby's controllership, the network's offering of feature and documentary programmes was thin and frequently unchallenging. Now there are more features than ever before – some more prosaic than others, some quite wooden – yet thankfully few are quite as backwards-looking and old-fashioned as the staple fare of Radio 4 forty years ago. And the very best retain the true power of radio-revelation; the power, as Michael Green's successor in the controller's chair James Boyle remarks, to change the way you look at things.

> Sometimes in radio you can just feel you've got to sit down and listen to it: just stare at the radio when you're hearing the voice. I often and often found myself sitting in a chair at the end of a programme just thinking . . . and just thinking . . . and just thinking. And then looking up and thinking, 'Wow!'

Rollercoaster *ride*

The mid-morning hammock problem (see Chapter Four) has always beset controllers of Radio 4, and each in his or her own way has tried to address it. Moving *Woman's Hour* was one solution, placing sit-com at the heart of the morning schedule is another. However, there was one fairly short-lived experiment that had all the best intentions but fell apart spectacularly. It was called *Rollercoaster*.

The year was 1984. David Hatch had recently assumed the controller's chair in succession to Monica Sims, who'd been promoted to Director of Programmes, and, not unnaturally, he wanted to make a mark quickly. Hatch, later Sir David, was a showman and had his feet firmly embedded in light entertainment from the start; he was also a very different sort of leader from Monica. 'It's quite difficult to run a channel working for the person who's just run it,' observed Hatch, 'because anything you touch is like touching their antiques or their photographs. So you have to be very bold, and I suppose that's why I did *Rollercoaster*, just to shake the trees a bit.'

Shake the trees he certainly did. I recall the sense of dread within Broadcasting House that the crafted documentaries we made were perhaps under threat – and all because Hatch attempted to do

Informing and warning: You and Yours

If the documentary side of Radio 4's morning has come a long way in forty years, the factual programme that shepherds listeners in an orderly and safety-aware file towards the weather and one o'clock news has changed remarkably little, at least ostensibly. It was fifty years ago that the Consumers' Association launched *Which?* magazine to report on the burgeoning market in goods and services, so it wasn't surprising that within a few years there would be a real desire to offer some form of consumer advice on Radio 4. Therefore, on October the 5th 1970, as part of the second wave of Tony Whitby's Radio 4

something about the 'missing' listeners of the mid-morning hammock, by turning a big block of airtime into a 'hosted sequence'. In fact, with hindsight, I think the idea of loosening the tight grip of the programme-grid is not a bad idea, though where and how it's done is crucial. *Rollercoaster*, however, wasn't the answer.

For a start it had an unfortunate name, with its implicit suggestion of downs as well as ups, not to mention bumpy rides. In the event, the switchback experience was Hatch's. His chosen presenter was avuncular Richard Baker from *Start the Week*. The programme might shake the trees, but the presenter could charm the audience birds out of them . . . or so Hatch imagined.

> Didn't lose any audience I have to tell you – it did absolutely fine. And it might have worked. It didn't. But to me it was good fun while it happened. I made some mistakes – I probably should have been even bolder and not had it presented by Richard Baker. Not that I don't like Richard Baker, I think Richard Baker was a wonderful broadcaster; but if you're doing an experiment which is going to shake the trees, you shouldn't do it with somebody who *is* the tree, if you know what I mean!

revolution, Joan Yorke presented the first edition of 'the Radio 4 series that tackles topics of direct concern to you'. The programme was and is *You and Yours*.

That first edition devoted itself to money – 'earning, saving and spending it' – and the show's concerns have an amazingly up-to-date ring. There's a thorough run-down on the current dos and don'ts about home ownership ('initial charges, mortgage arrangements, running costs'); there's an interview with the author of a new book on buying a house and – classic *Y&Y* fare this – an interview with the Chairman of the Building Societies Association. Pretty unexciting-sounding stuff, I have to say, which explains perhaps why so often the programme has ended up on the receiving end of critical press attention.

The problem with *Rollercoaster*, as so often with new ideas on the network, was the matter of tone: *Rollercoaster* didn't really sound like Radio 4 – 'counter-intuitive to the whole Radio 4 mindset, in my view,' agreed Gillian Reynolds of the *Daily Telegraph*, in a real lather:

> My back was up from the moment the announcer said, 'My name is x and I am your host.' And I would shout at the radio, 'No, you're not! You are in charge of this programme. *I* am the host. I'll say whether you'll stay or go. Or whether you're barred. You're barred! Out!' But David gave it a go because I'm sure he was being told that it was the great thing from America to have seamless sequences. And you can see the idea still has currency.

James Boyle, who spent a year undertaking painstaking and thoughtful analysis of the UK's listening habits in the late 1990s, calls *Rollercoaster* 'an honourable attempt, and it was often very, very entertaining'. The problem, he says, lay in the actual warp and weft of the network and the way listeners organise their day around it.

The first Tuesday programme focused on the world of kids: what was the changeover from primary to secondary school like?; Wednesday was pensions, Thursday, 'Your Health and Welfare', while the show wound its way towards the weekend with a leisure-filled Friday edition featuring two more favourite consumer standbys, the bosses of the tourist board and ABTA (travel agents). All that's missing is an item on new disability legislation and some early warnings about how to deal with capital gains tax and it might, I guess, have strayed from last week's schedule.

A week later and Radio Review Board gathered in Broadcasting House's windowless basement conference room B50 to discuss the first set of editions. There was a certain amount of damning with faint praise ('this "service" programme had started satisfactorily'), but Whitby was delighted: 'The programme's practical, down-to-earth approach was exactly right,' he observed. 'It dealt with matters which [are] of daily concern

> It was a programme without proper broadcasting definitions in the time sense, for an audience which is very conscious of time and very conscious of the use of its day. It *wasn't* that it was unintelligent. It wasn't that it didn't have vastly entertaining people in it and good producers, it was simply wrong for a network that's based on intelligent speech radio with boundaries.

> Yet David Hatch remained defiant about what he was attempting on the broader scale: 'You can either say, "Sit still and some of this will go away" or *really* throw it about to prove that you are vibrant and alive. And I took the view, "Let's throw it about" because I don't want us to just sink slowly into the sand and the waters go over the top. That's the end of Radio 4.'
> So who would have been his choice of host if he now considered Richard Baker too much part of the Radio 4 furniture? 'I dunno . . . the equivalent of a Jonathan Ross. Now that *really* would have shaken the trees!'

to ordinary people.' A month later, there was evident satisfaction in the way the new programme was performing, and, quizzed about the displacement in the schedule of old favourite *Down Your Way* by the new show, Director of Programmes asserted that 'It was simply a case of the better being the enemy of the good.'

This claim of excellence may come as something of a surprise to readers, given that the programme regularly attracts the venom of critics. Craig Brown moaned about *You and Yours*'s 'endless parade of officers representing different associations, all of which seem to be calling for an urgent change in the law . . .' and Peter Barnard, writing in *The Times* in 1995, targeted the show in similar vein. 'It cannot be too many years,' he wrote, 'before *You and Yours* has an item about the fact that Hampstead Heath tends to be windy and demanding that the Department of the Environment does something about it.'

Ten months into its first run and the new consumerist baby in the Radio 4 firmament was firmly established: 'one of Radio 4's recent successes' declared Review Board in August 1971, and so it has remained, acquiring a huge and faithful listenership. Today, the presenters – John Waite, Peter White, Liz Barclay, Sheila McClennon and Winifred Robinson – with nearly forty years behind them can afford to take the sniping (the 'bullied child in the BBC Radio 4 school', critic Gillian Reynolds called it) in their stride, and are happy to have fun from time to time with the more risible side of consumer journalism. Indeed, as a token of its power regularly to pull a big audience, James Boyle nearly doubled the show's airtime and folded into the mix coverage of disability issues (previously a separate programme with the brilliantly allusive title *Does He Take Sugar?*). On the other hand, although Peter White joined the *You and Yours* presenter team, his programme for the visually handicapped, *In Touch*, remains as a separate Radio 4 landmark.

How things have changed: 'I've grown towards *You and Yours*,' Gillian Reynolds told me. 'It used to be something we all said "Ach! horrible programme" (and too long at an hour since James Boyle's schedule revamp). 'Well actually, once you listen to it it's full of terrific stuff, very serious.' She hears 'good stories well done, hard-hitting interviews conducted with courtesy, a refreshed sense of Britain across its regions and not just as an offshoot of London'.

Those qualities were never better demonstrated than during the 2001 foot and mouth crisis, when the programme teamed up with *Farming Today* to offer a remarkable service of information and advice, and in one critic's words made 'a bit of broadcasting history'. In the face of a lack of openness by government, *You and Yours* mounted its own enquiry into the outbreak, with an impressive array of expert opinion and, with the toll of culled cattle rising daily, a studio audience of affected farmers.

'We could talk about this till the cows come home,' observed the government's representative on the panel. 'Or not,' was the audience's caustically witty reply.

CHAPTER SIX

1.00 pm: A nose for news

News and lunch have gone together since the beginning of broadcasting, though the numbers of listeners who are actually sitting down at a table with knife, fork and a plate of steaming steak 'n' kidney when the one o'clock pips squeak out from the loudspeaker must be dwindling somewhat these days. But there was a time . . . In fact, one of the first moments that I can recall as a teenager when a news programme stopped me in my tracks was over lunch. It was the spring of 1968; I'd rushed home from school for dinner, and then the voice of William Hardcastle boomed out of the radio: 'This is William Hardcastle withhh *The Wuuhld at One*, thirty minutes of news from Britain and around the world. First the news with . . .'

It was in retrospect an astounding year of many, many news-worthy events: that spring, too, there was the Czechoslovak revolution of Mr Dubcek; the Tet offensive in Vietnam had just started; headlines spoke of an incident with an American warship the *Pueblo*; and we all gasped when Robert Kennedy suffered the same deadly fate as his brother – all the more shocking when we heard Alistair Cooke on Radio 4 describing how he personally witnessed the assassination. Domestically, we learned of the sudden death of our Formula One hero, Jim Clark, while racism was all over the headlines courtesy of Enoch Powell and the Basil d'Oliveira affair in cricket.

In May though there was only one story dominating the bulletins day in day out. Paris was in crisis. The students of the Sorbonne were barricading their classrooms and every day the Champs Elysées was the scene of charge and counter-charge. It was as if all the social freedoms that had been won in that young persons' decade were momentarily focused in a small quarter of

'Before the news, the weather . . .'

News on Radio 4 has always had its distinctly formal feel. Although the dinner-jacketed tone has long given way to smart casual, the fact that it's a newsreader rather than a personality journalist who's in front of the microphone still offers a sense of cool detachment from the newsroom mêlée. Likewise, the weather forecaster, who on TV becomes a kid in a video arcade sending computer-generated maps swooping across the United Kingdom, tends to sound much more like the Met Office employee he or she is when delivering the forecast on Radio 4.

But there's a real problem with weather on the radio: how do you alert people that their 'bit' is coming up? On a flying map, you can see when Rob McElwee is going to point to the Isle of Man, or Humberside or Aberdeenshire. Radio doesn't have a map: it's a problem. 'The re-creation of the weather forecast was a very, very long job that worked, I think, extraordinarily well,' says James Boyle who, in 1996, took a good look at it all during his close scrutiny of Radio 4 and its listeners.

> The critical moment came when we were sitting in the Meteorological Office and one of us said, 'You know what? I start listening to the weather forecast and then I suddenly look up and think, "Damn, I've missed my area."' One of the meteorologists said, 'D'you know, that's true; that's a well-known phenomenon, academically.' And I looked up and I said, '*That* is what is wrong! I want you to tell me how to make a riveting weather forecast.'

the French capital. I was soon to go to university and study French, so I guess those rioting students caught my attention particularly strongly.

But what really snagged my imagination was one piece on *The World at One*. The reporter was David Jessel, later TV champion of the wrongly convicted on *Rough Justice*, but back in May 1968 he was the young correspondent sent to Paris by the *World at One* specially to cover the riots. The BBC of course

So they applied their minds to it: 'We went through all the options: you know, do you do it city-by-city? Do you tell people to take umbrellas? What words do you [use]? All of that kind of thing.' They don't do it by city, they do occasionally tell us to take an umbrella, and it all does sound a lot more logical and organised these days. But, I have to tell Mr Boyle, guess what, it's still easy to miss your area.

When it comes to the news bulletin itself, on the other hand, there's an inbuilt pattern of repetition that helps embed information more firmly in the mind of the listener. Often mocked, these repetitions aren't simply carelessness, but are there to reinforce and gradually amplify the information load for the listener.

Radio 4 news generally is a very serious business. It's entrusted only to senior announcers who don't take their duties lightly. Charlotte Green, beloved of the *Dead Ringers* pranksters and by self-admission an inveterate giggler, nonetheless approaches a major bulletin like the one o'clock with care. 'You've got to be very sure of your tone,' she says, 'and your ability to remain detached from what you're reading about; because it would be death if you allowed yourself to become sentimental or mawkish over some of the truly awful things that we are dealing with.'

Unsurprisingly, Charlotte has in her time had to deal with some terrible news stories, but in her first few weeks she had one, she says, which was 'a real blooding' for her: the Zeebrugge ferry disaster of March the 6th 1987, when the *Herald of Free Enterprise*, setting sail with its bow doors still open, capsized off the Belgian port with the loss of 193 lives.

☞

had their distinguished correspondent there, Erik de Mauny, who was as much writer as newsman; for an age it seemed he'd charted the ebb and flow of de Gaulle's fortunes in his deeply informed but lofty, old-style BBC journalist-diplomat manner. Jessel's reports, though, were different. They were urgent, they were dangerous and they were personal. Dammit the man sounded as though he'd only just graduated himself, and here he was coughing and spluttering into his microphone live from the

> All the human, truly dreadful human stories of loss, and people being
> trampled under foot, and it was every man for himself: that was
> fascinating professionally, but at the end of that shift I went home
> feeling utterly exhausted and very sad; that actually it need never
> have happened.
>
> I wondered how a newsreader, dealing with human tragedies like
> this, managed to stay detached? 'You have to be very concentrated
> and very focused,' says Charlotte, 'and in a way you develop tunnel-
> vision. You just concentrate solely on the story and you block out
> every sort of normal human response. You just concentrate on telling
> the story, factually and with as much authority as you can.'
> Sometimes though, even the Newsroom's serious mien can crack.
> Clearly the top stories in a bulletin pick themselves, but, towards the
> end of the slot, there may be room for a less pressing piece of news
> that's perhaps come in from an agency, as Charlotte recalls:
>
>> I know there was one that was very definitely put into a news bulletin
>> for me because the people in the Newsroom were pretty certain I

barricades as volley after volley of teargas was fired at the
students. He even used the forbidden 'I' of the first-person
reporter. Jessel was a hero.

And so henceforth *WATO* ('Wotto'), as most in the news
business call *The World at One*, became, if it wasn't already,
staple listening for me. It's hard today to convey just what a
landmark the programme was in the Radio 4 of the 1960s. That
pre-*Broadcasting in the Seventies* landscape was pretty
featureless, and *WATO*, like its sister programme *The World
This Weekend* (launched two weeks before the Home Service
became Radio 4), was a beacon: a burning brand of news and
views and colour and breathless informedness. It brought the
Vietnam war into our homes and got us to care; it taught us
what was really going on in Rhodesia, and it was on *The World
This Weekend*, later in 1968, that we heard the plaintive yet
determined voice of the Czech boy pleading 'to all students of

would get the giggles over it – an American girl who eloped with a much older man, and her name was actually Chastity Bumgardner; which I thought was a classic! No wonder she eloped – she was obviously desperate to change her name!

And then there were a couple of other occasions when simply an ordinary name caught Charlotte's attention, by virtue of being repeated ...

I remember once reading quite a lengthy, convoluted story in which this woman called Mavis Davis appeared. So about three or four times they used the name, and it got more and more surreal as I kept saying it. Towards the end of that I was having real difficulty, trying very hard not to laugh. And I can think of another one with Phyllis Willis, that was even more bizarre. You don't expect those to trip you up but suddenly, when you're saying them, they sound *extraordinary*! And the more you have to say it, the worse it gets.

the world' to remember the plight of his country: 'Don't forget Czechoslovakia!' – a feeble, fading signal rebroadcast to Sunday lunchtime Britain. Those words, first heard on August the 25th 1968, like Jessel's four months earlier, cut to the heart.

Beginnings

The World at One began in 1965 on the Home Service (then run by the brilliant Gerard Mansell), but anticipated the sharper agenda that was soon to become the style of Radio 4. As such it was one of the most powerful influences shaping the future of the network. 'That's the watershed of change,' says radio historian Gillian Reynolds, 'Andrew Boyle [the editor] and William Hardcastle [presenter] were the great revolution and they made radio think – they made all of broadcasting think –

about different ways of doing the news. And that hadn't been thought of before. It was *so* daring and it flew in the face of every piece of BBC editorial received opinion.' Indeed, 'they found a desert and created an orchard', in the memorable phrase of the distinguished journalist and long-time friend of the programme, Anthony Howard. Not surprising then that – with *The World This Weekend* launching just ahead of the new network and *PM*, from the same stable, a key part of the April 1970 schedule change – the *World at One* team were on the front row of the grid, setting the pace, at Radio 4's two most significant dates in its early history. How come?

Although, clearly, the programme was and is absolutely a team effort, the vision was one man's, and he was Andrew Boyle. It was Boyle's maverick genius, and refusal to kowtow to corporate traditions or to bow low before other BBC barons, that gave his stable of programmes its edge. Jenny Abramsky, now director of all BBC network radio, was recruited as a producer by Andrew Boyle, before later becoming *WATO*'s editor; she describes him as 'one of the most brilliant and completely terrifying and contrary people you could ever meet, but a genius'.

Boyle was always on the look-out for real talent, and in the autumn of 1967 he spotted a reporter on a one-month temporary contract working in the south-east newsroom. She'd not long arrived from South Africa and her name was Sue MacGregor. Sent off to Pinewood Studios to gather interviews about *Chitty Chitty Bang Bang*, then in production, Sue returned triumphantly bearing a tape of stars Dick van Dyke and Sally Ann Howes. That recording was 'somehow heard', she says, by Andrew Boyle, who was looking for another '"girl reporter" as we called ourselves, and I joined *The World at One*: it must have been just about as Radio 4 began.' MacGregor had never been a news reporter before and found the challenge of *The World at One* 'enormously exhilarating and exciting but also terrifying'. Boyle's was a big presence at the heart of a big, significant programme:

Andrew was one of the great old-style BBC eccentrics. He was rather ruddy-faced, a Catholic, very left-wing and an intellectual. He had a considerable brain, but whenever he explained what he wanted to get out of a feature or an interview you ended up more confused than you'd begun because he couldn't ever say it simply.

'And he used to tell jokes that were completely incomprehensible,' adds Jenny Abramsky, who'd only just abandoned the studio manager's world of sound balancing and tape editing for production, 'and he would have a whole load of people who just would laugh, and I had no idea what they were laughing at. He used to have this slightly manic laugh. He was mercurial.'

Newsrooms and the production offices of daily news shows are fascinating places, and to the outsider often slightly bizarre: a combination of tight deadlines, evolving and breaking stories, the noise of despatches constantly being tannoyed in, and always the competition to be first, both collectively and individually. Gerard Mansell, at whose invitation *The World at One* was brought into being, kept a very close eye on Boyle's baby, and often peeked round the office door:

It was chaotic, but it was organised chaos. Bill was sitting at one table with piles of newspapers and tapes and so on and Andrew in another corner, and producers and reporters rushing in with reports, and Andrew making his mind up about what the running-order was. And the running-order would always be changed before the programme actually got on the air, and it was even sometimes changed *when* the programme was on the air. Bill, sitting there with his huge, beetling eyebrows and massive frame in the studio chair, was totally calm. I've never seen Hardcastle lose his nerve, become panicky or anything like that. Creative chaos I think is the best way to describe it.

All of which left new producer Jenny Abramsky gasping a little at first, as she tried to puzzle out her editor's slang identifying the politicians who trooped through the *WATO* studio. For example:

There was [a senior politician] who had quite red cheeks so he was known as 'Purple Sprouting Broccoli'. So you needed to know what the nicknames were to actually be able to follow a conversation with Andrew. Because he'd just fling out these names right, left and centre. And all the people who worked with him all their lives knew exactly what he was talking about. Terribly public school in that sense.

There was, too, almost a sort of 'inter-House' rivalry about the way Boyle dealt with his fellow news and current affairs teams. 'Andrew was a mischief-maker,' Abramsky smiles as she remembers; 'He also had very little respect for many of the people who worked in authority in the BBC. He believed that the *World at One* team were the élite of the department and should be left to do their own thing.' As a result, a fierce rivalry developed between Boyle and the non-*WATO* corners of Radio 4 journalism; and sometimes it became, frankly, laughable. One famous occasion was when, Jenny says, he deliberately failed to pass on news which the programme had obtained that an industrial dispute currently paralysing the nation had unexpectedly been called off. And why? Simply in order to make the newsroom look foolish.

So the newsreader's headlines said 'The Post Office strike goes on', and [Hardcastle] goes 'The Post Office strike is *over*!' And Andrew was laughing! He was dancing around the office in glee! There was no thought of the audience. The audience was irrelevant – this was just a battle of wills to prove there were actually a load of fools running the BBC in that sense.

Sue MacGregor, newly arrived in the bureaucratic BBC, also appreciated just how old-fashioned the news hierarchy still was: 'very small-c conservative; everything was meant to be passed by line-managers, and I think that part of the reason for *The World at One*'s successes was that they were ignored.' Another factor was the huge amount of inside information that the programme had built up over the years, what today would be known rather grandly as a 'database'. In those days, it was a sheaf of papers that were jealously guarded: producer Jenny Abramsky found herself in charge of 'security'.

> And one of the key things was that no one could ever have access to the *World at One* contact list (which was an extraordinary contact list). So every night you'd take the contacts and they'd be locked away in case the *Today* programme would come in overnight and try to find one of 'our' contacts.

A hand-picked cast

Alongside Andrew Boyle, the other half of the *World at One* duo was the redoubtable presenter William Hardcastle (see page 164). 'They were very different characters,' remembered Gordon Clough, another of the roster of presenters, in a Radio 4 biography of Hardcastle from the 1990s:

> Except that they both had this great curiosity and a great liking for the deflation of pomposity and they were both a little bit naughty – they liked to see politicians coming to what they thought was an easy fence and falling flat on their faces. But that wasn't the entire purpose of this; the purpose was to get away from the rather staid, deferential manner of current affairs broadcasting and to get something a bit more like tabloid journalism.

A feature of the Boyle/Hardcastle era on *WATO* was the preference the programme had for using newspaper correspondents (Boyle's 'private militia', Anthony Howard called them) to comment on affairs, rather than the normal range of BBC correspondents. As Sue MacGregor observed

> They didn't like to use BBC correspondents – the Angus McDermids and the John Osmans and others – they were all fine correspondents, but they preferred the more personal take on a story; they thought that journalists, if they were not attached to the BBC, were able to speak more freely and to give their own

A radio colossus: Nick Clarke

When he died in November 2006, Nick Clarke was mourned, very publicly, in an extended edition of the Radio 4 programme he'd presented for thirteen years. He had served *The World at One* longer than its founder presenter William Hardcastle, and was held in a degree of affection that few Radio 4 presenters could match. That tribute programme, a marking of a passing almost unheard of for a broadcaster, was testimony to Nick's special place in the hearts of both listeners and broadcasters. Nick Clarke was, for many, the broadcaster's broadcaster. He combined virtues of courtesy and politeness with a rigour and toughness that was worthy of the programme's first presenter. Indeed, they both shared mobile and prominent eyebrows, the lifting of which signified much.

Unlike more look-at-me interviewers, Nick's technique was artful and thoughtful, like that of the dexterous cricketer that he also was, watching for the opportunity to steal a single with a deft push to leg. In an article on *WATO* in *The Times*, shortly after he took over, he wrote of the sort of non-confrontational approach to his studio guests that he enjoyed: 'This type of interview requires trust on both sides. It is, by definition, not a hectoring exchange. I don't like interruptions, either: I believe it's nearly always possible *pace* Lady Thatcher to find a pause, however microscopic, into which a question can be inserted.' He was erudite – he'd read French and German at Fitzwilliam College, Cambridge – and well read, with a deep well of considered culture. But he enjoyed having fun too, as another autobiographical piece illustrates: here he was remembering his days of student journalism:

kind of shading to the story in a more lively way than the more old-fashioned BBC correspondents did.

Thus, Anthony Howard in America or Stanley Uys, the *Observer* man in South Africa, and William Davis, who later edited *Punch* magazine, became regular contributors and, in

We used to climb in and out of colleges at night to get copy out of contributors. I was capable of a 2.1 but got a 2.2: I've no regrets; I could either have had the time I had – which I enjoyed – or have worked for a 2.1. But not both.

Until 2006, I knew Nick only as the enlivening voice of *The World at One*, *Any Questions?* and *Round Britain Quiz*, and from occasional encounters at departmental parties, where we would exchange ruderies about programme quality. However, in the last nine months of his life, I came to spend an inordinate amount of time in the company of this funny and warm and sometimes pernickety man. Not often, it's true to say, in person, but above all through the extraordinary recordings he made in concert with his wife, the film-maker-journalist Barbara Want, which became *Fighting to be Normal*, the Radio 4 audio-diary of his treatment for cancer. ('It's a very *rare* cancer. Well, we don't want any common-or-garden cancers.') It was a harrowing story, with moments that made me weep with the rawness of feeling that both Nick and Barbara permitted themselves on tape. Few are prepared to expose their suffering and their intimacy to public gaze in this way, and for me, as a programme-maker, it was a sort of ultimate journalistic honesty, a rare privilege to witness – but always, *always* deliciously spiced with a wry humour, even when talking about the tumour itself:

I called it 'the thing' or 'the beast' or 'it', and when it became known as a sarcoma I didn't really call it this, I preferred 'the beast'. It's a bit like that; it's inside you and it's gnawing away trying to devour you which it did a good job of doing. I quite like 'the beast'.

☞

Davis's and Howard's cases at least, Radio 4 stars in their own right. 'It got to where I was almost the *World at One* Washington correspondent,' once remarked Anthony Howard.

Boyle's other amazing gift was for spotting talent, and the people whom he recruited constitute a journalists' Hall of Fame all by themselves: not only Abramsky and MacGregor, but three

When eventually the cancer recurred and in a very few weeks took his life, the tributes were fulsome, from Tony Blair ('a true professional') and Margaret Beckett, the Foreign Secretary ('an inspiration'). Mark Damazer, Radio 4's controller, put it more explicitly and exactly, calling Nick 'a Radio 4 colossus. He embodied what Radio 4 stands for, and his audience knew and appreciated it. He was fearless, superbly informed, scrupulously impartial, and wonderfully charming.'

> His aim was to illuminate the issues that mattered – providing exposition and insight in equal measure – and he had his own unique way of doing it. Nick combined unremitting intellectual courage with unfailing courtesy. Always.

When Radio 4 repeated *Fighting to be Normal* as a tribute to Nick, his widow Barbara recorded a postscript – charting how their lives had evolved following its first transmission – of which this is part:

> He was so looking forward to going back to work; it meant so much to get back to *The World at One*. And on the day he went back to work there was an extraordinary leader article in the *Guardian*. It said 'In Praise of Nick Clarke'. He was so embarrassed when he read that! And everyone in his office had read this leader article 'In Praise of Nick Clarke' and they just took the piss; they laughed their heads off. Which was always the way to treat him.

other members of the 'girl reporters' posse, Nancy Wise, Wendy Jones and Margaret Howard, all of whom found fame both on and beyond the programme. And amongst the blokes, there could be another incredible group photo – Class of *The World at One* and *The World This Weekend*: Roger Cook, David Jessel, Stephen Jessel, Nick Ross, Jonathan Dimbleby, Julian Mannion . . .

'In my view, *The World at One* was actually the start of modern-day broadcast current affairs' is Jenny Abramsky's considered view, shared by many who were there at the time and watched the Andrew Boyle stable develop.

You'd never have had *Newsnight* if you'd not had *The World at One* and I think it was that critical in terms of broadcast journalism. And of course, if you look at the team that he got around *The World This Weekend*, these were people who became outstanding journalists; it was radio's *Panorama*. They'd do these extraordinary revelatory features, and that was very much the team that Andrew created.

Something for the weekend

'A listener wrote and accused me of indelicacy,' sighed William Hardcastle to *Radio Times* in September 1967, 'when I first mentioned that *The World at One* was pregnant', but, he pursued, 'I can still think of no better description.' The launch of a weekend companion programme to the daily lunchtime show was, as I've noted, carefully scheduled two weeks before the fireworks of the arrival of Radios 1, 2, 3 and 4. Not only did such timing avoid confusing listeners with too many changes in a single week, but it meant *The World This Weekend* got a publicity strapline on *Radio Times*'s cover pointing to Hardcastle's article, strategically placed just inside on page 2.

> It will not be what I have heard described as a 'radio rissole' – warmed-up material from previous programmes. Like its parent it will be based firmly on the essential and up-to-the-minute service of the one o'clock news . . . We will bring you famous names and voices; cartoons-in-sound to stress the absurd side of the news; and highly personal stories to highlight the human aspect. News in its endless forms and variations will be the business of *The World This Weekend*.

So, for forty years, *The World This Weekend* has been filling in the detail, the big picture and the deep background on every major news event and myriad minor ones – and also making the news. The cuttings file for items sourced from the programme

William Hardcastle: an unlikely star

'A great big teddy-bear' was how Clive Jenkins, the acid-voiced Welsh union leader, described William Hardcastle, star of *The World at One* and frequent ringmaster of Jenkins's on-air clashes with politicians. Others found Hardcastle less cuddly and never afraid to take an argument to a dissimulating interviewee. It was in his nature. Hardcastle had 'an instinctive ability to know what questions to ask', as Eleanor Ransome, journalist wife of Andrew Boyle, put it in her article for the *Dictionary of National Biography*, 'whether interviewing some quaking newcomer to the microphone or an evasive politician. With the latter his questioning was relentlessly persistent; but seldom rude and abrasive.'

   William Hardcastle was a print journalist through and through. He was a Geordie by birth ('always a burly Tynesider and proud of it' commented Prime Minister Harold Wilson in Bill's obituary) and had cut his journalistic teeth on northern local papers, then graduating to Reuters news agency. Reuters sent him to Washington, and the eight years he spent in North America turned him into the image of the brash, shirtsleeved American newsman, who loved his drink and his cigarettes and chased stories until he dropped. Back in London, Bill rose to become editor of the *Daily Mail*, but the desk job wasn't his style and eventually he was sacked. As one door closed, however, in 1965 arguably an even bigger one opened – into a whole new style of journalism, as the first and possibly greatest voice of Andrew Boyle's new *World at One*.

lists thousands of quotations that in their profusion offer a fast-forward transit through the ebb and flow of events: the Falklands . . . SDI . . . controversy over the *Real Lives* TV documentary . . . the Westland affair . . . *Spycatcher* . . . the Anthony Blunt affair . . .

   Interesting, that last one, because the man who unmasked the hitherto unnamed 'fourth man' in the Cambridge spy ring was none other than the creator of *The World at One* stable, Andrew Boyle.

'He was a large man with enormous eyebrows and specs,' smiles Sue MacGregor who worked alongside him, 'and I thought he was immensely old.' Certainly, overweight and growly, he seemed more than forty-nine, which was his age when Radio 4 began. Short of breath and with a slightly nasal voice, Hardcastle wasn't an obvious radio natural either. 'He was an *absolutely* unorthodox broadcaster,' observed the distinguished journalist Anthony Howard in a Radio 4 portrait; 'no one could have been *less* suited to do what the BBC used to call "microphone work".' These were, after all, still the days of Alvar Lidell and John Snagge, whose finely honed newsreader's style had accompanied listeners through the war. Sue MacGregor says:

> And *he* had not been trained by anyone about how to speak on the radio and his brain was always rushing way ahead of his tongue. There were spoonerisms all over the place and occasionally he even got his own name wrong: he once said, 'This is William *Whitelaw* with *The World at One*!' – which confused everybody [big laugh].

He was also hopeless at pronouncing names correctly, especially foreign ones; take for example this moment from the cue to an interview with Herbert Chitepo, then leader of the Zimbabwean ZANU party in the last days of Ian Smith's UDI.

> Last night, Herbert Chit . . . Chi . . . Chi . . . I'm sorry about this, Herbert Chitepo, Chairman of ZANU which is the illegal Rhodesian freedom
>
> ☞

Winding down

So much for the journalism. The atmosphere was more colourful, more folkloric, shall we say. 'It was a little bit like the radio version of Michael Frayn's *Towards the End of the Morning*, you know!' Sue MacGregor recalls. 'People worked hard but *actually* not as hard as they work now. We seemed to be able to burn the candle at both ends *and* enjoy ourselves!' Libby Purves, working at the *Today* programme end of the movement . . . arrived in this country. This morning I asked Mr Chi . . . Chi . . . Chitepo . . . I'm having great difficulty with his name . . .

And on another occasion, the name of a Soviet human rights campaigner so defeated him that he just drifted off into a bit of Bill-burble, live: '. . . Dr Andrei Cher . . . I honestly can't pronounce this word very well, Cher . . . Doctor bloblov . . .'

Hardcastle, though, had a sceptical tone which he could deploy to devastating effect; it made his presentation irresistibly different. 'You could almost hear the curl in his lip,' comments Sue, while critic Gillian Reynolds relished his energetic originality: 'The excitement of hearing Bill Hardcastle starting up *The World at One*, reading a menu . . . "Withhh, *The World at One* . . ." just reading the menu. You just felt so excited, you felt so up.'

Hardcastle himself once confessed in a radio interview that his unorthodox style stemmed from his love of the journalistic thrill-ride: 'the fact that I speak fast under certain circumstances,' he said, 'is obviously a natural thing which results from pressure of work, excitement; because I think it's worth saying that often *The World at One* is produced under fair pressure which I always invariably enjoy.' It was, of course, a two-way street: 'The listeners *loved* it,' confirms MacGregor, 'and they loved Bill, you know, for all his stumbles on air, they loved the way he interviewed people.'

That sheer joy at being able to have a go at pomposity or evasiveness led Hardcastle into some fearsome rows; as, for instance, when a disagreement with Oswald Mosley, former leader of the British fascists, became distinctly heated, and Hardcastle dropped his

newsroom, remembers a not dissimilar atmosphere a few years later:

In those days, news offices had bottles in them in case distinguished guests came in. And of course distinguished guests never did come in, so you just drank the bottle yourself. I remember one guy from the newsroom so drunk he was being helped out of the building. He said, 'No, no, no. My shift is *starting*!'

broadcaster's impartiality with the rejoinder, 'I didn't like your tactics in the thirties.' It was the sort of unvarnished opinion that journalists rarely openly voice on air, but exactly the unconventional quality that Gerard Mansell, as controller of the Home Service, had found attractive when he was commissioning *The World at One* back in 1965. 'I was struck by the pugnaciousness, the sharpness, the swift reflexes and the great journalistic experience,' Mansell is recorded as saying. 'He was a very big man, a man in his own right, a man with whom if you were going to have an argument you knew you would have an argument with an equal, and who could therefore take on politicians and other governing people as an equal.'

But the workaholic lifestyle of the programme and the responsibilities of nominally fronting eleven live programmes a week told on him. His regular stint on *WATO* was reduced from five to three, with other presenters taking the strain. In 1975, after a long and stressful Friday at the office and in front of the mic, and with tickets booked for a fortnight's holiday, Bill Hardcastle suffered a massive stroke. He died three days later on November the 10th. He was a mere fifty-seven years old.

Harold Wilson, then Prime Minister and known to be a regular listener who particularly enjoyed the Sunday *World This Weekend*, recorded this comment for Hardcastle's obituary that catches just a flavour of broadcasting's and Radio 4's loss:

> He always played it very, very straight with me and I would have said he was a character; the kind that in Lancashire is called 'jannock', a genuine character, a very big guy.

Everyone I spoke to underlined just how boozy the journalist culture was thirty, forty years ago. Indeed, as recently as twenty years back, 'nipping over to the Club for a quick half' – which inevitably ended up as several bottles of the disgusting BBC Club house wine, Sans Fil (= 'wireless') – was, even in the more sedate area of Features, almost a daily ritual. 'I'd never come across anything quite like it,' was Jenny Abramsky's astonished reaction when she arrived:

In the corner of the main office was a drinks cabinet, and as soon as *The World at One* was over, all the senior producers would go and they would pour out gins and tonics of which the glass had gin 80 per cent and tonic 20 per cent!

Meanwhile, supplies of cheap red wine were being sent for:

They'd say, 'Go out and buy the "gut-rot"'; they would then sit round the editorial table with the food that they'd had brought down from the canteen, drinking this wine while they planned the *PM* programme. Which they did in a wonderful alcoholic daze!

But was it befuddlement or a heightened sense of perception that the 'gut rot', or 'the red infuriator' that Sue remembers Andrew calling it ('because everybody got quite hot under the collar about whether the programme had worked or not'), engendered? Gordon Clough was firmly on the side of the drinker-philosophers:

It wasn't the bacchanal that that sounds; a lot of very useful talking went on in that period: the hospitality would come and Bill would say, 'Let's lock the doors and tie one on,' and we would sit and we would drink and discuss the future of radio until such time as the trolley was dry.

Stories, stories

It was with a certain sense of irritation amongst some of the team, when a story came up that featured not only booze but also women's rights, that it wasn't one of Andrew Boyle's 'girl reporters' who got to cover it. The affair was to become a landmark moment in the Women's Movement, when a group of women journalists challenged the discriminatory policies of the famous Fleet Street wine bar, El Vino's. 'I remember being furious that one of my male colleagues was sent,' recalls MacGregor.

Of course there were some jolly tough women journalists around in Fleet Street and they got a whole lot of other women to sort of besiege El Vino's one day: chairs flew and glasses were smashed and it got quite dangerous. Nick Barratt who went for *The World at One* was flung to the ground by a sort of bouncer, and you can hear his report where the tape actually grinds to a halt because the machine has been bust by one of the bouncers. Any one of us would have loved to have done that story.

Although the female reporters tended to be kept away from assignments where there was a possible risk of injury, there were, in the late 1960s and early 70s, plenty of powerful stories for them to get their teeth into – tough social issues to report – 'a lot of what we cynically used to call "bleeding heart stories"', remembers MacGregor. 'Listeners were for the first time taken into a sort of vivid picture of what it was like to be on the wrong side of the tracks in Britain.' Twelve months before Sue joined *WATO*, the BBC had broadcast the remarkable and epoch-altering *Wednesday Play* about urban homelessness, *Cathy Come Home*. Such social issues inevitably became urgent matters for politicians – and journalists.

We used to go to some of the real run-down council estates and talk to women about their income and how they brought up children on fourteen quid a week or something. And for the first time I learned what it was like to be poor in Britain. Having come from southern Africa, I suppose I naively thought white people were ipso facto better off. But they weren't, in Britain, better off than some of the poorer black people that I'd seen. I mean it wasn't stark, African poverty, but it was real grinding poverty, British style.

Sue MacGregor was not alone in bringing an outsider's clear eye to bear on British domestic issues: Andrew Boyle recruited a number of experienced reporters with roots in Commonwealth countries. 'We used to call ourselves the "colonial bunch",' remembers Sue MacGregor, 'quite a lot of ex-South Africans, New Zealanders, Australians. Sandra Harris came from

Australia, Roger Cook and Nancy Wise from New Zealand and I was from South Africa. I suppose we all had had good experience early in our lives by virtue of being there.'

And always *WATO*, in those early days, brought an irreverence, a Fleet Street brashness to the still staid Radio 4, witness one of Sue MacGregor's celebrated tales. The story goes like this: she was sent out one summer day by Hardcastle and Boyle to report on the sizzling heat that was enveloping the country ('It was one of those "phew, what a scorcher!" days'). Traditional BBC values would have reported the exact temperature reached on the Air Ministry roof and possibly mentioned tar melting somewhere in the Home Counties, but Bill Hardcastle wanted more graphic proof. Thus, Sue's mission: to attempt to fry an egg on the pavement in Piccadilly Circus, a convenient five-minute walk south from Broadcasting House. 'And I broke this egg on the pavement and of course it didn't fry; it just went into a glop on the pavement.'

Undeterred Sue had another couple of goes, but to no avail:

> So I nipped into Boots and bought a bottle of meths and lit it and then fried the egg. It made a splendid noise, and I remember at that point there were rather a lot of unwashed hippies gathered round the base of Eros and they got very interested in all these eggs and scooped them up and ate them. And when Bill discovered that I'd cheated he was *furious*. He reckoned that we'd let the listeners down. I thought it was rather funny.

Another factor that marked the programme out from the crowd in its first decade was the strength of its 'repertory company' of opinionated regular commentators – Malcolm Muggeridge, Woodrow Wyatt, Richard Crossman and Lord Bob Boothby – and its other regular presenters. William Davis and Anthony Howard both had illustrious careers outside broadcasting, but a *radio* man through and through was the less flamboyant, though much-loved figure, Gordon Clough.

Clough began on *The World at One* five months before the birth of Radio 4 and remained with the team, and especially on *The World This Weekend* for which he won a coveted Sony

Radio Award, long after Hardcastle's early death from a heart attack in 1975. A mile away from the latter's breathlessness, Gordon Clough possessed a warm, slightly snuffly voice and spoke Russian fluently, having previously worked with the BBC World Service at Bush House. 'He sounded so world-weary,' remembers critic Gillian Reynolds. 'You always felt this was a man who knew more than he was telling you.' Sue MacGregor evinces a similar affection for this short, slightly rumpled figure: 'Gordon had one of the great radio voices. When you met him he was . . . I wouldn't say insignificant-looking, but he looked like a little sort of professor of Russian. But Gordon was a wonderful presenter, and another person who died much too young.' 'Oh, I miss him. I miss his kind, actually,' adds Reynolds. 'I did feel that he spoke for *me*, because he wasn't a megastar Bill Hardcastle; he was a sort of working journalist who knew loads more than I'd ever know.' 'He loved radio and was the complete radio man,' ran the obituary when Clough died in 1996. 'The power of words was his craft, and he created pictures that left lesser performers gasping.'

There is a curious consistency in the fact that at least four of the people most closely associated with *WATO* suffered untimely deaths. Clough died at 61 (robbing at a stroke two other Radio 4 shows, *Round Britain Quiz* and the less enduring magazine about Europe *Europhile*, of their host); Hardcastle was a mere 57 and even Andrew Boyle only made it to 71. Then in 2006, *WATO*'s star presenter for fifteen years Nick Clarke (and another redoubtable *Round Britain Quiz*-master) died of cancer aged 58 (see page 160).

Special pleading

Where *The World at One* team really come into their own is in the set-piece specials and spectaculars that they have mounted over the years. Jenny Abramsky, working alongside fellow pro-ducer Helen Wilson (later to become controller Michael Green's second-in-command) was still very new to the show when the Watergate conspiracy began to catch fire. 'The break-in had

happened, but people hadn't realised how important it was –
and Andrew just said to the two of us, "You follow this", not
thinking it was very important.' In fact, as far as British media
were concerned, the story of the burglary and bugging of the
Democrat HQ Watergate building in Washington in June 1972
was largely buried in the hullabaloo surrounding Nixon's re-
election campaign and the landslide vote that brought him back
to office, sworn in the following January the 20th.

> And of course gradually, as '73 went on it became clear that it was
> more and more important and we started – we were young –
> coming in on our days off, and so, very often in the evenings we'd
> go into studios and do montages ourselves. We were collecting
> material from every American local radio station: we got the most
> amazing material. And by the time we got to July and August
> [1974], because we knew so much, we had effectively been given
> the responsibility for all of radio's coverage.

Jenny Abramsky and Helen Wilson started laying plans to
field the strongest analytical team they could dream up to
support the correspondents' reports when the Watergate wave
eventually broke. In the BBC's Washington office there was
Charles Wheeler, prince of correspondents, while on Fifth
Avenue, Alistair Cooke was in his prime as timeless historian of
American politics; and then there was Fred Friendly, the legendary crusading CBS television producer who helped expose the
Joe McCarthy witch-hunt trials of 1954.

On August the 8th 1974, President Richard Milhous Nixon
resigned.

> On that day we did a four-hour special with Charles Wheeler,
> with the great Fred Friendly and the great Alistair Cooke and with
> Bill Hardcastle in the studio; and we'd done a series of montages
> about Nixon and different aspects of Nixon's life. I remember at
> the end Fred Friendly coming on the line to Bill to say, 'That was
> a brilliant programme.' I still think it's one of the things that I'm
> most proud of.

In fact, there's nothing like a crisis to bring out the best in all broadcasters; we thrive on them. Even in the more sedate areas of factual and drama output, if there's the prospect of dropping everything to mount a special – a live outside broadcast, an 'instant' feature or a quick turnaround play based on contemporary events (such as Radio 4's recent *Fact to Fiction* plays) – then the rush of adrenaline as studios are readied, sound crews put on standby and writers engaged is irresistible.

However, it's in news and current affairs, whose natural diet consists of breaking stories and who are geared up to react at an instant's warning, that the fervour for special programming runs hottest. For the listener and viewer, on the other hand, it can be a more take-it-or-leave-it affair: the appearance of these news specials in the schedule tends to be greeted either as an invaluable extension of the normal coverage or (just as likely) simply as a damned nuisance, provoking the cancelling of some much-loved piece of regular programming. You only have to take a look at the internal overnight telephone log (which details all the calls received from members of the public) on the day after a programme-change to accommodate a special in order to get an idea which side of the fence listeners have come down on.

Thus, though it may not to the listener appear to be a huge change, 'clearing the schedule' to accommodate even something as limited as an extension of *The World at One* to 2.00 pm can be quite a big deal. The knock-ons may be horrendous. Series are interrupted, serial dramas disrupted, single programmes displaced or broadcast on Long Wave or FM only . . . Just one little half-hour special can, believe me, wreak havoc. These days, of course, since the advent of Radio Five Live in 1994, some of the pressure to clear the decks on Radio 4 has eased, but, as we shall see, it wasn't always thus. 'I can remember having terrible arguments with some of the News people,' says Monica Sims, who became controller of Radio 4 in 1979, 'who couldn't understand why I wasn't interested in the absolutely *latest* decision in Parliament or something. And I said: "They'll hear it in the six o'clock bulletin or one o'clock or whatever. We don't have to stop everything to say so now." And they would say, "But we *do*! Terribly important."'

Incoming

If the 2003 Iraq conflict was the broadcasting tale of the 'embedded' correspondent, the 1991 Gulf War was that of what many came to know as 'Scud FM' on Radio 4. It's a tale, as so often, of battles-royal between the advocates of news and news analysis and those who prefer a mixed diet even in a world crisis. Yet, despite its detractors and the pain it caused its controller, it was a triumph and paved the way to Radio Five Live and television's rolling *News 24*. Gulf FM as it was officially known was the brainchild of Jenny Abramsky, then Head of Radio News and Current Affairs:

> I suddenly thought we've got over 30,000 troops who were going to be out in that desert. If 30,000 troops have, probably, at least eight people caring about them back here, you start thinking, 'That's a lot of people who are going to be concerned about what is going on to their own loved-ones. Maybe this is the essence of "public service".'

Yet such ideas remain pipe-dreams until officially sanctioned. Today, establishing a new service would no doubt have to undergo the strictures of the BBC Trust and a 'public value test', but back in 1991, the deal was done in the executive offices of the Deputy Director General, the Managing Director of Network Radio and his Radio 4 controller.

> So I went to John Birt and said, 'I would like to suggest that we try to do something like this,' and he said, 'Terrific!' And I went off to Michael Green and David Hatch and they said, 'Yes.'

Crisis, what crisis?

Today the very DNA of Five Live is constituted to allow a special response to breaking news stories. On Radio 4, however, it's always been a different tale, and always one of clash of wills – the constitutional eagerness of the News Division to make a big splash versus the controller's measured and wider

Key to the operation was 'network splitting', the process by which Radio 4 offers a twin service on its FM and Long Wave frequencies: good old widely available Long Wave would carry the regular programmes of the network while FM, somewhat less complete in coverage and almost inaudible beyond these shores, would broadcast the war and war analysis. Sounds fair enough, doesn't it? Except that Long Wave never offers much better than muddy sound quality, and in mono. FM was then the only option for high-quality stereo broadcasting. Of course, technology has in fifteen years leapfrogged many of these problems and digital services offer all stations in full quality, but in 1991 the choice was stark; it was Hobson's choice; but in the end, they chose to put the war on FM.

Ten or so editors and producers were selected, and, starting on January the 17th, Radio 4 Gulf FM went on air as the first air strikes were hitting Iraq. Jenny Abramsky's dream was a reality: 'and I remember asking Brian Redhead and John Humphrys to stay, people like Gordon Clough, would they stay? And the idea was to fill in the gaps between *Today*, *World at One*, *PM* and *The World Tonight* and just keep going.' The team was joined by Nick Clarke from *WATO* and eventually from television by Nicholas Witchell and Nick Ross. With correspondents filing from all over the Middle East and round the world, linked with expert opinion from the BBC's former defence correspondent Christopher Lee (also star of the Falklands specials), the service became a highly professional operation. 'Scud FM', as it soon became known (after the ubiquitous Russian-made 'Scud' missiles used by the Iraqis), ran up to seventeen hours a day, with cramped studio 4C in Broadcasting House as its centre of operations.

perspective that takes in all shades of opinion. Is this crisis, the question is always asked, big enough to warrant the mayhem of disruption and displeasure that mounting such a special will occasion? And it's not quite so simple when the news hounds are baying at the door.

Michael Green, as we've seen (in Chapter Two), had to face hard questions from the Deputy Director General when he let

In the controller's office and that of his Managing Director, there was rather less excitement. There was a feeling, thinks Jenny Abramsky, that they'd been hoodwinked into agreeing the service: 'They thought I was only meaning the first twenty-four hours.' Michael Green puts the issue more philosophically:

> How does a network that is so diverse and anachronistic in an odd way, that has comedy and drama, religion and journalism; how does it respond to cataclysmic events like Gulf Wars and so forth. Well, the answer is: with great difficulty.

Battle lines in Broadcasting House were forming, not least because Green had a particular local problem: 'I had recommissioned a radio dramatisation of *The Forsyte Saga*, narrated by Dirk Bogarde,' he recalls. 'I mean, we'd spent a *lot* of money on this, and it was a stunning stereo production: it needed the FM to run it on.' Which, of course, was at that moment fully taken up with sand, Scuds and soldiery. 'They feared permanent damage to Radio 4,' declared Abramsky in a lecture she gave in 2002, 'but, in reality, their greatest fear was that, once established, the service would never come off. They had reason to fear.'

After about three weeks of Scud FM, Michael Green had had enough and went to the Deputy Director General. But Birt (who, you remember, had shown in the great storm of '87 how keen he was on rolling news) was adamant: Scud was a fixture and, he told Green, 'You can't have the FM back for this rather grand adaptation of *The Forsyte Saga*.'

Today end as scheduled on the morning of the 1987 hurricane. Two controllers and five years earlier, Monica Sims found herself in a similar crisis of her own when Argentinian troops disembarked on the lonely archipelago of the Falkland Islands. 'I can remember it all starting . . .' The ex-controller utters an audible gasp as she recollects the battle of wills to come. 'The News people wanted us to cancel everything in order to carry what was happening.' At the door stood the boss of 'the News

In the *Daily Telegraph*, Gillian Reynolds was agog at the 'war inside the walls of Broadcasting House. News has annexed territory from a network and shows no signs of willingness to surrender it.' Green and his MD, Hatch, radio men through and through, were set against two hugely powerful advocates of rolling news in Birt and Abramsky. 'It culminated in the Director General having to get involved,' the latter remembers, 'because there was John on one side and David Hatch on the other – two immovable objects as you might describe it.' DG at that time was the non-programme man who'd risen through the financial side of the BBC, Michael Checkland.

> His judgement of Solomon was that we would stay on air till the war ended, and we would have to come off as soon as the war ended. And I can tell you that when it was announced that there was a ceasefire David Hatch and Michael Green walked into the studio and said 'Right, you're off-air in two hours!'

That was March the 2nd 1991. In the end, the huge success of Scud FM wasn't lost for ever. By skilful shuffling of frequencies (and some heartache), and under a new Managing Director Liz Forgan, Radio Five Live was brought into being on March the 28th 1994, just over three years after Gulf FM had ceased broadcasting. 'I wasn't at all persuaded that news alone could sustain a 24-hour service on radio,' concludes Michael Green; 'sport was Liz's vision, and absolutely right, and has made Five Live what it is.'

people' – Editor, Radio News – Peter Woon (later to move on to run the TV operation), and sitting alongside Monica was her deputy and scheduler, Richard Wade.

I can remember Peter Woon coming into the office and I was listening to something. He was furious with me because I wanted to finish what I was listening to *before* listening to him! And, oh! they thought I was being *so* irresponsible! I remember Richard saying, 'Oh, I'm so *bored* with all this *Boys' Own Paper* stuff that you want to have non-stop' – I must say, quite a good way of describing it. But the News people were furious. Furious. Hated me. Well, in the end I had the last word, but they didn't like that of course.

It's not difficult to sympathise with Sims's dilemma here. Although clearly the Falkland conflict was a huge national and international event, there were for the controller other, more practical factors to weigh up. Firstly and quite simply, the islands were a very long way away, and the Ministry of Defence sat across the lines of contact and communication. Such news reports as were possible were subject to censorship, and news media were to a large extent reliant on the tantalising slo-mo delivery of the MOD spokesman Ian McDonald at regular press conferences. There was very little to fill the acres of time between these frustrating gobbets of pasteurised copy; so as far as Monica Sims was concerned, there was no argument – the schedule would continue, and be changed immediately if something important was reported.

I think as an ordinary listener, though I wanted to know those things, I didn't want them all the time thrust down my throat. Didn't see the need for it as long as Radio 4 could go to them when necessary or something new had happened. It's not that I'm not interested in news because it affects us all – just don't want it all the time! Other parts of life.

9/11

The events of 1982 are now over a quarter of a century old, and it's perhaps not so easy to remember how frustratingly unconnected the world was then. Correspondents were reliant on radio and telephone links from Royal Navy vessels to file their despatches (thus committing to posterity one of the great circumlocutory quotations 'I counted them all out and I counted

them all back'), and satellite feeds were rare and costly. Nineteen years later, when on a brilliant September New York
morning terrorists flew two aircraft into the towers of the city's
World Trade Center, we watched it all live. So what should
radio do? Special rolling programming was, as we'd by then
learned to say, a no-brainer for Radio 4 controller Helen
Boaden – but it's worth hearing her story in full because it shows
a very human side to the tough decisions senior broadcasting
executives have to take over news management.

In the UK, the September morning had already become afternoon and Boaden was at the pudding stage of a lunch meeting
at the Groucho Club in Soho. She was listening to a pitch from
Suggs and writer-comedian Andrew McGibbon for a new series
(which was commissioned in spite of what was about to happen)
when the Director of Radio called to break the news.

> Through Soho to Broadcasting House, on the phone constantly to
> my Head of Presentation and my Network Manager, working out
> what we were going to do in terms of what we needed to drop;
> and then talking to the head of Radio News about what would
> they do, making sure we weren't replicating Radio Five Live etc.,
> etc., etc.

First port of call, the Radio 4 continuity studio, 'and the first
person I saw was [announcer] Carolyn Brown whose dad had
died the week before; so she was ashen-faced – I gave her a big
hug. Then talked to everybody about what we were going to do.
And then just went up and listened and watched.'

Next came a quintessential Radio 4 moment, and one which
echoes vividly the dilemmas faced nearly twenty years earlier by
Monica Sims: 'The big decision was whether we kept *The
Archers*', and thereby bring the ship of Radio 4 back on to a
more normal course. Herein, too, lie some of the subtle shades
of difference between radio and TV, and between the audiences
for Radio Five Live and for Radio 4; it's not a bad demonstration either of the slightly curious and perverse way the
network works, to the frustration of 'the News people' who
sometimes see only the imperative of immediacy.

I made the decision we went with *The Archers*, and actually, when the *Archers* music came on after that completely traumatising series of events for anyone watching or listening, the relief that swept over me that something normal was still going on . . . And I got lots of letters from listeners saying, 'Thank you so much for just having some normality in what was the most abnormal day.'

CHAPTER SEVEN

2.00 pm: Life and death in the afternoon

Standing at the top of the afternoon on Radio 4 is a bit like reaching the summit of a good fell walk. You've scrambled up through the tough-going boulder fields of *Today*, made good progress across the gentler slopes of the talk shows, *Woman's Hour* and the features, and just about managed the perils and pitfalls of *You and Yours* and *WATO*. Now you're at the peak of the day; it's all easy-going from here, right down to that busy, humming place where you're heading – the *PM* programme away in the far distance.

Stretched out in front of you is the view – and what a view. That big thick patch of forest holds many mysteries and much magic and it dominates the view – or so, rather fancifully in this image, is how I'm imagining the riches of *The Afternoon Play*. It's still the dominant feature of the daily Radio 4 afternoon landscape throughout the week, and, in slightly different forms, at weekends too – and where else in the world can you find, seven days a week, such a rich and regular dramatic presence drip-fed into the cultural life of a nation? It's a genuine and, in these days of media profusion and straitened resources, a truly astonishing and little-trumpeted achievement.

Back on our two o'clock pinnacle, the view stretches out beyond the dramas into what's a bit like a rich British flood plain of cultivated fields, a patchwork across the week of excellent programmes that are as diverse as an agricultural landscape – a spot of medicine here, a patch of education there; on the left a swathe of living history, to the right, some gardening and a little culture. Scattered amongst these myriad items are a regular pattern of readings, tiny gleaming mini-features and, increasingly, of what's known to insiders as

Another age: Home This Afternoon

Teatime was traditionally children's radio time on the Home Service, but following the demise in 1964 of *Children's Hour*, Radio 4 families had only *Story Time* – half an hour's serial reading – to make do with on weekdays. The rest of the old 5.00 pm children's slot, and a chunk before, was occupied by a forty-minute live daily magazine programme, intended, paradoxically, for 'the older listener'. It was called *Home This Afternoon*, and featured a wide range of items and a set of accomplished and well-loved presenters: former television announcer and reporter Polly Elwes, was one. Then there was Ken Sykora, with his distinctive dry, light voice, and another amazingly prolific radio performer, the balding, bearded musician Steve Race. Steve was also chair of the long-running *My Music* quiz which started at the beginning of 1967, and was Roy Plomley's 'Musical Mistakes Man' in another long-gone long-runner, the game show *Many a Slip*.

Despite – or perhaps because of – the well-honed sound this trio of favourite presenters lent to *Home This Afternoon*, the programme was, heaven knows, quaint and frankly cosy. It wasn't going to frighten rabbits, let alone the horses. Try a few of these items for size: 'Sir Francis Chichester, Freeman of Barnstaple'; 'What shall we have for afters? – cordon-bleu dessert recipes'; traditional music from Norway; 'Mad Squire Mytton – a great English eccentric recalled'; 'Eve Machin on the entries in her autograph book'.

'narrative history'. These are the blockbuster partworks of the air that tell you everything you ever wanted to know about the history of Britain (*This Sceptred Isle*), about childhood, the British Empire, classical music and so forth. Simply constructed, with expert narrator and an array of fine actors, these programmes – and especially *Sceptred Isle* ('This Septic Tank' to its friends) – have been somewhat surprising hits in the recent Radio 4 firmament, and have made formal history a best-seller.

In *Woman's Hour* mode, the show would from time to time freshen up with a dose of regional voices, but mostly it was run by a team of talented youngish producers in London who would subsequently carve out distinguished careers in other Radio 4 incarnations. One of them was Rosemary Hart, six years later to become the architect and alchemist of the legendary *Kaleidoscope* arts magazine: 'Home This Afternoon was the inspiration of Jack Singleton; he was an amazing character – a real innovative producer.' Singleton's creation was clearly still a fond memory for Rosemary:

> It was a completely eclectic mix of all sorts of bits and bobs; Steve Race did a series on opera, and for some obscure reason was very aware that older listeners might not be completely comfortable with references to sex. He used to do storylines of various operas, so we had these awful expurgated versions of operas that he thought might offend the older listener!

The signature tune – it seemed everything had to have a signature tune back then – was just as a good 'sig' should be: memorable, distinctive and perhaps the minutest bit annoying. *Home This Afternoon*'s was all of these: it was the Clog Dance from the ballet music by Hérold for *La Fille Mal Gardée*, a percussive wood-block tapping along with a looping, scooping melody.

☞

Navigating the afternoon

This chapter, then, is a journey through this diverse landscape, starting with its old early-afternoon fixtures like children's programmes; onwards, then, through the whole rich history of radio drama; and we'll end up with a brief look at that spread of magazine programmes that immediately precede the *PM* programme, which is the subject of the next section of the book. Incidentally, if your regular date with *The Archers* is at lunchtime, I've not forgotten you; Ambridge and its denizens are to be found where the programme originated, at

The signature tune was a ploppety sort of thing, and we got a wonderful letter from a vicar and his wife who said that they just loved this and they settled down and always had their tea for *Home This Afternoon*. When the signature tune came on they hit each other on the head with teaspoons in time to the rhythm! But it was a lovely, lovely programme to work on. I went to Malta, Cyprus, and Portugal during the Salazar regime, which was interesting. We had to keep interviewing people in back alleys because they wouldn't talk to the BBC.

Home This Afternoon would periodically go on the road to do outside broadcasts from holiday camps or seaside piers – always a risk with a live show:

One year we had the OB in the Salvation Army hall in Oxford Street, and the Salvation Army in fact provided the audience. They'd no sooner all sat down than they suddenly said, 'Well, before we go on air, everybody ought to go to the facilities.' So the entire audience decamped into the bowels of this building. I thought we would never get back on the air!

Home This Afternoon was replaced in April 1970 by *PM*.

the top of the evening schedule, in Chapter Nine.

So what, then, is the texture of the afternoon on Radio 4? Well, as the overview that I've just given suggests, it's not homogeneous, and from the network controller's office it looks like a problem: how best to serve the listeners; indeed, how to publicise this fairly schizophrenic menu? Its very diversity reflects the fact that listeners' own lives are now taking more divergent patterns: many who got up with John Humphrys are still heads-down at work; those at home may be relaxing over tea or bent over an ironing board (a traditional view), but are just as likely off to aerobics at the gym, doing the weekly shop or preparing to collect the kids from school. The old long-outdated-if-ever-true 1950s view that placed *Woman's Hour* where women could put their feet up and listen comfortably, having done the chores, is entirely without value today.

And yet, until James Boyle took a hard and realistic look in the late 1990s at how his listeners *actually* used their days (see Interlude 4), the Radio 4 afternoon schedule still bore traces of thinking that was thirty or forty years out of date. It was an overgrown landscape of programmes, dominated by plays which were of wildly differing lengths. Now the afternoon is, even in the age of daytime TV, still an important time for radio listening, but it doesn't represent primetime in the way that the breakfast shows do. Radio 4's listeners drift away after *The World at One* and only come back in really big numbers for the 'drivetime' show *PM*. So trying to sustain the audience against the ebbing tide of interest and the counter-surge of re-engagement with real life is a perennial problem. The story of Radio 4's afternoons, then, takes us through some complex historical territory as we trek down from our lunchtime eminence towards our next big destination at 5.00 pm. So if you're sitting comfortably, I'll begin . . .

Once upon a time

For Libby Purves, as for me as a child in the 1950s, afternoons began with a bell-like signature-chime played on, I think, a xylophone, and the warm, comforting voice of Daphne Oxenford. '*Listen with Mother* was known as "tinky-tonk" in our family because it went "tinky-tonk, tinky-tonk",' remembers Libby. *Listen with Mother* was the story programme for the under fives and had been a piece of the Home Service's family silver for more years than anyone could remember. Every edition would begin with the same ritual formula: 'Are you sitting comfortably? [PAUSE] Then I'll begin.' 'But,' says Libby, 'every time they said "Are you sitting comfortably?" we would all shout "NO!!" And she would say, "Then, I'll begin" and that was the big joke!'

Listen With Mother followed the lunchtime *Archers* at 1.45 and charmed us with stories like 'Pussy Simkin goes to Town' or

'The Little Red Hen's Secret'. With the bloody demise of *Children's Hour* in 1964, the programme for the under fives was left vulnerable, but it managed to keep going, under the protective wing of Schools Radio department for another eighteen years. In September 1982, however, this little infant, long dwarfed by the grown-up programmes towering above it on both sides, was axed. Dealing the fatal blow was, ironically, the former head of Children's television and now controller of Radio 4, Monica Sims. 'I must say *Listen With Mother* was a frightful nuisance in the Radio 4 schedules,' she told me. 'Really made the audience, or a lot of the audience, switch off.'

Little room for sentiment there. The demise of *Listen with Mother* caused a degree of fairly predictable nostalgic wailing, but to be truthful, the programme had, in the harder-nosed and more tightly organised network that Monica Sims had inherited, long been an anomaly and, as she observed, a substantial thicket of brambles blocking the listeners' path through the afternoon landscape. In any case, Sims had far tougher and more significant skirmishes to deal with, and one in particular that endangered the very existence of the network itself.

Rolling news ... again

Margaret Thatcher arrived at Downing Street just five months after Sims took over at Broadcasting House in late 1978, and radical ideas were soon to be in vogue. Likewise in Portland Place: following *Broadcasting in the Seventies* had come the Annan Committee scrutinising the whole rapidly evolving radio and TV landscape; now came BBC Radio in the Nineties, another searching enquiry that set out to think the unthinkable – and this one was designed actually to dismember Radio 4.

The twin driving forces, as so often, were money and the audience's appetite for news and current affairs. Commercial local radio was burgeoning, a new TV channel (C4) was being mooted; why not, it was suggested, follow the trend towards simpler, generic radio and make the strange, illogical hybrid Radio 4 a rolling news station (a perpetual theme, it seems, in this book), with the remaining non-news programmes offering what was called a 'sustaining service' for BBC's underfunded local stations? 'Oh God!' remembers Monica Sims with a touch of horror in her voice, 'that really was a terrible nightmare; we were in dire straits, you know, and there were serious moves to get rid of it.' So was this, I wondered, more than just another piece of kite-flying about Radio 4? 'It was, yes, very much in danger,' asserts Monica; 'the thought of turning it into a round-the-clock news programme was, I thought, the most awful prospect.'

With hindsight, the excision of the Radio 4 riches that are largely the subject of this chapter – the plays and features and magazines, not to mention the conversation programmes and debates – would today be considered a hanging offence. In 1980, however, the 'crown-jewel' status the network possesses in the BBC nowadays was far from the prevailing orthodoxy. 'We had some very, very eminent listeners who could, if necessary, make a bit of a fuss in Parliament,' Monica Sims recalls, 'so it was not to be dismissed, but you could not win an argument in terms of sheer numbers as you could in television.' And as far as senior BBC management was concerned that was the end of it. 'It was thought to be a bit middle-class and toffee-nosed and therefore not a really important way of reaching the great British public. I suspect that that was a general view from some of the people who were involved in the governance of the BBC.' In the end the apocalypse was avoided; but the idea of rolling news, as we've seen, rolled on.

Despite the riches that Tony Whitby had bequeathed to the schedule, Monica Sims's time at Radio 4 is rarely talked of as a golden era for the network. Radio 4 still had too many old properties like *Listen with Mother* clogging up its schedules to allow it to adapt to the evolving audience. All a bit unfair, considering the fact that she successfully fought off the network dismemberment plan, and even more so when you remember that Sims oversaw three of the network's triumphant all-time hit shows that marked in some ways the first real lifting of the gloom of unfashionableness that had long enveloped the network. *The Hitchhiker's Guide to the Galaxy*, the Angus

I'm afraid we seem to be having a little trouble . . .

Live broadcasting without the safety-net of a tape loop or time delay always produces unintended horrors; for internal consumption they usually end up in the sort of compilations that bored studio managers assemble during night shifts, the 'bloopers' tape. So there was the unfortunate announcer who had to read a news story about elephant dung, and failed to make the finishing post without corpsing helplessly, and the celebrated occasion when the Radio 3 Proms announcer had to fill for aeons when the piano at the Royal Albert Hall became stuck during a platform rearrangement. 'I remember on Black Wednesday when we left the ERM,' says former chief announcer, Peter Donaldson. 'In the *Six O'Clock News* there's always a financial report and we'd begin it: "In the City share prices this, share prices that." And of course, on this particular day, I said, "In the Shitty . . . City . . . share prices have plummeted!!" I got three letters saying how right we were!'

Then there was the financial journalist with the broken headphones who once struggled for at least ten minutes to make contact with his interviewee in Sweden, while listeners could perfectly well hear – though the interviewer couldn't – the man vigorously replying to every plea (and eventually a burst of song) coming from the journalist in London: 'Hello, Stockholm!' is a Radio 4 legend amongst bloopers.

The other enemies of the live broadcaster are the broken lift, the misread clock or just bad timing that result in a vertiginous rush to the microphone and subsequent uncontrollable breathlessness. Peter's colleague Charlotte Green knows all about it.

I'm reasonably fit, so I try to move rapidly but not rush, so that I'm almost on the point of being out of breath, but not quite. Actually

Deayton and Geoffrey Perkins comedy *Radio Active*, and *Lord of the Rings*, which became one of the network's most successful drama productions, all showed the potential of Radio 4 to develop cult programmes, and to do things quicker, cheaper and better than TV.

fairly recently there was a mix-up in the schedule, and the schedule said we were in studio S1 for the ten o'clock bulletin when in fact we were in S2. So I managed that with forty seconds to spare, up a flight of stairs; and I was trying desperately to get my breath back for the start of the programme – just about managed it! But it's not the best way to begin a live broadcast.

Usually the disasters are genuine accidents, though setting fire to scripts while they're being read was at one time a favourite test of the 'con' announcer's nerve. Part of his or her routine duties is of course to be standing by, ears cocked, to pick up the pieces when things fall apart so badly that they can't continue. 'I'm afraid we seem to be having a little trouble with the studio at the moment, so in the meantime, here's some music . . .' is, as avid listeners know (don't we all love it when things go wrong?), the signal for mayhem somewhere. So here on cue is Peter Donaldson again, with the tale of a truly heroic performance by one of his colleagues, Pennie Latin in the Radio 4 Continuity studio, who had to cope single-handedly with an incident that's gone down in recent Broadcasting House legend. It involves, perhaps inevitably in that repair-ridden building, the plumbing and a bit of shoddy workmanship . . .

Some workman on the eighth floor, even though the radiator was hot, decided he would cut the pipe with an angle-grinder. So eight floors of water cascaded through the broken pipe into all the wiring, putting the whole of radio off the air. Except, for some reason, the microphone in Radio 4 Continuity. Pennie wasn't able to play any of the trails, the programmes couldn't be played, but the microphone was live! And she talked for seven, eight, nine minutes – a wonderful feat!

Drama in the afternoon

Plays have always been part of Radio 4's afternoon sequence, though not always in the same place. In the early days, they sometimes popped up for half an hour at (the memorable start-time of) 12.27 pm. Thus, in autumn 1967, Radio 4 at lunchtime was up to episode 12 of a 48-episode adaptation of *The Forsyte Saga*. It's perhaps worth noting here what a text for the time this little fact is. With TV in its pomp and church pews emptying to watch Kenneth More and the Porters, Eric and Nyree Dawn, strut their stuff on Sunday nights on BBC2 (first shown in early 1967), radio simply tags along, following rather than leading its powerful younger sister medium; it would be a couple of decades at least before that order of things was reversed.

As in the TV version, the leading parts in the radio *Forsyte Saga* were played by stars; but down the cast list are some of the best-known and best-loved acting names of the time – Grizelda Hervey, Gudrun Ure, Beth Boyd, Garard Green and Preston Lockwood (who'd known children's fame as Dennis the Dachshund in the *Toytown* stories on *Children's Hour*). These actors crop up all over the schedules like clues in an Agatha Christie. One of the reasons was what's still known to people in radio as 'The Rep', a troupe of actors on long contract to the BBC. Nowadays shrunk to a handful of names, the Radio Drama Company as it's officially known, was, in its heyday forty years ago, perhaps as many as thirty strong. For drama directors, it was, as the great drama and features producer Piers Plowright observes, both a blessing – and a curse:

> Sometimes they were a bit abused because they wouldn't get many interesting parts – directors would buy in the big stars and they'd be doing the little parts. But of course you knew they were the same actors – 'He was a cardinal last week and now he's being a costermonger!' It was very much like a repertory theatre, and you'd expect to hear the same voices; that was half the pleasure of it.

Selecting names from the wealth of talent that regularly trooped through the radio drama studios – such as Carleton Hobbs, Maurice Denham, David March, Mary O'Farrell, Godfrey Kenton, Rolf Lefebvre, Richard Hurndall, Diana Ollson, Peter Woodthorpe and many, many others – is an invidious task, but one name is perhaps worth a particular mention. Mary Wimbush played so many roles that it's perhaps unfair to single out her last and most prominent incarnation. This was Julia Pargetter in *The Archers*, Nigel's venerable mother from Lower Loxley Hall, a part she played from 1992 until her death in 2005. 'Mary Wimbush was my favourite, I loved Mary; Mary goes back to the beginnings of drama as an art on radio.' For producer Ned Chaillet, who directed her in many plays, the multi-faceted Wimbush (she was the lover of playwright, poet and BBC man Louis MacNeice) was a very special talent:

> Her presence! She'd got a wonderful voice, great intelligence and the greatest thing about Mary was you knew she had *lived*. The audience didn't necessarily know that she had lived with Louis MacNeice but they knew that she had *lived* and she had a wonderful, wonderful character. At the end, she was recording for *The Archers*. She finished her take; she went into the room and had a cigarette, and, alas, died.

Inside the baron's castle

Drama Department was a venerable part of the oldest of the old BBC. Well into the 1990s, it still cultivated a slightly raffish reputation of bohemian extravagance, of expense accounts running into tens of thousands for fictitious projects (*The Celtic Twilight* was one often mentioned) against which to settle monstrous bar bills. One venerable head of Drama is reputed to have caused a huge internal row when he carried off all the remaining cases of wine at the end of the joint Christmas party with Light Entertainment department and stashed them in his cupboard. When the talk was of 'BBC baronies', the great semi-autonomous institutions within the fabric of the corporation, Drama Department certainly had a lot of weaponry.

It also had a huge and justified reputation. The very greatest names passed routinely through its studios – Pinter, Stoppard, Minghella to name just three of dozens of major writers;

A tale of three productions

'We will broadcast at least 730 hours of original drama and readings' in a year, declares Radio 4's official policy, so it's of course an impossible task, when contemplating the output of *forty* years of Radio 4 drama, to do other than sample. Here then are three anecdotes plucked from the many I've gathered that illustrate just how far Radio 4 people go to get inside the imaginations of their listeners.

Let's begin with a scene-setter from Piers Plowright. It concerns that great institution of the old Radio 4, *Saturday Night Theatre*, that he'd listened to as a boy: 'You know the famous line actually heard in one of those plays: "May I top up your sherry, inspector?" Nobody's ever said that line, I shouldn't think, except on Radio 4 *Saturday Night Theatre*!' When he came actually to producing it ('so clangy', he confesses) Plowright found himself caught up in a mystery, but, bizarrely, a completely unintentional one . . .

> It was adapted from some elderly detective novel that was so peculiar that we were getting near the last day of recording and somebody suddenly said, 'But . . . the solution to this is *impossible*!' And we realised that the play – maybe the novel – just didn't make any sort of sense. You just had to carry on; and the inspector would open the door and say 'Gotcha!' But why he'd got the person nobody really knew . . .

The creakiness didn't always lie within the scripts, either; performances and studio effects could sometimes be less than

Gielgud, Branagh, McKellen, Dench – a random quartet among hundreds of superb actors – all regularly popped up for a couple of days in the Broadcasting House studios and gathered among the throngs having lunch in the eighth-floor canteen. Drama was also very much not simply a metropolitan power; in Bristol, Edinburgh, Belfast and above all in Manchester were princes-of-the-blood owing strong allegiance to London; even Birmingham,

convincing and it sometimes took a fair bit of suspended disbelief to convince the listener that studio 8A really was, say, the great steppes of Russia . . . For the production story that Ned Chaillet relates the studio was, on this occasion, to be transformed into the Gulf of Mexico, with, no doubt, lots of sea and boat FX.

It was an adaptation of *The Old Man and the Sea*, Ernest Hemingway's celebrated novel about the Cuban fisherman who hooks a giant marlin and battles for three days to bring it aboard his small boat (memorably filmed in 1958 with Spencer Tracy in the central role). For this Radio 4 adaptation, Ned wanted an equally starry name. 'I was thinking of doing it with Anthony Quinn who was Mexican American and had a lot of other things going for him.' But before casting was complete, word of the production reached the (even bigger) Hollywood star, Rod Steiger; '"I'll have to do it. He'll fuck it up!"' Chaillet reports Steiger as saying, 'and so he cast himself.'

But Steiger was a film actor with very decided ideas about how to play a scene; not a small problem for director Chaillet who had just two working days in the studio to get the definitive incarnation of the Old Man, his battle with the fish, and the dispiriting return to port with the shark-scavenged carcase . . . He asked around the circuit, and Simon Callow, who'd directed Steiger on film, said he'd had the same problem: in his case Steiger would only do big close-ups. However, Callow also gave Chaillet his solution – capture everything: 'They'd do set-ups and they'd say "This is for lighting" so they could get medium shots' and so on until they got enough versions to offer the range of cutting options they needed. Chaillet followed suit:

☞

with *The Archers*, was a force to be reckoned with. Additionally, the sheer volume of output, running into hundreds of hours of plays every year, meant that in staff numbers alone Radio Drama carried huge clout.

Life within the confines of the department during the first two and a half decades of Radio 4 was still reminiscent of the sort of clubby, autocratic, prank-filled, arty atmosphere typical of many

The only way to get alternatives was to record everything – rehearse, record that. And he would come up [too close] and give you exactly the performance *he* wanted, whereas you needed a little depth. But the great stories he had . . .

My third tale of Radio 4 drama features a certain well-known boy wizard. It's Christmas 2000 and new controller Helen Boaden is looking for something blockbusting for her seasonal schedule: 'I want people to know that we're here,' she explained to me, 'so you need a few big splashy things.' And pretty well the splashiest thing at that moment for a Christmas treat was *Harry Potter and the Philosopher's Stone*. The first hurdle was author J.K. Rowling's agent: 'He said "I don't want it to be done in parts." And of course initially I thought "Oh that's a bit of a problem." And then I just had a bit of a brainwave which was let's do it all in one. This Boxing Day.'

And so plans were laid; Stephen Fry would read and Radio 4 would do one of its fork-in-the-road tricks with Potter occupying the FM while regular programmes continued on Long Wave.

I worried about people who didn't want Harry Potter who'd feel very short changed by having to get everything else on Long Wave, and

corners of the 'old BBC'. The poet and Radio 4 broadcaster Michael Rosen joined the department as a high-flying young recruit in 1969, and vividly remembers the atmosphere at the weekly meetings:

These were chaired by the great Martin Esslin who used to sit there, speaking in his very strong mittel-Europa accent and saying, 'Too yoo tsink zis iss a highbrrow play or a mittelbrrow play or a lowbrrow play?' And then sitting round the room [among others] you had Bill Ash who was, rather incredibly, on the General Executive of the Communist Party of Great Britain (Marxist-Leninist), who used to nip out of the BBC in his lunchtimes to go over the road to the Chinese Embassy, and who used to sit in the canteen and tell us of the glories of Albania.

then I worried about would people know where to find it on Radio 4?
But we did draw in for a period at least people who'd never come to
Radio 4 before. We had people ringing up the BBC and saying, 'What's
Radio 4?'

Until the Christmas line-up was published, Boaden knew it all had
to remain very hush-hush:

I kept that so secret! For a gabby person I was unbelievably secretive
about that. People were floored! It was great! [big laugh]. It was great
revealing the secret at the last moment!

And then the headlines; it was literally front-page news, a dream
coup for the new controller and a real radio event. Overall, too, the
audience was thrilled; though it wasn't all unalloyed joy: 'Got loads
of hate-mail when it was announced; I mean really vicious hate-
mail,' which astonished Boaden. 'You know, "You bitch! All you care
about is the young"; stuff that was incredibly hurt and angry. It was
a good sort of birthing into being loathed by members of the public!'
she adds with a huge guffaw.

Esslin, an Austrian-born academic and critic (he coined the
term 'theatre of the absurd') fled to Britain before the Second
World War, eventually joining the BBC to rule Drama
Department with a firm hand for fourteen years, until 1977.
Little surprise then that one of the famous graffiti adorning a
studio sound effects door read 'Martin Esslin has bad Brecht'.
Esslin could be, says Piers Plowright 'totally ruthless, but was
kind; knocked a few heads together'. He was, too, 'the best of
the "robber barons", fighting for his territory, following and
defending his men, for *ever*!'
Esslin's men – and to the newly recruited Plowright it seemed
that almost all the production staff at that time, with one or two
exceptions, were men – could be pretty wild: 'I remember
particularly Martin Jenkins and Gerry Jones, younger pro-

ducers, who were a wonderfully raucous pair and the walls were *covered* with nudes – they all had to be taken down later!'

For on-duty actors, lunch would usually be, as I've mentioned, a big, noisy table in the canteen; but evenings meant everyone over to the BBC Chandos Street Club. Propping up the bar would often be director David Johnston: 'He lived in Brighton,' remembers fellow producer Ned Chaillet, 'and had been Terence Rattigan's boyfriend. He was the most outrageous comic, camp person, but he was also incredibly intelligent and did wonderful script work.' Johnston was one of the stalwarts of the 1970s and 80s; from an earlier, yet grander (pre-Radio 4) era were still to be found legends like R.D. (Reggie) Smith. Smith did, however, reach his apogee on Radio 4 with the famous dramatised account he made of journalist (and fellow great imbiber) James Cameron's heart operation, *The Pump*, which won the 1972 Prix Italia.

Thus, convivial, connected and charming, Radio Drama Department even twenty-five years ago, as Mrs Thatcher began to modernise Britain, was living on borrowed time. Take, for example, the 'working day' of another venerable departmental figure with a sumptuous pedigree (poet, Cambridge medievalist and first producer of Tolkein's *Lord of the Rings*), Terence Tiller. Piers Plowright met him in Broadcasting House in the 1970s.

> Terence would arrive on a Green Line bus from Luton at about seven in the morning, go to his office where the curtains would be drawn. He would probably translate *Beowulf* or something and then have a little look at a script. At twelve he'd go to the Club and he would be there till about three; and he'd drink about eight or nine pints of beer or Guinness. Then he'd come back and put in some sort of work for another hour, and he'd catch the four o'clock Green Line bus back to Luton. That was Terence's day.

Despite what appears in retrospect as a rather dissolute atmosphere, fine and lasting work was being done with the greatest playwrights and the creamiest of acting talent. Plowright singles out director Richard Wortley's *Lord Nelson*

Lives in Liverpool 8 about a young black man on twentieth-century Merseyside who identifies with Horatio Nelson, and *On a Day in Summer in a Garden* by Don Howarth in which the central characters are talking dock plants who offer a wry commentary on the humans. 'They speak perfectly ordinary English. All the humans go "bbwllwblgwwlwgwldl"!'

Maurice Leitch, Guy Vaesen, Kay Patrick, Robert Cooper, Richard Imison, Jane Morgan, Martin Jenkins and Glyn Dearman are a randomly selected handful of the famous London director names that stud the chronicles of the literally thousands of hours of drama broadcast in its forty years by Radio 4. During the old 'barony' regime, two big men with flamboyant style led the department to glory and into the annals of BBC Radio anecdotage. Ronald Mason and John Tydeman were larger-than-life characters of the old school; John was also a brilliant director with one of the most illustrious records in the business, yet he'll perhaps be forever remembered for having brought a young man aged 13¾, name of Mole, A., to the public's attention via Radio 4 for the first time.

Beyond the capital, Bristol, Glasgow and Belfast all had their drama luminaries, and in the north of England – and especially in Leeds – the name of Alfred Bradley still shines particularly brightly. Alfred was a maverick who fostered talent with a distinctively northern grain – like Alan Ayckbourn, the wonderfully funny Henry Livings and gritty realists such as Stan Barstow and Alan Plater. Gillian Reynolds calls Bradley's talent-spotting operation 'a sort of guerrilla unit' based in Yorkshire. 'He worked his own patch, he knew how to pull the strings and he did it, not for the pleasure of the power, he did it for fun! And for the greater joy of the listener.' One of Alfred's regular showcases for his discoveries was *The Northern Drift*, that I recall as a wonderful anthological mix of poetry and playlets where, amongst others, Livings and his singer-songwriter friend Alex Glasgow would conjure touching and hilarious sketches of north of England life.

Alfred Bradley now has a writing prize in his name, and one of the early winners was a Tyneside-born playwright, Lee Hall, for his first play *I Luv U Jimmy Spud*. But if Hall's first piece carried off a shelf-full of prizes, his next, the story of a seven-year-old autistic girl dying of cancer caught the attention of the audience like virtually no production since Adrian Mole. It was called *Spoonface Steinberg* and was a sensational hit for Radio 4 in 1997. An hour-long monologue, it was the perfect vehicle for radio: 'It had so many hundreds of affected people calling the BBC and writing,' recalls Chaillet, 'that it was repeated fairly immediately and sold in vast numbers. That's the kind of impact you can have.'

It was the making of Lee Hall; *Spoonface* was remade for television and Hall went on to write the much garlanded film *Billy Elliot*. But *Spoonface* remained best as a radio play, where all the work was done at the point where the words, and the voice meet the imagination of the listener. We're back where we started this book, playing dramatic games with the mind. Ned Chaillet says:

> And let's not forget, radio is able to create in the audience the greatest kind of imagination of events. A sex scene on radio is usually nothing more than maybe someone kissing the back of their hand – but the letters you get from outraged listeners! It's because their imagination is so unleashed by being alone with the radio; and I love that impact. And the ability to move.

Coming up next on Radio 4 . . .

One of the benchmarks radio people often use to assess the impact of a programme, how effective it's been in moving and captivating its audience, is the 'car park test'. Were listeners 'unable' to leave their vehicles before the end credits rolled? It must be a hit! It's a crude guide, but a powerful one nonetheless. For the Radio 4 announcer Peter Donaldson, arriving for an afternoon shift in continuity, it became a bit of a ritual:

> The car park used to be below our studios and, if I were listening to the *Afternoon Play* and enjoying it, I was not going to leave my

car until the play had finished! So I flashed my lights from the car park up at the studio, which people got to know was 'Donaldson's here but he ain't coming in till the play's over!'

Continuity announcers are in many ways the unsung heroes and heroines of Radio 4, stitching all the other bits of the network together so that it forms a composite, coherent whole. Rarely do they become real stars: 'We're not *presenters*,' Peter asserts. 'When I was Chief Announcer there were people I turned down for the job of announcer because they were too big. I said, "You have a presenter's presence. An announcer has to be far more subtle."'

And yet, by virtue of their very continuous presence on air, they become the familiars of the audience, the reassuring voice letting listeners know subtly and undemonstratively that life is continuing, that Radio 4 is there, come what may: Peter Donaldson remembers: 'Tony Whitby once said to me that no one should be an announcer for more than five years, and I said, "I beg to differ, because I think it takes at least that amount of time to build up a rapport with the listener." I know what *he* meant, but it takes that time for the listener to get used to you, to like you or to loathe you.'

And as Professor Laurie Taylor, another broadcaster who has spent pretty well all four decades of Radio 4 in and out of the station's studios at one point or another, has analysed, that familiarity is part of the whole grammar of the network. The audience is cautious over new arrivals, careful to examine who it is they're welcoming into their home. By dint of having served the network so long, Taylor qualifies therefore as a 'safe pair of hands' for listeners and for controllers alike. When he eventually pulled the plug on *Anderson Country*, Michael Green turned to Laurie to pick up the pieces in *The Afternoon Shift* (see page 200).

These days, he tills one of those rather neat fields I talked about right at the beginning of this chapter: *Thinking Allowed* is one among many shows making up the latter end of the afternoon. This isn't an exhaustive list and many come and go periodically, but they include old favourites some of which have

Country matters

Just once in while, Radio 4 makes a big, public cock-up. It's not usually as bad as the press would have it, nor is it usually a really big deal; but because Radio 4 serves so often as the chat-room for journalists and much of the Establishment, trouble at t'mill can soon become a campaign, and a great big juicy stick for those who dislike the BBC to beat it with. In the four decades of Radio 4, however, there can be no single programme that's come in for the sort of vicious ad-hominem critique as did that mid-afternoon initiative called *Anderson Country*.

The man at the eye of the storm is, I should say immediately, a good colleague of mine. Gerry Anderson has been responsible for some of the most remarkable broadcasting about his native Ulster that Radio 4 has transmitted; his several talks series which I was privileged to produce were remarkable; from *Surviving in Stroke City* to *The Road to Nowhere*, via *Gerry's Bar*, they told sly, anarchic stories of Northern Ireland that feel to listeners like the *real*, the normally unspoken truth.

But, for years, Gerry's day job has been talking the citizens of Derry through their mornings on BBC Radio Foyle, and more widely (on television too) presenting programmes across the whole of Northern Ireland. 'The first moment I heard Gerry Anderson on Radio Ulster,' remembers the radio critic Gillian Reynolds, 'I just fell in love with not just the voice but the airy way he talks about things, and the way everything knits up in his world, and he makes strange conjunctions and strange connections.'

So it wasn't a bad thought to book him as the voice of a new show being dreamed up to 'do something' about those troublesomely

been around for years like *The Food Programme*, *Gardeners' Question Time* and *A Good Read*. Then there are others like *Word of Mouth* which have a pedigree of fifteen or so years; yet others date from the Boyle reform, such as *Open Book*, *Material World* and *Ramblings* with, finally, some much more recent creations, including *More or Less*, *Home Planet*, *The Film Programme*, *Questions*, *Questions* and *Travellers' Tree*.

messy afternoon schedules that used to exist on Radio 4 before James Boyle knocked them about a bit. The year was 1994 and in January, the Media *Guardian* headlined 'More shockwaves on the way for conservatively-inclined Radio 4 listeners'. In February 'the easy-going pattern of their afternoons is to be disrupted' by the arrival of a new 'flexible, unpredictable, topical magazine', to be named – after its presenter – *Anderson Country*. The programme, an hour long, would run daily at 3.00 pm. 'It was a risky venture editorially anyway,' observes the then controller Michael Green, 'because it wasn't prescriptive.'

> It was an attempt to say, 'Here we are in the middle of the afternoon; we've been lectured at pretty relentlessly all day. Let's try and tap into the byways of human life.'

Despite his impressive record in live broadcasting, the appointment of Gerry Anderson was a risk; not least on account of the endlessly debated matter of the tone of Radio 4. The hard truth is that local radio phone-in hosts and Radio 4 presenters have little or no tonal overlap. Where a laid-back, let's-explore-that-topic feel is just what a gently freewheeling local talk programme requires, Radio 4's listeners are used to having their presenters' thoughts ordered, shaped and organised. When Radio 4 does relaxed, it's often more *intellectually* so than structurally. Hence casting Gerry as host was a bit of a gamble. 'I mean we piloted it ad nauseam,' says Michael Green, 'and there was a great debate about was he right? Well, eventually, we went with it. You take some risks, don't you?'

☞

All in all, this elaborate patchwork of programmes that nowadays fills up Radio 4's afternoon landscape offers us money, medicine, food, gardening, books, science, language, maths, geography, history, travel . . . or, indeed, with *Questions, Questions* simply provides 'answers to those intriguing and seemingly imponderable questions which dog our daily life'. Well, that's got it all pretty well sorted, hasn't it? Don't have to

'This is a fine time to be Gerry Anderson,' Catherine Bennett was writing in the *Guardian* within a few weeks of the launch. 'In the last five weeks he has been transformed from a popular regional name into a focus of national lamentation . . . *Anderson Country* has become the most reviled radio programme for years.' Marion Greenwood, as chief press officer for Radio 4, had her work cut out: 'It was too big an ask, an hour-long programme with one voice,' she says with a resigned shrug, 'and it might have settled down, but some sections of the press just wouldn't let it lie.' Indeed they wouldn't. '*Anderson Country* must go!' screamed the *Sunday Times*; 'I am going to smash up my kitchen unless someone does something about Gerry Anderson. A fatwa would be a start' shrieked the *Independent on Sunday*.

'It got very personal,' remembers Greenwood, 'and it must have been terrible for him.' Gillian Reynolds, while not dissenting from the general view, was regretful more than angry: 'No one was more profoundly disappointed than me because I was just such a fan,' she told me. 'They'd taken this cheery singing bird out of the hedgerow – he sings, he's not scripted – and they sat him down with a script and they timed him. Death. Death.'

After a year, the axe fell on the beleaguered *Anderson Country* and its host. He was replaced by Mr Safe-Hands, Laurie Taylor, and the show was renamed *The Afternoon Shift*. *The Shift* was never a

go far to make sense of everything: just tune in to Radio 4 every afternoon. Forty years ago, apart from the drama and the Schools, it was just acres and acres of . . . music.

Who said the network had dumbed down?

Words and ideas

To round off this chapter, and by way of a prelude before the frenzy of *PM* and the *Six O'Clock News*, a taste of just two of those programmes chosen at random, one that dates from James Boyle's era and the other from a previous age. And here I

gold-plated hit, but at least it wasn't drawing down irate listeners and doomy headlines on Radio 4 and Michael Green. What then, with a good bit of distancing perspective on the affair, is the controller's view of it all? Pretty negative, I'd say.

> On the two counts. Wrong man for the course, wrong jockey, and I regret that because it tarred his reputation as a fantastic broadcaster for a period. And secondly a programme idea that perhaps was too diffuse, too spongy, too disparate – just a bit unmanageable for a daily strike.

Finally, James Boyle's 1998 network springclean carried off *The Afternoon Shift* too, but created a real diamond-encrusted hit in *Home Truths* that owed not a little to the tone so eagerly sought by his predecessor:

> Still quite discursive, you never quite knew what would fetch up, very much down the alleys and the ginnels of life, really. And that had been exactly the same ambition for *Anderson Country*. So one knew it would work, sooner or later, and I think that much more discursive kind of broadcasting now has a place in Radio 4 in a way that it perhaps didn't before *Anderson Country*.

apologise if your favourite's not had a mention; as you can see, the riches are just too vast for me to be comprehensive. So here goes. *Thinking Allowed* is Laurie Taylor's programme about sociology. It's his field and, although Laurie's a consummate broadcaster, it's not a soft listen, more what Michael Green once graphically called a 'hard chair' programme ('I had nearly twenty-five minutes talking to Ronald Dworkin about the development of democracy'). Despite its clever-clever title, you find wit, interaction and ideas, not to mention the odd joke. Take this anecdote that Laurie tells:

I had a letter from a student the other day who said, 'I was

amazed to hear you on your programme the other day saying you
were glad to be here . . . I was a student of yours in the sixties at
York . . . I should have thought at your age, you must be glad to
be anywhere!' And that's the sort of stuff that you get!

Laurie firmly believes that the audience is, in the internet age,
more sophisticated in the way it responds to such sit-up-and-
listen fare; thus, returning to his desk from the studio Laurie
finds '. . . emails have come in immediately after the programme
saying "the problem of this principle . . . the problem of
that . . ." You'd never have that in the past.' This connection
with the audience, their desire not just to make their opinions
felt but also to contribute experiences and expertise, is one of
the big evolutionary stories of broadcasting over the last forty
years. Once, Radio 4's programmes loftily broadcast down to
the masses. But, first phone-ins in the late 1960s and since the
mid-1990s email and text-messages have changed all that to
create what, rather blandly, is known as 'interactivity'.

Some shows have been doing it from the start. *Word of
Mouth*, another of Radio 4's afternoon delights, canvassed
public opinion from day one, seeking listeners' favourite words.
Since then, the audience has voted for Britain's wittiest person –
the most recent winner was the late Linda Smith – and, perhaps
most imaginatively, their words for things that don't have
adequate names. One favourite: those employees who stand
outside offices smoking a quick cigarette – and a big round of
applause to the ingenious listener who came up with
'snoutcasts'. Think about it.

Michael Rosen is the current and third presenter to have held
the chair, the first being Frank Delaney whose original idea
Word of Mouth was, and then Russell Davies. Although
Michael Green, when he first welcomed the show on to his
network, said he hoped it would field all the listeners'
complaints usually directed at him about bad English on Radio
4, Rosen points out that *Word of Mouth* isn't judgemental.

It's not concerned with putting people right and telling them that
they're wandering about with wrongheaded notions. It's saying,

hey, wow, isn't it weird! Let's look at the way in which people name perfume. Years ago it used to be Chanel No 5, now it's called things like Sssshh or Joop Jump. Why's that? Or why is it that people seem to say 'that' instead of 'which'? What happened to 'which'?

I wondered, finally, whether Michael Rosen had any favourite moments? So many, he says – like going golfing for language on the links with Jimmy Tarbuck and Henry Cooper – but one really stood out; it was shortly after the Iraq war and Kate Adie had joined another expert to discuss the language of post-war situations: 'We talked about "occupation",' remembered Rosen, 'and about the language that was used after the invasion of Germany and the occupation – was it "occupation"? Was it "liberation"? Was it "reconstruction"?' But then Adie mentioned another post-war term, 'fragmentation'. 'And lo and behold,' Michael says gleefully, 'four or five years later what are they talking about? *"Fragmentation* of Iraq" – we're not talking politics, we're talking *language*. And I'm thinking, "Wow! Bloody hell. Kate Adie was on to that"!'

Boyle's law

Twenty-eight years to the week after Tony Whitby introduced his radical shake-up of Radio 4, his successor but six James Boyle undertook, starting in April 1998, a similarly revolution-ary step – but where Whitby had just three and a half months to invent his new shape, Boyle spent eighteen months thinking and rethinking the network. It was the most detailed piece of research ever undertaken on Radio 4, and involved not only a close inspection of the audience's living patterns (we got to know which bit of *Today* most people cleaned their teeth to) and the programmes they enjoyed, but also the minutest scrutiny of how every component of the network meshed with the next, how programme ideas were chosen and commissioned, and how the whole thing was to be paid for.

I distinctly recall the sense of excitement combined with trepidation within radio production departments as Boyle set to work. Commissioning editors were appointed to oversee the new Radio schedule and we learned a new piece of jargon: 'day-parting' – each of the new commissioners was in charge of a chunk of the day. It was regime change, and to those of us who'd spent a long time in a more familial if haphazard relationship with the network it felt very strange. For the first time, money was managed as part of the editorial process, so that some slots were deliberately assigned relatively low budgets in order to keep the programmes uncomplicated – and more appropriate to the degree of attention listeners could afford at that time of day. It sounds crude, but it was incredibly effective, and forced programme-makers to think inventively about how shows were produced, and concentrate on how the audience actually listened.

Despite the odd turkey (the quizzes and the late night sport weren't big successes) the overall marrying up of programme shapes with listeners' lives was quite brilliant, and the schedule that Mark Damazer works with today is very largely still the model engineered by Boyle. Take for example the moment in the Radio 4 day that we've arrived at in this story, the afternoon. Today, Damazer has a well tended orchard of programmes, neatly organised in rows, drama here, magazines over there, a bit of storytelling in the other corner, all tidily squared off. But it was not always so.

To those who ran the network in the 1990s, Michael Green and James Boyle, a glance at the afternoon schedule must have felt like a gardener surveying several centuries' growth of brambles – the roots were deep and the trunks thick and spiny. Yet the heavy-duty hacking had, just had, to be done: 'trying to get to grips with the schedule and sort out the afternoon', is how Marion Greenwood, former head of publicity for Radio 4, and for more than two decades very close to the controller's office, puts it.

> That was this terrible, terrible mess, because every afternoon you had programmes of different lengths so you had no idea: Monday was a sixty-minute play, Tuesday was a thirty-minute play, Wednesday was a forty-five-minute play, Thursday was a forty-seven-minute play and Friday was an hour. But Monday's was a repeat of the *Saturday Night Theatre* and on Friday afternoons I think at one point we were repeating *Classic Serial*.

As a result, programmes that followed the play had a variety of start times. Back in the days of the Home Service, a less ordered view of the schedule was normal; listeners would seek out what they wanted to hear, having first consulted *Radio Times*. However, by the 1990s, even die-hard Radio 4 listeners found what Boyle described as the 'medieval town-plan' of irregular programme lengths and styles pretty puzzling. 'It made it very difficult to talk about the afternoon,' remembers publicist Greenwood, 'because there was a different feeling and texture every afternoon. You'd go from *Analysis* – really heavyweight documentaries – to something really light the next day. It meant that you couldn't make that appointment to listen.'

It fell therefore to James Boyle finally to grub out the brambles and tidy up the Radio 4 landscape: and not least to challenge the barons of Radio Drama to a fight – a fight which as controller he must at all costs win. Boyle told me, 'I remember the great Michael Green – Michael Green was my hero as controller – Michael said to me, "Don't try to commission drama".'

Here we need to touch, albeit briefly, on internal BBC politics. Until James Boyle formally instituted a commissioning editor for his drama output, the process of choosing which plays got the go-ahead was, at best, a shared exercise with Radio Drama department. At the other end of the scale, the controller simply provided the airtime while Drama took all the decisions. Henceforth, however, Drama Department would, in effect, no longer be in control of its output. If Radio 4 didn't fancy another potboiler *Afternoon Theatre* it would no longer commission it. This was heresy.

James Boyle was a man with a plan: 'I had a personal sense that Radio 4 was in danger,' he told me. He was worried the network wasn't giving listeners *what* they wanted *when* they could listen to it; and he was also bothered about cash. 'Believe me, at that time an accountant's view of drama was that it just wasn't value for money: you just looked at it and you could see that it wasn't holding its listeners.' Boyle knew there were those in the highest echelons of the corporation who would be doing the maths; by taking commissioning for drama back to the centre, he reckoned, he could offer a degree of protection. 'So I was going to be commissioning it.' Battle with Drama Department was joined:

> The worst thing I heard was a man saying to me, 'Why do you have to have all this business of commissioning systems and drawing people in from Manchester and so forth? In the old days we used to do this in the pub. We'd go round to the George and we'd talk about a programme . . .'

(The George pub in Great Portland Street was a legendary haunt

of BBC drama people and poets like Louis MacNeice and Dylan
Thomas.)

> I said 'Well, for those of you that live on the Central Line that's
> fine, but what about people that live in Cardiff, what about the
> woman in Norwich who's talented but has got two kids at her
> ankles, what about Newcastle? We cannot go on commissioning
> from just the same sixty people every year; we've got to find new
> talent.' It was about finding new talent, new talent, new talent,
> and doing justice to the fact that *everybody* in Britain owns Radio
> 4. Not just the people that can go for a pint in the George.

And it wasn't just *how* plays were commissioned that got
Drama staff cross, but *how long* the actual pieces ran on air.
Henceforth, decreed Boyle, he'd transmit nothing longer than
one hour, thus sounding the death-knell for the beloved ninety-
minute play: Ned Chaillet, the award-winning drama producer
and former critic for *The Times*, recalls with a sad shake of the
head: 'James Boyle decided that the audience didn't like them
any more.' He accompanied James during his public consul-
tations and, perhaps unsurprisingly, found listeners who were
sympathetic to the Drama Department line: 'They said, "We *do*
like them! We wanna know why can't we have them?"'
Speaking ten years on, Chaillet is still grumbling:

> Now we're dominated by a 45-minute slot which is *The
> Afternoon Play* and it's very hard to have a full narrative in 45
> minutes. You can do it but it's not that easy. It's too long to be a
> short story and it's not long enough to have a proper, full
> narrative.

James Boyle's new schedule came into being on April the 6th
1998. ('We were going to do it the week before,' grins Marion
Greenwood, wryly, 'and then realised it was April the 1st and
thought that was not a good idea!) Although the axe didn't fall
quite as press leaks predicted (*Farming Today*, *Midweek*, *Start
the Week*, *You and Yours*, all survived) the changes were
substantial and, unlike Tony Whitby's relaunch, the whole

business was played out in the full glare of the modern media spotlight. There were dozens of new programmes – *Broadcasting House, The Archive Hour, Live From London* . . . – new start times, and new presenters for old favourites. Several programmes (*Week Ending, Kaleidoscope* and *Does He Take Sugar?*, for instance) disappeared, while *The World at One* and *The World This Weekend* were shorn to thirty minutes. Weekday lunchtimes were now shared with a raft of new entertainment programmes – 'Those 1.30 pm quizzes were *awful*,' confides Marion Greenwood with the benefit of hindsight.

Not all though. The lunchtime guesswork also embraced one of Radio 4's best loved and enigmatic puzzle-programmes, *Round Britain Quiz. RBQ* is a veteran of the Home Service and has barely changed its cryptic format since it began in 1947. Its crossword-like clues elicit either bafflement, or, as so often in the case of Irene Thomas who became a minor star as a result, stunning elucidation that leaves the average listener like me gasping 'But . . . How? . . . What?' Lionel Hale, Anthony Quinton, Gordon Clough and Nick Clarke all chaired the programme over the years, which now inevitably sports its erudition online as well as over the air.

Some of the biggest and most prominent of Boyle's changes were to the network's drama schedule: gone was creaky old *Saturday Night Theatre* while *The Monday Play*, the home of 'full-length' (i.e. long), serious-minded drama, now became *The Friday Play*, and would henceforth only last an hour. Classic serials moved to Sundays, and in the afternoon of every day of the working week, stripped and stranded at 2.15 pm after *The Archers* was *The Afternoon Play*, forty-five minutes of daily drama, dependable and accessible.

In the event, the day of the launch fell somewhat flat. I clearly remember colleagues turning to one another and saying, 'What was all the fuss about?', a response shared by some of the press. However, many verdicts were less generous, and although some reviewers were glad to see the back of programmes they loathed ('Whatever else you say about the new Radio 4 schedules, you have to admit that they don't include *Week Ending*' wrote the *Independent*), the replacements that weren't up to snuff came in for a hammering. Initial response from the audience was likewise mixed, and though listening figures leaped to begin with, they fell back as the effect of all the press hype drained away. 'He just didn't have the programmes,' points out Gillian Reynolds, while acknowledging that some radical surgery was required, 'and it was apparent the first week. You'd turn on *The World at One* and it was shortened, and you'd think, "Awww, I really miss that ten minutes." And here would be the most God-awful quiz show; five ghastly quiz shows across the week – "Oh, no! oh, no!"'

Six months on, the *Guardian* was reporting 'leaked figures for July showed that Radio 4 listening dropped by 10% year-on-year. The 1.30 pm quiz show suffered particularly . . .' By October 1998 the audience for Radio 4 had dipped steeply, with half a million fewer listeners tuning in. Questions were being asked. However, as the poor performers among the new shows fell away (who now remembers the end-of-evening sports show *Late Tackle*?), and some excellent replacements came on stream, and, above all, as listeners adjusted their mind-sets, the figures began to recover. The *Broadcasting House* programme on Sunday mornings, after a shaky start, is now a firm favourite, and *Home Truths*, John Peel's cosy Saturday confection became a multi-Sony Radio Award-winning triumph.

What endures above all else ten years on is Boyle's *shape* of the network. It was clever and intuitive and is one of the reasons why, once the shock of the new had worn off, the network has continued to maintain extremely healthy audience figures of between nine and ten million a week. Although there's been some shuffling of the cards in the afternoon schedule deck – a magazine replaced here (*Veg Talk requiescat in pace*), a new baby there (all hail *Last Word*) – James Boyle's main building blocks between Ambridge and *PM* remain in place.

Shortly after the revamp, Jenny Abramsky took over as Director of Radio, and, while applauding the new shape, was distinctly cool about how it was introduced. It was all too much, too quickly, she asserts, and had Radio 4 listeners had somewhere else to turn, as ten years later they now would, they mightn't so readily have found their way back into the Radio 4 fold: 'I think if you suddenly wholesale-change it, and think that the audience will appreciate and thank you for it, then you're making a big mistake,' Abramsky observes.

> I suspect if this were to ever happen again, they might have somewhere else to go, and I would caution any controller of Radio 4 not to do it so – the word is not 'cavalierly' – but not to do it without that understanding of just how hurt the audience feels about the way it is treated. Even if what you're doing might be the right thing, sometimes the way you go about doing it needs to be different.

Speaking now, a long way removed from the hub of radio operations, James Boyle is pretty unrepentant: 'I did know . . . that it had to done quickly, that it wouldn't be popular . . . But I was the person from outside to change it.'

> And if you want me to stand up for myself and say, 'What did he bring that nobody else brought?' I think I brought bottle. Because I looked into people's eyes and I said, 'We're gonna do this.' I really did get very upset looking at a number of folk . . . who were just swindling producers and listeners by ignoring things they knew to be wrong and not doing anything about it. So if you want me to be self-inflated and put on a kind of big ostrich-feather hat, yeah, it's the one that says, 'He's got bottle.' I did have bottle; that's what I supplied.

CHAPTER EIGHT

5.00 pm: Informing and entertaining

'It's *PM* . . . at five p.m.' William Hardcastle's breathy voice, with that momentary pause for drama, heralded for five years until his untimely death in 1975 the start of Radio 4's first ever drivetime programme. What followed was the jittery, Morse-code-like metallic signature tune, courtesy of the BBC Radiophonic Workshop with its four ding-dong notes and then the voice-over: 'This is William Hardcastle . . . and Derek Cooper . . . with the programme that sums up the day; and your evening starts here . . .' Sig tunes were still a programme essential forty years ago: *Woman's Hour* had one – and changed it from time to time – *Kaleidoscope*, the long-running arts programme had one, as did *Down Your Way*. *Today* experimented with musical stings and even Radio 4 itself in its first six months had a little flirtation. Hard to imagine today, yet in March 1968 Radio Review Board minutes reported that the experiment with 'short musical sequences prepared by the Radiophonic Workshop' was proving 'very effective'.

The signature of the BBC's Radiophonic Workshop on any theme music was at the time de rigueur for the hip and the cool. On television *Dr Who* had famously used the workshop, and so later did a number of Radio 4 programmes, not least the science magazine *New Worlds*. Little surprise therefore, when a bright shiny fanfare was required to announce Tony Whitby's new current affairs programme for the early evening, that the programme team turned to the men and women with the oscilloscopes, synthesisers and wobbulators. It was exceptional though, because at a time when sig tunes were everywhere, other news programmes didn't have them, apart from *Radio Newsreel* whose old military march 'Imperial Echoes' disappeared – with

Charlotte Green's delights

Comedians need a straight-man, and topical comedy needs its straight-faced feed, so who better than radio's corps of newsreaders to provide the service on shows like *The News Quiz*? For two or three it's become a minor career option, so when called upon Peter Donaldson, Harriet Cass and Charlotte Green are only too happy to slip off the straitjacket of seriousness and don the smart-casual of comedy. 'I love *The News Quiz*,' says Charlotte, who's been doing it for nearly twenty years: 'They are always trying to make me laugh, and usually giving me particularly risqué clippings to read that set me off!! But I love that.'

There has of course been a long tradition of the formal announcer voice being parachuted into the lunacy of radio comedy: the Goons did it, and newsreader Douglas Smith ('I, Douglas Smith . . .') famously played all sorts of strange roles in *Round the Horne*. But Charlotte Green very definitely plays herself when appearing with Sandi Toksvig and the *News Quiz* regulars.

> It's like being with a really good, witty, funny group of friends and just sitting round the table enjoying a good bottle of wine and having a really, really good laugh. I adore it, and for me that's the icing on the cake.

The biggest joke on Radio 4 newsreaders came of course not on *The News Quiz* but on *Dead Ringers*, in which Charlotte's alter ego is incarnated by impressionist Jan Ravens. These days, Ravens's target is Fiona Bruce of BBC1's *Ten O'Clock News*, but the first to receive the

the programme – in the new schedule. Thus, on April the 6th 1970, to the first public airing of those Morse-code twangings, *PM* took to the air. It had three regular presenters to begin with: William Hardcastle, not unnaturally, given that *PM* came from the *WATO* stable and, alongside him, two other experienced broadcasters: Steve Race, who had been, you'll remember, one of the stalwarts of the magazine that *PM* now displaced called

newsreader-as-vamp treatment was Radio 4's Green: 'I mean it's wonderful: how can you complain about being sexed up like that? It's absolutely wonderful!' gushes Charlotte, a little overcome.

Dead Ringers was one of James Boyle's innovative commissions to fill the gap left by axing *Week Ending*. 'I remember the instant that I knew I had the replacement,' James Boyle smiles as he recounts the story, 'driving along in the car, I put this tape on. It was *Dead Ringers*, and I just listened to the person beside me roaring with laughter.' At that moment, he knew where satire needed to go on Radio 4: 'We're not talking about Westminster Village, we're talking about people who have a knowledge of cartoons on television, people who know Rolf Harris. It's just a better, more modern frame of reference. And it just worked in spades.'

Steve Punt agrees and points out that even more than Rolf Harris, the *Dead Ringers* team had very specifically the world of Radio 4 itself at its heart.

> You know, it doesn't take an Einstein to realise that impressions are good on radio, but it just hit the network like a bomb! Because of that genius idea of doing impressions of Radio 4 people who you certainly weren't going to get from anyone else. Charlotte Green and Brian Perkins – brilliant!

So mild-mannered newsreader 'Brian Perkins' became a no-nonsense, don't-mess-with-me mobster type to match the come-hither seductiveness of 'Charlotte Green':

☞

Home This Afternoon; and Derek Cooper, who would eventually find a permanent home as the elegant, knowledge-able presenter (with a voice as rich as the finest burgundy) of *The Food Programme*.

PM was a vital part of Tony Whitby's new current affairs pattern for Radio 4: each weekday, there were now five sequences: the four successes were *Today*, *WATO*, *PM*, and, at

It is quite extraordinary if you go to drinks parties or dinner parties, I think people half expect me to be this extraordinary sort of vamp and femme fatale who is truly moving around every man within Broadcasting House and Television Centre, sort of ticking them off, you know. And I'm not really like that at all!

Charlotte told me that she especially enjoys the extra roles she's asked to take on because it's 'a very welcome antidote' to the grimness of the rest of the news she has to report. However, there was in recent years a special bonus, and one, tragically, she can no longer enjoy. Linda Smith, voted by Radio 4 listeners the wittiest person in Britain, was a regular on *The News Quiz* and Charlotte got to know her well and love her company, as all of us did who had the luck to work with her. 'In a very witty, funny programme she just added another layer; she shone,' remembers Charlotte, 'and I used to really look forward to being in the Green Room with her because she was *as* funny if not more so before we went on as she was on the actual show. So she was a very big favourite and it's terribly sad that Linda is no longer with us.'

10.00 pm, *The World Tonight*; the fifth programme, *Newsdesk*, timed at 7.00 pm and hosted by Gerald Priestland, completed the line-up and was the only one of the quintet not to survive. Here it's perhaps worth noting just how radically loyal listeners had seen their 5.00 pm fare change in six years: *Children's Hour* had vanished, to be replaced, first by a magazine for elderly listeners and now by breathless Bill Hardcastle. Some gear change.

The menu in *Radio Times* for *PM*'s first edition advertises 'the latest news, the evening press . . . and the people and the talking points of the day.' Sounds not too dissimilar to the sort of show that Eddie Mair anchors nearly four decades later. In fact, editor Andrew Boyle stuffed the show full to bursting with items that seemed perhaps more in keeping with the general-interest magazinery of *Home This Afternoon*. 'He fell into the trap that almost everybody falls into when they're suddenly given a very large space of airtime on Radio 4,' explains Jenny Abramsky, who later also edited the programme; 'They're very frightened that you can't fill it, and so they have lots and lots of fixed points. So there used to be a review of the evening papers; there used to be "What's on television tonight?"; a guy used to come up from the City, and of course there was the sports spot. He had Steve Race and Derek Cooper taking it in turns to do those kind of "soft" items, while Bill did all the hard things.' So how did Hardcastle, Cooper and Race shape up?

Gillian Reynolds, in those days writing for the *Guardian*, thought *PM* to be one of the less successful innovations, a fact noted when Review Board took a first look at the show after three weeks. However, despite some carps, they felt that 'Hardcastle had got the programme off to a really professional start', though there was, interestingly, some criticism exactly along Jenny Abramsky's lines.

A month later and the florist's was doing a busy trade, with bouquets on offer from every quarter: 'a very good magazine programme of the kind that was wanted at that time of day' . . . 'a very attractive programme'. Tony Whitby, especially thrilled, crowed that, despite the radical change of fare at 5.00 pm, the listening figures had increased 'so substantially that it must be presumed to be providing the right selection of items'.

What I, as an ordinary listener, particularly love about *PM* is its sheer style. Whether it was William Hardcastle, Jeremy Vine, Robert Williams, Susannah Simons, Gordon Clough, Valerie Singleton, Chris Lowe, Nigel Wrench, Eddie Mair or any of the many others who've carried that early-evening agenda, the show always has a sense of excitement about it. More tabloid, more chatty, more down-home with less lofty Westminster punditry, more the feel of an evening newspaper; and launched – why not? – by a sig tune. In the end, there were three versions over the years – the last from 1996 was upbeat and tuneful, with big drumbeats and an overarching trumpet solo – but all of them made the programme feel *exciting*, and quite different from any other news show on Radio 4. The sig finally disappeared during the period of mourning for Princess Diana in 1997 and never came back.

Priestland's pulpit

By *PM*'s six-month anniversary, its teething troubles banished, Review Board could only praise its 'stylishness' and 'sure touch' (and cracking audience figures). *Newsdesk*, the new show at 7.00, on the other hand, had a rather less convincing start. It was a very different sort of programme, with a host who offered opinions and context for news stories – the first such on the BBC, Review Board noted. Gerald Priestland, the corporation's highly regarded former Washington correspondent was the main anchor, and a brilliant one. 'This marvellous programme . . . was a sort of discursive version of the news,' Gillian Reynolds recalls: 'He would ask hard questions, but not in a sort of "poky", antagonistic way; and often get quite cross. And I loved his style because it made me think.'

Early internal reaction was noticeably less warm. Tony Whitby sent an urgent memo to his assistant head of Presentation:

> Of all the Sequences the least successful in audience figures is *News Desk*. I would like to give it . . . a substantial burst of trailing. Could I suggest something on the following lines to be dropped in before the 8.00 am News: 'Tonight at 7 o'clock – the day's events as seen by Radio 4's newsman Gerry Priestland . . .' The characteristic adjectives to go for are 'cool', 'relaxed', 'witty' and 'comprehensive'. The personality of Priestland should be played up.

By the time they returned for another go in February 1971, Review Board were more smiling. Clearly Whitby's trailing strategy was working as audience numbers were heading north healthily – but, following an occasion when Priestland was unavailable, he warned that 'It could not survive long in its present form with a stand-in presenter.' It was a prescient observation and, as it turned out, *Newsdesk* was the only element of the new current affairs line-up *not* to survive intact across the forty years. Of course, Gerald Priestland himself more than survived, becoming closely associated with religious broadcasting during the 1970s, adopting Quakerism and finally taking the role of the BBC's religious affairs correspondent in 1977 (see Chapter Eleven).

Despite appearances of continued healthy existence, *PM* itself went through a patch of distinctly uncomfortable turbulence during the mid-1970s when Ian McIntyre, the former *Analysis* presenter turned controller, took a slice out of the programme (along with *Today* – see Chapter Two) and replaced it with an archive miscellany called *Serendipity*. Inevitably, given the storms the cuts caused, *PM* eventually got its time back, but Jenny Abramsky, suddenly promoted in the wake of the management upheaval, to editor of *PM*, remembers with some heat the critical vengeance wrought on the programme at a subsequent Radio Review Board.

> It was absolutely terrifying. We'd just done our first programme at the restored length and Ian McIntyre slammed it, completely slammed it. It was the first Review Board I'd ever been to and of course I was defending it. In the end I said, 'I have no doubt that it will increase the audience from the programme that it has replaced' and Ian McIntyre said, 'I have no doubt it won't!' So I said, 'Right! Let's bet!' And we actually took a bet – I won!

New laughs for old

One of the striking features of how both Home Service and Radio 4 programmed their early evening is that wherever there was a heavy-duty bout of news and comment, there too would go something lighter to brighten the mood. So the Radio 4 of autumn 1967 had News-and-*Radio-Newsreel* at six, followed by a regional news magazine and *The Archers* at a quarter to seven, with a thirty-minute slug of comedy on the hour. There, antique but much-loved shows like *The Clitheroe Kid* or *The Navy Lark* mixed it with those rather dismal manifestations of radio's late-1960s low ebb, the remakes of TV hits like *Steptoe and Son*.

Just a classic minute

'And as the Minute Waltz fades away . . .' Nicholas Parsons gets yet another edition of the timeless Radio 4 gameshow under way. What a strange confection this programme is: a perfect example of how a classic formula has not only stood the test of time, but subtly changed within. *JAM*, as insiders know it, first appeared as part of the new Radio 4's first winter schedule in 1967. Produced by the extraordinary David Hatch, who also gave Radio 4 its other longest running comedy show, *I'm Sorry I Haven't a Clue*, the new panel game was invented by Ian Messiter – who remembered an old school-master of his, Mr Jones, whose favourite punishment was making pupils speak for a minute without hesitation or repetition. The formula, though, of *Just a Minute* is only half the magic. The other half lies in perfect casting and careful interpretation of the rules of the game – 'controlled (!)' as *Radio Times* used to put it – by chairman Nicholas Parsons, who's still on board after forty years.

The programme soon evolved a classic line-up, with parsonical Derek Nimmo (Rev. Mervyn Noote in the hit 1960s TV sit-com *All Gas and Gaiters*, whose radio incarnation David Hatch also produced) paired with lugubrious Clement Freud. Clement is today the only surviving member of the very first edition, from an era when he was famed not for his work as a Liberal MP (that came later) but as a food writer and, in the game's first year, as the voice of a legendary dog-food commercial.

Actress Andrée Melly was also on the first panel and returned regularly, but the programme's classic-gold guest-list featured fellow actress Sheila Hancock paired with her friend and confidant Kenneth Williams. With the ponderous, bewildered Peter Jones

And thus the pattern continued until Tony Whitby's 1970 springclean. Now, one of the many consequences of *Broadcasting in the Seventies* was the ending of the original arrangement of radio by national regions. At a stroke, the old North of England Home Service, Welsh Home Service or, for Bristolians like me, the West of England Home Service, and the

(famously The Book in *The Hitchhiker's Guide to the Galaxy*) also a regular panel-member, *Just a Minute* soon became a hilarious fixture in the new Radio 4 schedules. Williams, who by the end of the 60s had lost his muse and mentor Kenneth Horne, was having difficulty finding a suitable new radio comedy vehicle to replace *Round the Horne*; but his regular appearances on *JAM*, and his feigned indignation – 'and to think I came all the way from Great Portland Street to be insulted like this!' – became a much-loved turn.

Just a Minute points of course don't really count, as Parsons desperately tries to rescue real low-scorers from ignominy; but the key to building a big total is sneaking in with a 'successful challenge' just before the whistle is blown for the full minute, at which, as Parsons ritually announces, 'You have one point for a successful challenge and another for speaking when the whistle went . . .'; and then it's into the next round and 'Kenneth, will you speak for one minute please on . . .'

As the early stars have left the *JAM* stage others have taken their place: Paul Merton, a childhood fan is now a resident panellist, alongside Tony Hawks, Stephen Fry, Sue Perkins, Jenny Éclair and others. But it was Kenneth Williams, rudery to the fore, who was always my favourite as he got furious with Freud and played the game by outrageously dragging out every syllable of every word with Laurence-Olivier-like precision . . . only to go off into a hissy fit and bring the house down.

And if you think it's all just a game . . . when an in-house Radio festival edition was staged recently, the knives were out as Radio 3 Controller Roger Wright went head to head with Mark Damazer of Radio 4. In the end, after several extra highly contested rounds, Nick Parsons had to declare a winner . . . and it wasn't Radio 4.

rest, disappeared, and henceforth BBC Local Radio, kicking off in Leicester in November 1967, carried the torch for non-metropolitan Britain. For the dynamic controller, this meant (apart from a lot of complaints) the removal of a troublesome regional opt-out and the consequent opening up of a priceless half-hour slot bang after the six o'clock news – and as I've indicated, once you've got the audience thoroughly gloomy with the state of the world, it's not a bad plan to give them a good laugh immediately afterwards.

Here, however, Whitby played a cautious game. He didn't risk the new satirical show he'd commissioned in that exposed slot; that was kept well out of the critical glare, late on Saturday night. His first offering of 6.15 pm 'entertainment shows', as *Radio Times* called them, was largely the mixture as before: *Stop Messin' About* with Kenneth Williams (half-heartedly trying to do *Round the Horne* without Kenneth Horne, who'd died the year before); cosy, unchallenging parlour games like *Twenty Questions*; as well as more anarchic fare, albeit cross-repeated from Radio 2, in *I'm Sorry I'll Read That Again* – again. This show was radio's standard-bearer for the intelligent zaniness that would on TV produce *Monty Python*. *ISIRTA* starred future Radio 4 controller David Hatch, John Cleese, Tim Brooke-Taylor, Graeme Garden, Jo Kendall and Bill Oddie and with its funky gibbons, Lady Constance, elderly retainer Grimbling and the Angus Prune Tune was a breath of modernity amongst the fusty games and TV rip-offs.

David Hatch, who sadly died while this book was being prepared, was a brilliant young Cambridge graduate who'd immersed himself, alongside many other future 1960s stars, in the famous Footlights comedy club; he'd even done a stint on Broadway, touring a Footlights revue called *A Clump of Plinths*. When he was recruited in the mid-1960s by Radio Light Entertainment, however, he discovered a cobwebby, much less thrilling environment, furnished metaphorically at least with empty in-trays and telephones that didn't ring any more.

> It was a very successful department, but it was a dying department, because the department I'd joined had producers who were used to the days when radio was king. By the time I got there television had superseded them, and they found that nobody was coming anywhere near them and they were mystified by this.

There were, of course, still some bankable properties: *Round the Horne* continued to pull huge audiences for its last (1968) series, while *The Navy Lark*, *The Men from the Ministry* and *The Clitheroe Kid* had life enough left in them. But alongside those favourites that still raise a period giggle today on BBC7, creaky vehicles like *Twenty Questions* and *Petticoat Line* continued to fill large stretches of the Radio 4 schedules.

Petticoat Line (what a title!) was a frankly ghastly all-woman panel show 'in which we air the differences between men and women' as the opening announcement went, 'about women, by women, and of interest to men and women'. It was chaired by the crystalline-voiced actress Anona Winn, also a regular on *Twenty Questions*. 'Anona Winn always seemed just like my father's sisters,' shudders Gillian Reynolds, 'all of whom wore particularly scenty face powder so that when you kissed them you got this particularly florally scent and this particular texture on your cheek from kissing them – not somebody whose company I would search out.'

Anona would lob listeners' questions at a panel of showbizzy women that invariably included ancient ex-music hall star Renee Houston with the growly Scottish accent, actresses like Eleanor Summerfield or Bettine le Beau and the Cockney domestic-turned-writer Margaret Powell, she of the screeching peals of laughter. The questions were often ostensibly straight enough – 'My husband's mother wants to come and live with us . . . How do I get out of this without causing bad blood?' – but the answers were designed only to raise a giggle. 'I remember going to *Petticoat Line* down at the Playhouse Theatre and indeed I'm not sure I didn't produce a couple' – from the director's booth, David Hatch couldn't believe his eyes:

> It was an amazing sight – Renee Houston on the left, Anona in the chair, all of them in hats! And an audience in the Playhouse of probably 500! All in hats! You know it was a wonderful sight!

Radio audience shows are free, and whether the recording took place at the Playhouse or at the 'Paris' studio, just south of Piccadilly Circus (see page 224), there'd always be a hard core of regulars in the stalls: 'I mean my parents went to see *Beyond Our Ken* at the Paris,' remembers Steve Punt, star of Radio 4's

Paris in Piccadilly

'Make it like the Paris' was the plea from Radio Light Entertainment producers when the Radio Theatre in Broadcasting House took over as their recording studio for audience shows in the mid-1990s. 'The Paris' was the sentimental home-from-home of Light Ent., a curious, rather dingy basement studio, located behind an unobtrusive entrance in Lower Regent Street, thirty seconds' walk south of Piccadilly Circus in London. Its original incarnation was as a cinema showing continental movies, but from the 1940s and for as long as most people in the Radio 4 era can remember, it was the studio of the stars – from *ITMA* and *Round the Horne* to Radio 1's *Mary Whitehouse Experience*. 'We *loved* going down to the Paris because it was an "event"' – Richard Edis produced countless shows there – 'you physically had to leave Broadcasting House with your programme boxes and go down to Theatreland.'

Likewise, performers had a soft spot for the scruffy studio with its worn seats, because it had 'atmosphere': 'It was a brilliant room for comedy,' Steve Punt remembers, 'it has a low ceiling which is always good, felt really enclosed', just like the club venues the new breed of 1980s stand-ups were used to playing.

> But it also had such a sense of history. I remember telling my parents we were recording the show at the Paris: 'Oh, the Paris!' Because they used to go and watch shows there in the early 60s.

The Paris was ostensibly far-from-ideal: the studio was in the

The Now Show, 'and they said the situation was much the same [as at the Playhouse]. There's a regular audience there and performers begin to spot the regulars who're all in the front row. I think you can sense when an audience is enjoying something, and it somehow permeates through the radio.'

Familiarity, dependability, bankability – regular and returning comedy gives a network like Radio 4 not only its texture, but its big draws, guaranteed bums on seats. However, while the

basement and tube trains rumbled through beneath the floor. 'Backstage was pretty disgusting,' Richard Edis recalls, 'I mean in the summer you could smell the sewers'; whilst in the wings, guests jostled for space with all the impedimenta for recording radio comedy. Gillian Reynolds once guested on Roy Plomley's old Radio 4 panel game in which he'd read out passages with mistakes in them:

> I did *Many a Slip* in the Paris, and you could have a good play with the variety door [sound effect] before you went on . . . *Many a Slip* was quite hard: it was Tim Rice, David Nixon, Eleanor Summerfield, me and Roy Plomley – and David Nixon used to do this trick of pouring out water in front of the microphone which made everyone want to go to the loo!

'All the ghosts walk at the Paris' says Edis – and note the nostalgic present tense of his reminiscence – '*Hancock's Half Hour* was done there; all the *Round the Horne*s were done there; *The Navy Lark*, *Educating Archie*; there were some *Goon Show*s done there . . .' For young performers like Steve Punt, whose first ever Radio 4 show, *Live on Arrival*, was broadcast from the studio in 1988, this accumulation of show business heritage was a bit intimidating 'because as you walked in there was a huge collage picture of everyone from Ted Ray and the cast of *ITMA* through Kenneth Williams and Kenneth Horne and all these people. . .'

There was a sense of history about the audience, too: in the front row, week-in week-out, sat the regulars – 'what we used to call the

☞

Radio 4 audience is small-c conservative, it can also be radical and anarchic, and in order to keep all constituencies as happy as possible, controllers must somehow balance that mix. So today alongside the raw, fresh-from-the-Fringe comedians heard at 11.00 pm, sit *I'm Sorry I Haven't a Clue* and *Just a Minute* – old, bankable shows that started four decades ago and which have brilliantly done what other, creakier vehicles haven't managed – re-invent themselves.

"Tesco carrier bag brigade"' according to Sally Grace: 'They came to everything, probably one sandwich short of a picnic but they were so loyal! And they always had to sit in exactly the same seat.' Listen to enough archive recordings and you can even recognise the distinctive cackle of one stalwart audience member called Joyce: 'Joyce came to everything, and you felt that you knew her. And every show you did, the same people would ask for your autograph – they'd only had it the week before from another show!'

The Paris was vacated in 1995 and returned to its landlords, with the Radio Theatre taking up the role as BBC Radio's comedy central, but I've not met anyone who knew it who hasn't a hankering for the Paris. And David Hatch made a more serious point about it, which has a message for all of us who work in the business.

> I believe that the Light Entertainment producer is in a better position than any other producer, because he actually goes out in front of the audience and says, 'Welcome to the Paris studio; this is what we're going to do.' At the end he has to go up in front of them and say, 'Thank you very much'; and on his way back to the [control] cubicle, he is abused if it's awful. So he knows, you know, what the audience thinks! In Light Entertainment you do face the audience live, all the time, and that's actually a jolly good discipline.

Clued up

In 1972 David Hatch was in at the birth of *I'm Sorry I Haven't a Clue*, which owed not a little to its soundalike predecessor in which he'd starred. '*Clue* of course came about because Bill Oddie and Graeme Garden who wrote *ISIRTA* – I think we'd done 110 programmes or something – said, "We can't go on writing this for the money we're getting."' With *Python* and *The Goodies* now absorbing many of the talents from *I'm Sorry*, any new radio programme would struggle to compete, 'and Radio wasn't gonna up their fees'.

Yet the fertile minds loved the zaniness and the speed of making radio comedy, 'and so Graeme rang me up and said,

"Let's go and have a chat."' They met outside the Guinea pub not far from Hatch's office at Aeolian Hall, 'and he said, "I tell you what we can do – we can have the same crowd and we will *invent* it. There'll be no writing involved; we'll come up with some *silly* rounds and we'll do it as a sort of panel game, but it'll have the same anarchic feel to it."' Hatch told me neither he nor Graeme Garden could ever remember who first suggested that Humphrey Lyttelton be the show's chair 'but he was inspired, whoever's idea it was!'

With its rituals and regular panellists and rounds, its suggestive script, the lovely Samantha and its tradition of bad puns, not to mention Mornington Crescent, *Clue* has become a minor cult. 'Graeme had actually come with his ideas for some of the rounds, some of which still exist. So you could see that'd work, and that'll work. So there was enough that was built-in not to be too terrified.'

The crowd that turns up for recordings of *Clue* has always been amongst the youngest and most raucous for radio comedy shows: 'There is that thing with radio comedy that the audience enjoy watching something that isn't meant to be watched,' says Steve Punt, who regularly records *The Now Show* in front of a live audience: 'The tangible slight sense of disappointment that Samantha *does* actually exist, but in fact she's just the scorer – she's not really *Samantha*. In fact she's a programme assistant with a stopwatch!' And boisterous audience participation has been a feature of *Clue* since the beginning. At first, it slightly intimidated Humphrey Lyttelton who was then more familiar with the intimate world of the jazz clubs in which he performed; as his first producer David Hatch remembered.

> We did the pilot at the Playhouse in front of an *I'm Sorry I'll Read That Again*-type audience and Humphrey Lyttelton was devastated. He was standing in the wings going 'What is going on?' I mean there were 600 people in the Playhouse for a pilot programme. He thought, 'I do not know what I'm getting into.'

Something like a 35-year run to date, in fact – but as Hatch confessed, *Clue* wasn't an instant success: 'It went *half*-well. I suppose I recorded over an hour and had to cut it back, and cut it back, and cut it back to make anything vaguely broadcastable. But it was broadcastable.'

Gradually the 'antidote to panel games' – a deliberately parodic take on all those dusty programmes that Hatch was so keen to replace – grew away from the *I'm Sorry* model. Cleese had never been part of the *Clue* line-up, and Jo Kendall soon dropped out as later did Bill Oddie. From different walks of comedy Barry Cryer and Willie Rushton joined the team, and so, until 1996, the cast and crew of what has become Radio 4's most enduring comedy property was set.

Like *ITMA* (*It's That Man Again*) for wartime listeners, *Clue*'s cult status in part derives from known routines – the gags about Samantha, the does-it-really-mean-something? daftness of Mornington Crescent, the ruderies aimed at pianist Colin Sell and above all the *Round the Horne*-like double-entendres of the script. Fundamentally, however, *Clue* is about the funny men who make the madness happen. So when Rushton died in 1996, questions were inevitably asked about the show's future: 'There was the thought "oh, well, that's it. No more *Clue*,"' recalls Richard Edis, a long-serving producer in Radio Light Entertainment, 'and somebody at the time said, "Well, wait a minute, we can get people like Graham Norton in and Jeremy Hardy and Andy Hamilton and Stephen Fry . . ."' and so, as with the network on which it's broadcast, subtly the programme refreshed itself for another generation of fans.

The heart of the show since that pilot edition three and a half decades ago is the dead-pan Humphrey Lyttelton: 'If you gave him the Argos catalogue he could read it and make it funny,' says Iain Pattinson, who these days writes the script. 'He always sounds as though he'd rather be doing something else, which is also why he's so funny,' Edis adds. '*Clue* has now become the *Round the Horne* de nos jours with the smut. Let's be honest it's filthy.' Too many gags to enumerate linger in the aficionado's memory, but I recall the huge laugh that greeted Humph's straight-faced account of scorer Samantha's recent purchase of an ice-cream – she was, he said, 'going to spend the evening licking the nuts off a large Neapolitan'.

With Pattinson on board as resident writer and, for many years, producer Jon Naismith in charge, the show forges forward with Humph proudly standing at the prow – 'not just a magic voice, but a magic persona: my desert island voice' according to Gillian Reynolds. But for how long? 'Barry Cryer said to me, in a rare lugubrious moment,' she adds, '"Well, when Humph goes we all go. We could survive the going of Willie; it could survive without me. It can't survive without Humph."'

Makeover radio

I'm Sorry I Haven't a Clue is an absolute one-off, and because it lives – as does the very best radio comedy – in the imagination of the listener, it could never make the leap to television. Think about it: four ageing comedians sitting on a stage with an octogenarian jazz trumpeter making up sexy fantasies about the scorer and timekeeper? Likewise, even the lunacies of the crew of HMS *Troutbridge* in *The Navy Lark* depend on *not* being able to see Leslie Phillips yet again navigating the vessel into the harbour wall: 'Left hand down a bit' and the almighty sound effects CLANG are powerful enough triggers for the listener's imagination. Not surprising also then, that when TV tried out *Just a Minute* for a handful of series in the 1990s, despite the classic ingredients, the magic didn't really work and the show was swiftly dropped.

In the past twenty-five years, however, as comedy itself has become hip and joined the music and club scene, more and more television successes have been bred on Radio 4. What a reversal from the days of sloppy radio remakes of *Steptoe and Son* and *All Gas and Gaiters*! Partly it's of course to do with cost. As Steve Punt has remarked, you can create an Egyptian desert full of thousands of slaves with a bit of rhubarb-rhubarb and a couple of sound FX CDs. It's also to do with the niche effect of Radio 4: new comic talent can be brought on like seedlings in a greenhouse very effectively through the various Radio 4 slots – late-evening for the risqué and raw; 6.30 pm for the mainstream

TV-hits-to-be. *Little Britain*, of course, but also *Goodness Gracious Me*, *The League of Gentlemen*, *Dead Ringers*, *People Like Us*, *Knowing Me*, *Knowing You*, and, more recently, Stephen Fry's comedy drama about a P.R. company, *Absolute Power*, and *That Mitchell and Webb Look* have all emerged from Radio 4's seed tray, and, while less obviously a direct lift, *Have I Got News For You* is also acknowledged as having originated with Radio 4's *News Quiz*.

Sketch shows and shows that rely on impressions make the leap with just a little refocusing of the characters, so in the TV *Dead Ringers*, Fiona Bruce and Kirsty Wark take the place of Charlotte Green and Brian Perkins on Radio 4. Other transfers have needed more radical surgery. *Broken News*, the TV spoof of endless rolling news services like CNN and News 24 in fact has its spiritual origins, though heavily adapted, in *The Sunday Format*, one of the cleverest ensemble sketch shows of recent years on Radio 4, whose target was not TV but the world of Sunday newspapers, their glamorous columnists and faddy features. Ten years earlier a similar, subtly adjusted transfer had taken place when Chris Morris's *The Day Today* grew naturally out of Radio 4's zany, news-magazine spoof *On the Hour* ('first on the scene of major disasters!').

If by the 1990s, the escalator from Radio 4 to BBC2 and ultimately to BBC1 was well established, a few years earlier there had been a number of wobbles. One radio hit that didn't follow that BBC path was at heart an old-fashioned parlour game, but exploited the phenomenal growth in stand-up talent and cleverly used their quickfire improv routines. The brainchild of Dan Patterson and Mark Leveson, it was called *Whose Line is it Anyway?* and (as with *Clue*) the dead-pan and put-upon chairmanship of Clive Anderson was the key to the chemistry. Michael Green, who'd not long taken over as Radio 4's controller, attributes the show's success in part to the changes he made to the schedule.

The renaissance in the late 80s, early 90s of comedy was partly to do with scheduling: opening up the late evening, sort of eleven o'clock time. When you could say that those who'd had their

cocoa and would be upset by the more risqué stuff could turn off
now – you're allowed to switch off now – and develop some new
ideas at that time.

Whose Line? launched on Radio 4 as long ago as January
1988, and David Wade greeted it warmly in *The Times*: 'I
believe this show just might develop to equal *The News Quiz* or
I'm Sorry I Haven't a Clue . . .' Too right. 'I went to most of the
first series,' remembers Steve Punt, who twigged early on that he
was watching a phenomenon: 'Something was changing, and . . .
the audience knew they were ahead of the curve. Radio 4 had
found something here that no one else in Britain had seen', in a
word, improv.

> And I think it was one of those shows that really set people
> thinking that this network is actually ahead of where the TV
> companies are in what they're prepared to put on.

A mere nine months later, the programme transferred almost
unchanged to Channel 4 where it ran and re-ran for years, and
then leapt the pond with great success to run for six seasons in
America. 'Red faces at the BBC' trumpeted headlines as yet
another Radio 4 property slipped from the corporation's grasp,
close on the heels of Stephen Fry's spoof investigative series
Delve Special which, re-invented as *This is David Lander*, also
emerged on Channel 4, 'pinched lock, stock and producer' as
the *Sunday Times* put it. As we've seen, by the time *On the Hour*
transmogrified into *The Day Today*, BBC television executives
had learned their lesson.

You can't beat the original

There were two shows which successfully made the leap to TV
from Radio 4 during the late 1970s and early 80s, yet which in
both cases had slightly compromised outings on the box.
They're today considered amongst Radio 4's biggest comedy
triumphs, the sort of programmes about which fans like to

whisper 'but they *really were* better on the radio'. They were *Radio Active* and *The Hitchhiker's Guide to the Galaxy*.

Hitchhiker is now a cult classic, not only of radio (the novels came later) but of broader popular cultural trends, no less, to be studied in university courses with titles like 'Fantasy and Utopia'. But cults – *Hitchhiker* became an album, a TV series and ultimately a feature film – often have very ordinary and unpredictable beginnings, and while it would be nice to say that Radio 4 had spotted its universal potential, it would be wrong. What the BBC provided was the sort of creative freedom that ten years previously had spawned the anarchic lunacy of *Monty Python*. So, as all but the few know, *The Hitchhiker's Guide to the Galaxy* was the creation of an offbeat young writer called Douglas Adams, whose brilliant idea came to him at the age of nineteen when he was touring Europe.

> I was lying drunk in a field in Innsbruck and I had a copy of the *Hitchhiker's Guide to Europe*, and it seemed to me, as I watched the stars swirling around my head, that somebody ought to write a *Hitchhiker's Guide to the Galaxy* as well. Little thinking actually that it would be me.

The radio series first emerged, amid a flurry of comings and goings of huge creative talents, in the form of a pilot episode. The producer was Simon Brett, then working full-time on the eccentric Nigel Rees show, *The Burkiss Way . . . to Dynamic Living*. (Though *Burkiss* is now remaindered in the BBC7 schedule, Rees is of course still going strong on Radio 4 with the evergreen *Quote . . . Unquote*.) Brett cast three young Cambridge Footlighters: Simon Jones (who'd known Adams there), Geoffrey McGivern and Mark Wing-Davey in the leading male roles of Arthur Dent, Ford Prefect and Zaphod Beeblebrox. For the dead-pan straight, yet surreal, narration (funny how this is becoming a theme) from 'the Book' itself, the team chose one of the country's best loved voices, Peter Jones.

However, even before the series got the green light, Brett left the BBC to write novels, and in stepped a clever, just-down-from-uni producer called Geoffrey Perkins. It wasn't, though, plain-sailing as Adams deadlined and over-deadlined through the writing schedule. To the rescue came Douglas's old Cambridge buddy John Lloyd, another young recruit with a bright future ahead of him, who helped him finish the scripts.

It was, to say the least, a complex production – I can remember the buzz around Broadcasting House as stories were told of the lengths to which the studio managers and composer Paddy Kingsland of the Radiophonic Workshop had gone to cook up the phenomenal sound effects – but eventually on Wednesday March the 8th 1978, with barely a fanfare and certainly no raised glasses of pangalactic gargle-blaster for the press, an engineer pressed the start button on the tape machine in Radio 4 Continuity. A burst of the Eagles' 'Journey of the Sorcerer', reworked by Kingsland, and *The Hitchhiker's Guide to the Galaxy* slipped on to the air.

'*Hitchhiker* certainly was a breakthrough. Terrific!' – the speaker is Monica Sims, who joined Radio 4 later the same year to preside over the second series of the show. 'It was great fun to go to the studio and hear what was happening. I must say I was very nervous about it at the beginning; I wasn't at all sure we'd done the right thing. I mean some of the audience simply didn't like it at all. Wrong sort of humour for them.' For schoolboy Steve Punt, though, it was dead right.

> *Hitchhiker's Guide* hit my mid teens, and it was a huge cult thing at school. That was something that made a lot of boys at my school, who would otherwise have been listening to the Stranglers, go and find where Radio 4 was on the dial. It felt like this was a new generation finding its voice on the radio.

The humour was dry, knowing, cool; it laughed at staid old values (Arthur Dent belongs to a very English tradition of put-upon heroes), 'and the actual production – the sound effects – didn't sound like the BBC clink-stirring that you associate with radio. It was creating a whole world. Because of course they were all very young – Geoffrey Perkins and Douglas Adams were mid-twenties – and it had that quality of kids in a toyshop, as it were.'

Above all, it was just plain funny; like so many fans, I remember collapsing in a sympathetic heap the first time I heard Marvin feeling depressed ('And then of course I've got this terrible pain in all the diodes down my left side . . .'). Young Steve Punt too . . .

> It helped you understand that stuff you read about people listening to the *Goon Show* under the blankets in the 50s. By that I mean the sense of privacy that a radio cult [has] as opposed to blaring out from the TV with everyone sitting watching it.

Which was part of the problem when it came to turning a hit that had used so many resources in the listener's own mind into something that worked on the box: not only did Zaphod have two heads, but now had to be *seen* to have two heads. The result: enormous production difficulties and blazing rows. In the end, the TV *Hitchhiker* wasn't a flop, even though fans felt it just wasn't as good as the original and so there was no second series.

At exactly the moment John Lloyd and his ex-Cambridge team were despairing over putting the galaxy on our screens, a group of largely Oxford-educated talents was assembling the pilot for Radio 4's next big success. Unlike the comedy drama of *Hitchhiker*, *Radio Active* was a traditional sketch show, albeit with a loose narrative structure; subtle difference. In the staff of a fictional local radio station (purportedly allowed to simulcast for thirty minutes a week on Radio 4), it had a cast of very distinctive characters. They had silly names (with groany puns on parts of a radio studio) like Anna Daptor and Mike Flex and did silly things like staging Radio Active's Mass Debate, a special event that had the unfortunate result of causing severe embarrassment every time someone announced 'You're listening to Radio Active's Mass Debat . . . ing competition'.

Plenty of innuendo and smut, then, but touches of Python in the comedy too, as well as echoes of *Not the Nine O'Clock News* which had started the year before in 1979. Having assured his place in *Hitchhiker* history, Geoffrey Perkins now became the production genius behind *Radio Active* and played

Mike Flex, while the other writer on the show, Angus Deayton, was another Mike, Mike Channel ('Hello Mike' – 'thank you Mike'). Over fifty episodes were made and it's invidious to single out any one element, though I loved *The Martin Brown Show* ('all Martin's usual features including "Lose the Record", "Find the Record" and "Put the Record on at the Wrong Speed" . . .') and the ever more operatic theme-music heralding the station's commercial breaks. There were spots by gruff 'Honest Ron' (with his silly jingle, brilliantly spoofing low-rent radio ads of the time), and sacred interventions by the station's pastor, the Right Reverend Reverend Wright ('with the top ten commandments as voted by the *Radio Active* listeners').

Unsurprisingly, *Radio Active* transferred to television, though not until 1990 and in a necessarily heavily adapted form, featuring satellite news station *KYTV*. However, it never had the same freshness on TV and, although it ran for three series, the team were already spreading their comedy wings and *KYTV* never became the television classic that *Radio Active* had been.

Taking a pop

One aspect of 1980s television comedy that the BBC signally failed to dominate was satire. It was the young Channel 4 (launched in 1982) that captured all the headlines and kudos for its technically brilliant and editorially razor-sharp takes on the decade of Margaret Thatcher in *Spitting Image*; indeed, Steve Nallon's celebrated voice of the Prime Minister became almost as well known as the original. Radio meanwhile made its own satirical sallies via *The News Huddlines* on Radio 2 (from 1975) and on Radio 4's venerable *Week Ending*, but the contrast with Channel 4's take was increasingly stark, as Steve Punt, who cut his broadcasting teeth writing material for *Week Ending* now acknowledges: 'Once you'd seen *Spitting Image*, *Week Ending* felt incredibly tame, because in a sense *Spitting Image* rewrote the rules.'

Part of the problem was again to do with the differences in the relationship between television and its viewers and radio and its listeners. Strong language has always presented a particular problem on radio. There's no image, of course, to defray the effect, and add to that the acknowledged intimacy of the medium and the effect of unexpected strong language can be not unlike the proverbial slap in the face. Which, according to Steve Punt, results sometimes in strange tensions:

> You'll be told, 'Oh you can't say that on Radio 4' and you think, 'but the audience last night were watching *They Think It's All Over* or *Have I Got News For You*, let alone the kind of stuff that's on Channel 4 on Friday nights.' And you think, 'It's an absolutely different world – have you ever *seen South Park*? Do you know what comedy *is* now?'

Which was the problem specifically, says Punt, with *Week Ending* by the time the audience for satire had had its eyes and ears stretched by *Spitting Image*.

It wasn't always thus for *Week Ending*. Late on the first Saturday in April 1970, as a key element in his new schedule for Radio 4, controller Tony Whitby unveiled a show that was ground-breaking and original. *Radio Times* even published a little Michael Heath cartoon of a man with his jaws closing on the tail of a dog, presumably to illustrate the old maxim that 'dog bites man isn't news, man bites dog *is*'. Michael Barratt, presenter of TV's *Nationwide*, was the slightly strange casting to host a look back at 'the funny side' of the week's news. The two producers credited, both prominent in this chapter, were Simon Brett and (it's that man again) the creator of *Just a Minute* and *Clue*, David Hatch. 'We'll be taking a look back at the previous week's news with a slightly jaundiced view', writes Hatch in a preview column; looking in the other direction was Basil Boothroyd, debonair humorist and editor of *Punch* magazine who'd been a Home Service regular for decades. He was on hand to present 'Next Week's News', a feature of the show that became the long-runner of the series across twenty-eight years.

Review Board as usual had mixed feelings. Tony Whitby, it was his baby after all, was lavish in his praise ('some comic inventions of a very high order'), but the head of Further Education likened listening to the show to 'drinking a glass of warm, flat beer' after a good dinner party. Simon Brett defended stoutly: the lack of audience (and thus studio laughter) might have seemed disconcerting at first; Gerard Mansell, Director of Programmes, thought the new show was getting better all the time and was 'worth persevering with'. That'll be a yes, then.

Quickly the programme evolved into a more secure format: Barratt left, as did Boothroyd, and the show settled into a routine based round regular performers like Bill Wallis, David Jason (a stalwart for many seasons) and even Nigel Rees, with Bill McGuffie providing the music. 'They were superb,' recalled Hatch, 'and what they loved about it of course is that we'd probably do 35 short sketches (of which 20 made it into the show), but it required them to do thirty voices in a morning.'

Week Ending ran for over forty weeks a year, with just a break for the summer parliamentary recess, and therefore had an almost insatiable appetite for new sketch material and especially for short topical jokes known as 'news-lines'. It quickly acquired the reputation as the best place to sell a gag, and so, unsurprisingly, it was where Steve Punt of Radio 4's *Now Show* started submitting jokes, while still in his second year at Cambridge.

> And then one week one of them was used, and I got a cheque for about seven quid! Which was astonishing; because I thought, 'I've earned some money from writing. I can't believe it! This is great. I must carry on doing this!'

Which, like so many others, he did. Rob Newman, David Baddiel, Rory Bremner, Richard Herring, Stewart Lee, Guy Jenkin, Andy Hamilton, Ian Brown and Peter Baynham, amongst dozens of other well-known names, came and wrote in the smoky atmosphere of the Writers' Room (see page 238). *Week Ending* was recorded in the Paris studio, and always without an audience, but the writers 'used to turn up at the end for "Next Week's News" to see if their lines had got in,' actress Sally Grace remembers. 'They used to come in like hungry

Creative space

It was smoky, crowded and full of the sorts of people who would have had Lord Reith sounding off testily. Yet for a period in the 1980s it was the crossroads of UK comedy talent that the Algonquin Round Table had been for the literati of 1920s New York. 'The Writers' Room' in the BBC's radio comedy HQ at 16 Langham Street acted as hostel, coffee bar and telephone exchange for aspiring gagsters seeking to kick-start their careers on radio shows like *Week Ending* and *The News Huddlines*. Steve Punt was one: 'The Writers' Room was basically used as an unofficial club for comics, and although in the modern BBC it was clearly financially unsound, it actually paid off hugely in terms of the – what do they call it? – hidden benefits or "soft power" or something.'

Light Entertainment producer Richard Edis watched the tide of hopefuls who turned up every week: 'It didn't matter who you were, if you thought you had an idea for a sketch, or you had a script you wanted to be looked at, then you were at liberty to come to the Open Meeting, which was on a Wednesday.' The result of this largesse was the lengthy litany of writers' names ('the rollcall of the First World War dead' Spike Milligan is supposed to have called it) at the end of *Week Ending*: 'With news-lines by . . .' 'People used to say, "You've gotta be joking; there can't be that many"; but there are!' says Sally Grace, who often had to read them out. 'And I wanted to say every week ". . . and Uncle Tom Cobbleigh and all"!'

The Open Meeting was intended for novices and the aspiring. What you really wanted to get to, says Steve Punt, were the *Tuesday* meetings, for 'commissioned writers':

wolves to see if they could eat for the following week, depending on whose next week's news-lines had been chosen!'

Just as the writers came and went, so did many members of the cast. Sally, on the other hand, joined *Week Ending* in 1983 and stayed until the programme was finally axed in James Boyle's schedule revamp of 1998. Her entrée came when she

> Which basically meant that they'd nick all the best stories. And then
> on the Wednesday, they had what was called the 'non-coms' meeting
> which was literally anybody, open house, where you could just turn
> up, and any news that was left you could pitch in with an idea for.

'And this is how they got started,' says Edis, 'with a one-line gag
and then it might be a 30-second quickie and then they'd suddenly
get commissioned.' As far as listeners are concerned, of course, the
attention is all on the stars and the stories, but when it comes to the
programme-makers it's the quality of the writing, the inspired
lunatic leap of the imagination, that is priceless: 'We exist to discover
new writers – *particularly* new writers. Without writers we are
nothing' was David Hatch's doctrine when he was the boss of Light
Entertainment.

Before he became a radio performer, Steve Punt was one of those
fledgling jokesmiths who, while still a Cambridge undergraduate,
was already turning up on Wednesdays for the Non-Commissioned
Meeting: 'Which was insane: you'd be left with only the really small
stories. So people would be going, "Well there's a story on page
eighteen of the *Telegraph* today about a dog someone's fitted a
wheel to, and it's really quite funny!" And the producer going, "Well,
it might make twenty seconds . . ."'

It all sounds a little bit dog-eat-dog and unglamorous, but in the
early 1980s, when club comedy was just setting out on the path to
the multi-million-pound industry it is today (Jongleurs, for instance,
opened its first venue in 1983), the Writers' Room truly was,
according to Punt, for a moment at least, the creative hub of the
comedy universe:

☞

was asked to deputise for another stellar comic talent who was
looking towards the other side of the Atlantic to develop her
career. The producer called her up:

He said 'Sally, Tracey Ullman who's doing it at the moment is in
America for a couple of weeks.' Would I cover? And they just left

They would all go in there, raid the stationery cupboard and use the phone. In those days the BBC would let you dial out and the famous thing I always remember is people using the phone in the Writers' Room to book their gigs for the next few weeks. But a lot of teaming up and a lot of ideas resulted from that, and it was a real nerve centre because a lot of the writers were also doing stand-up. It all coincided with a bit of an explosion of the London comedy circuit.

If you made the grade on *Week Ending* and *Huddlines* and got enough material commissioned, you had access to radio writing's top table, the Commissioned Meeting. Beyond that, the stars. Right. But, says Steve, there was nonetheless something a bit special about what went on in the dingy room in 16 Langham Street; it was, not to put too fine a point on it, a place where dreams could come true . . . Dan Patterson, the co-inventor of *Whose Line is it Anyway?*, once famously said: 'radio is the only place where you can get on the air what you've heard in your head.' And that has to recommend itself.

me there for fifteen years! I went in for a fortnight and they forgot about me!

The early line-up on *Week Ending* had been exclusively male, but Sally came in at a time when there was a real requirement for female vocal talent: 'I had Thatcher,' she smiles, and, adopting her best Margaret Thatcher voice, continues:

The blessed Margaret, what would I have done without her? And we just had huge fun with her. I remember Bill Wallis; some of our most fun scenes were shouting at the Dispatch Box when I was she and he was Neil Kinnock. We used to have some hilarious times – I ruined so many takes through laughing!

The programme was originally a late-night Saturday show, but eventually moved to a Friday slot, which meant that sketches, news-lines, cast had to be firmly in place for an early start at the Paris on Friday. In the early morning of Friday October the 12th 1984, a bomb exploded at the Grand Hotel in Brighton where members of the Conservative Party were staying for their annual conference, killing five people and injuring dozens more. 'We just had to throw the script in the bin,' remembers Sally, as producer Paul Spencer tried to work out what to do next.

> We had a wonderful writer called Richard Quick [who] always used to do marvellous poems, and Paul grabbed him by the throat and said, 'Look Richard, you've got to go away and write a poem to acknowledge what's happened.' And he did and as I recall Bill Wallis read it.

By the 1990s, however, *Spitting Image* had long been the popular benchmark for satirical comedy, and *Week Ending*'s gentle brand of parliamentary parody was no longer anywhere near sharp enough. It was high time to put the animal down: 'The mangy old cur has been blundering into the furniture, coughing up hairballs and puking on the carpets for long enough, and somebody has finally decided to take the kindest way,' wrote Robert Hanks in the *Independent* when James Boyle signed the warrant for the show's demise.

For the last edition, called *Week Ending Ending*, David Hatch returned to read the rollcall of writer credits at the end of the show and Jonathan James-Moore, the enormously loved Head of Light Entertainment, came back to sit in the director's chair. Then there was the inevitable wake; and in keeping with such occasions in big bureaucratic organisations, things didn't go quite according to plan. 'Broadcasting House had become a no-smoking building,' Sally Grace's husband, producer Richard Edis recounts, 'and of course all the writers were there puffing away, and everybody had got pretty merry by this time' ('or maudlin' adds Sally).

> – [Edis] And a fire officer came in and suddenly announced at the top of his voice, 'There are people smoking in this building, and

unless these people stop smoking immediately I'll have to clear the theatre!'

– [Grace] Jonathan was just making his speech and I was about to be presented with a rather large floral arrangement, tears coursing down my cheeks. And in the middle of this, this jobsworth comes in. He couldn't have picked a worse moment if he tried!

– [Edis] I was standing next to a writer called David Spicer, and when the security man went off, David just turned to me and said, 'I wish I'd written that!'

Since the ending of *Week Ending*, keeping the Radio 4 satirical flame alight have been the impressions of the *Dead Ringers* team (though their graduation to TV has meant that they rarely put in an appearance these days on Radio 4), and *The Now Show*. It's anyone's guess whether the *Now* team of Steve Punt, Hugh Dennis, Marcus Brigstocke and Co will last as long as the *Week End*ers – unlikely I'd guess because they'd be smart enough to bale out while the show's still flourishing – but the programme has now established itself as a modern classic, has been around for the better part of a decade, and is greeted, when it's occasionally gone on tour, with the same sorts of packed houses and raucous audience participation that attend *Clue*.

A turkey and a little peach

Radio 4 entertainment is so often defined by its long-running shows, *Clue*, *Just a Minute*, even *Brain of Britain*, that it's sometimes easy to forget the shows that haven't stayed the course. Who now, other than veteran critics, remembers a Radio 4 sitcom set in I think a chip shop, and called *The Spam-Fritter Man*? Oddly enough, I do, though only because of its gasp-inducing lack of popularity as judged by the audience Reaction Index or RI: measured out of 100. Gillian Reynolds listened as a critic and the memory still makes her cringe: 'possibly the

worst comedy programme ever in the history of British radio!'
David Hatch commissioned it:

> It got an RI of 34. It came from Manchester. I thought it was a
> great title, and the producer had told me something about it, and
> on it went. It was . . . it was horrendous! But, you know, lots of
> things are horrendous, that's OK. I think I took it off halfway
> through.

On the other hand, there are those little successes on Radio 4
about which cognoscenti nudge each other and say, 'Yes, great,
but do you remember, before he was famous . . .?' Amongst
these I'd count *Lines from My Grandfather's Forehead*, which
was a short-lived gem of a chamber sketch show, first aired in
1971. Surreal little items alternated with language-stretching
poems, with Ronnie Barker both as performer and writer,
playing word games long before the 'four candles/fork 'andles'
sketch was ever dreamed of. Radio Review Board liked it a lot:
Gerard Mansell, Director of Programmes, loved the eccentric
title which was in keeping with the series' 'very individual type
of humour, quite unlike that of any other radio or television
programme'. The head of Radio Training department went
further: *Lines*, he said, was 'more imaginative than any ten
ordinary' programmes.

But just as the show was first being nurtured on to the air, so
was another show, on BBC1, also starring Mr Barker, together
with the other Ronnie, and only two series of *Lines* were ever
made.

CHAPTER NINE

7.00 pm: Business in Borsetshire

Gently, Simon lifted the middling-sized cardboard box on to the table. It could have contained the presentation shield for a winning darts team – that sort of size – but it was much heavier than that, denser, its contents sealed with ageing tape, corners tattered. But it was unopened. I felt a bit like Howard Carter taking the bindings off a mummy, well just a bit; this was, after all, a warehouse in Brentford, not the Valley of the Kings. Stripping the sealing tape from the box, Simon revealed within a stack of anonymous-looking LP bags, with the familiar labels of the BBC Sound Library peeping through the portholes. This, he explained, was part of a consignment of BBC records from forty or so years earlier that had been manufactured for despatch to places like Canada and New Zealand. They were for use by the Transcription Service, which made available BBC programmes to radio stations in the Commonwealth.

So far so prosaic, but what I was actually looking at was a lost part of my life – and part of the history of Radio 4 – because this box, and the others stashed on the shelves, contained all 2,670 episodes of *The Archers* broadcast between the late 1950s and the end of the 1960s – over ten years of doings in Borsetshire. Births, deaths, fires, robberies, mayhem from Mods, accidents which befell Ambridge's finest, characters now long forgotten, a decade chopped up into segments lasting fourteen-and-a-half minutes – it was the lost history of Ambridge.

Of course, those episodes lived on in people's memories, and in the famous card and computer files charting every character and twitch of the storyline and kept safely in the *Archers* production office. But the actual programmes, the *sound* of the 60s in Borsetshire had, apart from a handful of episodes retained in the Archives, disappeared almost without trace. It was a decade that I had lived, in part, through the voices of the population of the fictional village: all through my schooldays, *The Archers* was a daily ritual at home, and those characters became part of my life too.

Thus it is, even now, for the millions of regular listeners who tune in just after 7.00 pm to this strangely addictive soap opera – and no matter how many times I walk into drama studios, see the scripts, watch actors kissing the backs of their hands to simulate a passionate embrace, I still find my disbelief suspended by *The Archers* on the wireless. I know the trick, yet am still drawn into it. Likewise actress Sally Grace, a passionate *Archers* fan: 'I absolutely love it – you can paint your own pictures; I know exactly what everybody looks like, and I don't like looking at pictures of them in the *Radio Times* because they're not like that at all. I know exactly what the dining room at Home Farm's like; I love Lynda Snell's "Morning Caroline . . ." I'm just an addict.'

So here, as I listened through the LPs for a Radio 4 programme about that lost *Archers* era – *Ambridge in the Decade of Love* – were names which in September 1967 were still familiar: Doughy Hood, Mrs Turvey, Greg Salt, Tony Stobeman, Reggie Trentham, Len Thomas the shepherd, Jess Allard, Zebedee Tring, Aunt Laura, Admiral Bellamy, PC Geoff Bryden, Rita Flynn, Polly Mead . . . I had to remind myself that they were just actors reading lines, and all long since consigned to radio history.

But when 'Snowball', the new baby Jill has just given birth to, is finally named ('Well, you know,' says Phil, 'I still like David'), the dynasty is assured, and the earliest seeds of painful twenty-first-century plotlines are set in motion. Listening to the brash, rude Brummie of Jack Woolley rolling up in his limo to berate local gentleman landowner Charles Grenville ('You can't hinder me, Grenville, your sort are on the rapid decline!') one casts one's mind forward to today's sad, shuffling, forgetful Jack. So too, the day in 1965 when Irish farmhand Paddy Redmond turns up at Hollerton Junction, intent on carving a swathe through the young women of Ambridge, reminds me he it is who

An Archers *explainer*

The Archers, 'an everyday story of country folk' as for many years it was described, has been broadcast regularly since January the 1st 1951 which makes it the world's longest-running radio soap opera. It's set in the fictional Midlands village of Ambridge, in the county of Borsetshire, and was characterised in an early on-air introduction thus:

> The village of Ambridge lies in the heart of the English countryside, midway between the towns of Borchester and Felpersham. It houses a typical rural community, and in spite of modern advances in agriculture and transport it has somehow still managed to stay unspoilt . . .

The serial is still built, as it was for the spring 1950 pilot run which was transmitted only in the Midlands Home Service, around the farming Archer family and their relatives. The family's HQ is legendary Brookfield Farm and its well-frequented kitchen ('I'll just put the kettle on, Walter; you'll stay for a cuppa, won't you?'). In the pilot, however, the farm wasn't called Brookfield and the drama was billed as *The Archers of Wimberton Farm*. Networked on the Home, the serial soon acquired a huge following for the doings of Dan and Doris Archer, the original central family, their three grown-up children Philip ('Phil', still played by Norman Painting who was in the first episode and also wrote many under the pseudonym Bruno Milna), horse-loving Christine and publican Jack who ran the Bull.

Dan and Doris's children, grandchildren and great-grandchildren still are the heart of *The Archers* ('In fact, putting it bluntly, Ambridge is

will father Adam, one of the modern serial's central characters and the first of them to come out as gay.

A lot of water has flowed down the Am . . .

This long lifetime where characters live, love, succeed, fail and perhaps disappear for years only to re-emerge a decade

lousy with Archers,' as Jack once explained), though there have been hundreds of other major and minor characters over nearly sixty years.

The programme's orchestral signature tune, the most famous on Radio 4, is called Dum-Di-Dum-Di-Dum-Di-Dum, or, more officially, 'Barwick Green' (a 'maypole dance', from the suite 'My Native Heath'). It was written in 1924 by a prolific Yorkshire-born composer, Arthur Wood, of whose other works virtually nothing is now performed. Scene transitions in early editions were marked by suitably dramatic musical bridges; and at really, *really* exciting cliffhangers and crises, listeners were alerted to the final flourish by the sig's peal-like descending sequence of musical phrases which crept up underneath, to climax in the famous bouncing theme. A weirdly nautical version for accordion heralds the Sunday omnibus edition which was for decades also introduced with a quaint, educative seasonal 'country note' delivered by Ambridge's game-keeper and Doris's brother, Tom Forrest.

So central to British lives did *The Archers* become at one point, that Frank Marcus's play about characters in a radio soap, *The Killing of Sister George* (and Robert Aldrich's subsequent 1968 film), derives much of its dramatic framework from the Radio 4 programme, though Aldrich transposed it to TV for the movie version.

Fictional Ambridge was loosely based on the Worcestershire village of Inkberrow, family home of Godfrey Baseley, the programme's creator, which boasts a pub called 'The Old Bull'. Besides the Bull pub, other notable features of Ambridge are the river Am and Lakey Hill (both great places for pondering life). The village shop-

☞

later, is one of the great strengths of a long-running daily serial like *The Archers*: 'It's a modern programme with a proud history,' Vanessa Whitburn, editor of the show for approaching two decades, tells me. It's their mission statement, in fact:

Not only verbally in the programme, quite often, when people remember things, but in the sense that we try to grow out of what

cum-post office is still going strong, another good gossipy meeting place, as are the kitchens, yards, fields and milking parlours (great for those utilitarian agricultural messages) of the various farms – Brookfield, of course, Home Farm where the Aldridges live, the Grundys' former home Grange Farm (now occupied by Oliver and Caroline), and Bridge Farm, home of organic farmers Tony and Pat. Grey Gables is a rural hotel-cum-banqueting suite boasting health spa, quality dining, family rows, culinary crises (and, from time to time, some high drama) for the wealthy of Ambridge.

Big-town shopping is offered by county-town Borchester (featuring Underwoods 'Borchester's most varied store') and to a lesser extent by Felpersham, though increasingly a trip to Brum is often the best option for a spree. The myriad characters trooping through the serial's studio each week are too numerous and too diverse to discuss in detail, but today's patriarchs are Phil and his wife Jill, their children, twins Shula and Kenton, David (now at Brookfield) and latecomer Elizabeth. Their partners and children provide some of the serial's central dramas, so David and his Geordie wife Ruth have in recent years had marital difficulties; Shula (how many Shulas do you know?) is today married to Alistair, but her first husband was Mark Hebden, killed in a terrible car crash in 1994.

Unreliable Kenton, long one of the 'silent' characters and living away, is now returned to Ambridge though still behaving pretty waywardly, while sister Elizabeth is married to Nigel Pargetter, and chatelaine of Lower Loxley Hall. The Jack Archer side of the family is the other main arterial road for storylines. Jack is no more, but was for years behind the bar at the Bull, with his wife Peggy, still played by June Spencer as she was in 1950.

has happened to our characters over the years, so we don't plonk things on top!

This sense of its past threading through the lives of the present characters makes *The Archers* very special among soaps; it gives it both a level of depth only *Coronation Street* can perhaps emulate, and an almost real-time evolution that lends an extra

Their children, daughters Jennifer and Lilian and son Tony (during his childhood years always known as 'Anthony William Daniel') and their associated partners and progeny compete for dramatic centre-stage. Adam Macy, Jennifer's celebrated 'illegitimate baby' from 1967 is the serial's most prominent gay character.

Jack Woolley, Brummie entrepreneur, erstwhile owner of the *Borchester Echo* (once a useful BBC spin-off souvenir product) arrived in his big car in the 1960s to put the wind up traditional Ambridge-ites. Long married to Jack Archer's widow Peggy he's in the middle stages of Alzheimer's and no longer owns Grey Gables. Prominent non-Archer characters are Sid Perks, landlord of the Bull, Caroline Sterling, née Bone, and of course the Grundys: grumpy old Joe, his son Eddie and his wife Clarrie, and their two sons Ed and William who don't get on. Their partners and offspring again keep the soapy pot bubbling merrily.

The serial has always had a range of elderly eccentrics who pop in and out, though tediously wispy old Walter Gabriel seemed never to miss an episode for several years early in the life of Radio 4. Finally, Ambridge has always had a busy-body who'll turn up just when no one wants her. Once it was Aunt Laura, who eventually fell in a ditch and died in 1985; today it's the wonderful, awful Lynda Snell, organiser of everything and with a hide as thick as that of the pet llamas she keeps.

Oh yes, and there *is* a real place called Ambridge. It's a noisy spot situated not on the gurgling Am, but the Ohio River, a couple of miles from Pittsburgh airport in the urban fringes of the Pennsylvanian former steel capital. It's named, unromantically, after the American Bridge Company.

layer of reality to what is, after all, just another radio drama. Laurie Taylor has said it takes years for radio listeners to accept novelty, and therefore perhaps the slow cooking of character within *The Archers* makes it ideally suited to the medium. Felicity Finch has been playing the part of Ruth Archer, David's wife, for twenty years and tends to agree:

I think part of the appeal of the programme is that the characters grow old within it – the listener is growing old with those characters, if you've been listening for a long time. You realise that Phil and Jill are of a particular generation and they were once like Ruth and David . . .

And so, deep in that archive store in west London, here are Jill and Phil, played then as now fifty – yes *fifty* – years later by Patricia Greene and Norman Painting. They're checking out their bawling baby twins, Kenton and Shula ('only crying in sympathy, Jill; dry as a bone!').

Another familiar voice, tracking pretty exactly the forty years of Radio 4, is Angela Piper's. Angela plays Jennifer Aldridge, a rather grand, deeply annoying character ('Jennifer Aldridge does come in really, really handy as a figure of hatred!' according to Libby Purves), but these days she's distinctly put-upon since becoming the victim of her husband Brian's roving eye. A few years back, Brian had an affair with Siobhan Hathaway who subsequently gave birth to the male heir Ruairi he'd always longed for. Now Siobhan's dead and Ruairi is motherless . . . and for those whose memories stretch to the earliest days of Radio 4, the ironies are legion.

Back then it was Jennifer, Jennifer *Archer*, Jack and Peggy's daughter, whose rebellious 1960s soul ('I'm a beatnik at heart!') had led her astray. It was the scandal of the year: an illegitimate baby, in Ambridge! But who was the father? Jennifer wouldn't tell, not even sister Lilian. Jack was furious and threatened to throw his daughter out; Doris Archer, matriarch of the clan, was shocked to the core ('Why, you must have taken leave of your senses! There's never been anything like this in the family – not in the Archers!').

A bare month and a half before Radio 4 was born, so was Adam – but while the great *Broadcasting in the Seventies* debate was raging around the corridors of Broadcasting House, wayward Jennifer was beginning yet another love affair, with her sister's boyfriend Roger (no wonder Lilian ended up with a drink problem). The decade of lurve ends with big family reconciliations and the wedding of Jennifer and Roger Travers-Macy. But it wasn't to last . . .

In soap-land, it never does. Life can't just go on boringly for the next ten years without much happening. 'It must have dramatic peaks,' agrees editor Vanessa Whitburn; and she's had plenty to choose from in the past few years – Ruth's breast cancer, Siobhan's affair with Brian and subsequent death, the Grundys' eviction, not to mention Ruth's very sudden affair with Sam the herdsman. 'And what we do after a dramatic peak . . . (and we had one with "would Ruth sleep with Sam?"; and she didn't) . . . what we're looking at now over a longer period of time is how David comes to forgive her. So the ongoing nature of the programme is its own strength, I think.'

Yes, well, up to a point. Here, I'm going to be thoroughly unfair and do a bit of cruel fast-forwarding through some of the stories, hitting, naturally, only those peaks. Cast your mind gently back, therefore, over the last four decades in Ambridge, and it does, I have to say, seem to have been a singularly sensation-racked place. Who now remembers Elizabeth being rushed to hospital after eating grain that had been dressed with mercury (1973)? Or the robbery at Grey Gables when victim Jack Woolley, also rushed to hospital, didn't regain consciousness for days? Then again, do you recall when Phil's entire herd of pigs was slaughtered because of an outbreak of swine vesicular disease at Hollowtree? Or Joe Grundy's 1975 pop concert at Grange Farm, or unfortunate Jill's thyroid deficiency a year later that kept her (guess where?) in Borchester General for three weeks? And you can guess, if you don't remember, where Neil ended up two years later still when he contracted Weil's disease. For Tony, on the other hand, it was tetanus that laid him low in 1980 and that caused him to hit the bottle. And how about this one that I'd completely forgotten: Jack Woolley's 1988 heart attack; and, hello, who's this administering the kiss of life? Lynda Snell! Truly, Ambridge is a very special village.

Sudden lurches in the storyline can make *The Archers* feel rather uncertain, a little unsure of itself. (The year Radio 4 was born saw one of the least convincing of the lot with the Ambridge equivalent of the real 1963 Great Train Robbery – the Borchester mail-van robbery – starring Nelson Gabriel in theatrical beard and stocking mask.) Likewise, many felt that

Ruth's affair with Sam was a zig-zag too far, too out of character, too unpremeditated – though it certainly got the listeners and the press talking (see page 262).

Ambridge woes

There was, however, a great deal more uncertainty all round about the serial forty years ago. It was hugely popular, but the network sounded still just a bit sniffy about having such a big populist property on their books. Just before the new schedule of spring 1970, Review Board had a go at virtually every aspect of the show, criticising the unevenness of the scripts and the acting, with Tony Whitby weighing in heavily: 'The programme changed gear very badly from time to time,' he complained, and production occasionally was 'awful'. Douglas Muggeridge, controller of Radios 1 and 2 meanwhile chipped in with criticism of the 'over-sensational' plots. Everyone nonetheless patted themselves on the back for *The Archers*' regular five million listeners and for the new younger age-group the soap was attracting.

Now one of the eternal truths of soap operas, it seems, at least according to the media press, is that they can't always be great: watch the ebb and flow of popularity between *EastEnders* and *Corrie*, the regular oscillation between too much sensation and too much dull dreary ordinariness. That's one of the givens; so build a big sensational story (remember Susan Carter and the 'Free the Ambridge One' campaign of 1993?) and the press will get on to it and, if you're lucky, it'll be front-page news – but don't expect to be loved by those who prefer a subtler, more realistic tone. 'When I arrived,' – Helen Boaden became controller in early 2000 – 'we had this terrible "summer of sadness" where all these storylines collided; so we had the Grundys being evicted, Ruth's breast cancer and then the ferrets being killed, and everywhere I went people said to me, "This is absolutely hopeless; it's become *so* gloomy, you know. We don't want to listen any more."'

Helen is a radio person through and through and cared passionately about the listeners' intimate relationship with the serial. So, following that overload, which she'd inherited, she decided she'd involve herself more closely with the way the narrative developed. 'I used to meet with Vanessa (who I think is a fantastic editor) and we'd go through the long-term storylines to make sure a) that it felt true to the characters and b) that you didn't have these unfortunate collisions,' because the Radio 4 listener, ever alert, will sniff out the faintest false note.

> So there was one point where [Vanessa] wanted to have a murder, and I forbade her, because I said there are so few murders in rural villages, if we have one it'll distort Ambridge for ever.

So mail-van robberies are OK, armed robbers, fine, numerous fires, heart attacks and violent deaths in cars and – notoriously in the mid-1990s – a car *and* a horse, all do the job. But murder no. 'Actually, I think *The Archers* can handle any story,' editor Vanessa Whitburn is emphatic: 'It's how you do it, the tone and the reality of it, which is important.' And she's got the whole history of Ambridge at her fingertips with which to make her case: so, for example, genteel rogue Nelson Gabriel's involvement in the 1967 mail-van robbery was out of character, whereas a quarter century later, violent crime came more naturally, she feels, to the nefarious Clive Horrobin:

> I could believe that Nelson, who ran an antiques shop by the time I inherited the programme, would have done the odd tough if not dodgy deal on an antique set of tables or something, but I didn't believe that he would actually cosh someone in order to get that table! Which is why when we did the village shop raid, Clive Horrobin did it – he's a much more damaged individual!

Ah yes, the vexed issue of plausibility – ratcheting up the tension without stretching credibility to breaking point. They used to do it on the show by giving the most innocent line at the end of an episode a really ferociously dramatic tweak: 'No, Dan, not . . . the silage?!' Dum-de-dum-de-dum-de-dum . . . And when Review Board paid another of its regular visits to Ambridge about eighteen months after the last lambasting, it

Faking it in Ambridge

I know the diehard *Archers* fans will hate to admit it but, despite the resemblance of Inkberrow to Ambridge, the Borsetshire village doesn't really exist. So, as it's a fictional place, existing in a parallel version of central England, I suppose it's OK not to be too concerned about the weather – but considering that the programme is set around ploughing, sowing and harvesting, you'd have thought that there'd be constant reference to the state of the sky. Trouble is, if you're recording the show a month to six weeks ahead of transmission, even with the very best long-range forecasts in the world, you've only got three choices – ignore the weather, get it wrong, or just be so vague you'll be right, whatever happens. 'Borsetshire has got to have a bit of a micro-climate!' insists editor Vanessa Whitburn. 'Luckily we live in a country where there are several climates going along anyway, so we get away with that. But it's a killer!'

The wise solution, says Vanessa, is: keep it vague. 'We don't tend to have a lot of *extremes*. You will also notice that when people are getting their harvests in they tend to say, "*All being well*, we should finish next week." We never say we have definitely finished.' But surely *The Archers* is famous for its ability at very short notice to slot in what's called a 'topical insert' when some really big unexpected event takes place?

> If it snows you cannot do a 'topical insert'. Because if it snows, every scene outside is affected in some way by that: you can't just pick three scenes and have the snow. I think the hardest thing of all, being *Archers* editor, is when you get very, very thick snow in the Midlands.

was these feeble cliffhanger endings they particularly took exception to. They then criticised the dialogue, with a management-level cat-fight ensuing over the credibility of the speech patterns of the rural characters. This was of course the era of Walter Gabriel whose vowel-gargling ('me ol' pal, me ol' beauty') seemed even more ludicrous each year. Review Board

The best thing to do at that point is go on holiday somewhere warm, because you can't win!

Another sort of reality-warp is the parallel time zone that the actors inhabit because of the advance recording schedule. So Ambridge is already preparing the bonfire night party and chestnuts when our summer is drawing to its end and, bizarrely, pulling crackers and roasting turkeys while the rest of us are still collecting spent rocket sticks. For Felicity Finch (Ruth), Christmas with kids Pip, Josh and Ben is also a slightly weird affair because not only is it *not* Christmas, but, often as not, there are no kids either. 'Until recently, all three were these disembodied [pre-recorded] voices that are played in. They're recorded with real children, very well, but then they're played in like a sound effect.'

Now, the dark art of sound effects is these days pretty well documented, but the *Archers* collection runs to more than 4,000 and is the most comprehensive set of farmyard noises in the world. Yet when it comes to certain scenes, 'spot' or practical effects performed at the microphone are still best. So what price a bit of ironing in the cowshed, Ruth?

One of the funniest things for me – and I always think it's the best sound effect – is, when you shut a pen for cattle. To get that clank we use an ironing board. I love it! It's my favourite sound effect because it's just so bizarre. It's just fantastic. So everywhere the cattle are, when we're doing those scenes – the cowshed or out in a field – there's an ironing board standing there; and we don't think twice about it!

☞

were as one in agreeing that *The Archers* needed more realistic dialogue, and storylines that moved the middle-aged and upper middle-class villagers to one side in favour of younger characters. However, the audience, said veteran producer Tony Shryane with a sigh almost audible across the years, didn't like the younger characters and complained. There had, he smiled,

And as for that critical dramatic moment that's a favourite of the agricultural soap, the troublesome delivery at dead of night . . . 'The birth of calves or lambs is always hysterical because the person who's doing the sound effects is always up to their elbows in yogurt and rubber gloves; and there's a soggy towel that has to drop at the right moment.' And Felicity Finch's own radio maternity was hardly, er, hygienic:

> When I gave birth to Pip, I was on a very dirty mattress with a very dirty something on top, doing it lying down, trying to get as much reality into that as possible.

It's a convention too that, when radio actors have to play a scene featuring a baby, it's helpful for verisimilitude to have a real, baby-shaped object to pass from one to another. In *The Archers*, it's a grubby old pillow: 'and of course this pillow gets dirtier and dirtier as it goes down the years and at some point someone will have scribbled a face on it. And at some point somebody'll suddenly kick it across the studio or do something revolting with this baby! And it *has* just been a baby – and suddenly it's not any more!'

even been allegations about the use on the show of a 'four-letter word': 'Anxious scrutiny of the script concerned had indeed revealed the offending word; it was "twit".'

During the fun-loving 1960s, despite the appearance of The Swingalongs (Ambridge's answer to the Beatles!), *The Archers* was slow to wise up to the way young people's tastes were changing. Rebellious youth, when it didn't take the form of Jennifer and her baby were leather-clad bikers roaring through the village setting the cut-glass accents of the worthies a-tutting. A decade later, even as Radio 4 was at last modernising, the centre of gravity was still middle-aged to elderly, certainly compared with today's strong cohort of youngsters. 'There was definitely an underlying threat to *The Archers*.' No wonder that when she took over as controller, Monica Sims was worried about her nearly thirty-year-old once-great soap:

It was thought to be representing a society and a time in the life of the country that was now over; that it was all now completely finished. It wasn't the way people behaved in ordinary life. It was an idealised picture of society that no longer existed and therefore there wasn't really room for it in an up-to-the-minute, news-dominated network which should not go in for these comforting, old-fashioned story-based serials.

Coronation Street and *Crossroads* ruled the roost on television and life in rural Ambridge really felt not only physically far removed from the lives of urban Lancashire and motel-land, but also socially. Sims, however, was stout in her defence of her ageing serial:

I said: 'But people *like The Archers*; why should it be taken away if it's something they enjoy?' OK, it wasn't modern drama by any means, it wasn't particularly inventive, but it had good, solid performances and characters whom the audience enjoyed getting to know. OK, sometimes they may not get it quite right, but what was the point of removing something that had become a natural part of the network? It only took up a quarter of an hour. So I couldn't see the point of getting rid of it, in spite of the scorn that was poured on it for a time.

But if you sample one of the episodes that the BBC Archive chose to keep from the late 1970s, you get an idea of what people were worried about. In one sense it's not entirely typical as it includes a dramatic moment (the death of a character, albeit not a central one); elsewhere, though, it's ho-hum humdrum: the archive synopsis tells the story . . .

Walter arrives; discussion of the Church Appeal. Jethro & Sid outside The Bull; Sid's pigeons; Eva arrives; gets lift home from Jethro. Brian & Tony watching TV; discuss death of Tony's cows; Jenny & Eva get children ready to go out with their father, Roger. Tony & Peggy: discussion of Tony's farming problems; Bill arrives. Phil & Christine – family chit-chat; George. Jethro, Tony . . .

New lives, new life

A change of editor, sharper storylines and a more contemporary relevance gradually turned the ship around, but, personally, I think the single saviour of *The Archers* was Eddie Grundy. Eddie turns up shortly after this episode and is young, vaguely dodgy, but also rather lovable and fairly hopeless. His dad Joe was a misery guts and never fun, but Eddie fancies himself; he is in his own way Ambridge's Del Boy. And, above all, he is funny. The advent of a degree of irony and characters that actually made you laugh gave the serial a completely fresh dimension. Amplify that with the still wonderful character of wits-end Clarrie and a whole new dramatic front is opened up in Ambridge, which today has built into a rich dynasty of younger, less predictable characters.

Vanessa Whitburn also points to something altogether more subtle, which concerns the construction of the narrative. Her example comes from the lead-up to the 15,000th edition landmark reached in 2006, when the surprising affair between Ruth and Sam was at its height. The writer, observes Whitburn, used Lynda Snell's rehearsal of the Christmas pantomime to offer a discreet commentary on the affair:

> And Lynda was saying things about the 'romantic idyll of Snow White' . . . talking about 'the nature of true love' and 'the nature of fidelity'. Now that I think is when we get the wit of the programme right: slightly arch. It's very funny and it's something *only The Archers* does. You won't see that kind of thing in *EastEnders* or in *Coronation Street* because it's word-based. It's a literary thing, and of course radio drama is word-based.

One index of the programme's attention to detail is the care taken to get the way the characters greet one another just right. It's not enough to say 'Morning, David'; you have to get the relationship dead right – there are millions of us out there listening for the false or inappropriate note. Former Radio 4 publicity chief Marion Greenwood is quite a fan and has a fine ear for nuances: 'It was very interesting that change in language.

Clarrie [Grundy] now calls Jennifer 'Jennifer' not 'Mrs Aldridge'
– that class thing is breaking down a bit. Because you just feel it's
probably untenable now.' So the days of Ned Larkin doffing his
cap to Dan and going all grovelly have gone; well, almost. It must
be very gratifying to Vanessa Whitburn that her listeners actually
notice these subtleties because they're a personal passion of hers:

> And then there's something even more subtle which is lovely
> which is Clarrie, for example, who *sometimes* calls Brian 'Brian'
> and *sometimes* calls him 'Mister Aldridge' depending on how
> confident she's feeling. And then there are lovely little textural
> subtleties, like Caroline will call Jack 'Jack' when she is with him
> socially, but in front of the customers at Grey Gables she'll call
> him 'Mr Woolley'. Quite right too!

Perhaps the biggest reflection of social change in recent years
has been the tendency of soaps both on TV and on radio to
feature gay characters in prominent roles. In the past, Shane the
barman at Nelson's wine bar and Jean-Paul, for twenty years
chef to the stars at Grey Gables, were both 'gently gay', but
never really emerged from the ranks of the non- or almost non-
speaking characters. Now, Adam, forty-odd years after the
kerfuffle surrounding his birth, has entered into a civil partnership with Ian, Grey Gables' chef since 2003. It was the wedding
of the year and aroused, perhaps inevitably in as venerable an
institution as *The Archers*, not a little controversy. But tut-
tutting about Ian and Adam's relationship was not confined to
the audience: Whitburn had ensured that Ambridge-ites were a
fair reflection of the broader contemporary reality. 'We have a
certain sprinkling of homophobics in the programme – Brian
and Sid; and Peggy finds it tricky.'

Sid Perks, now publican of the Bull, is an interesting example
of the way characters in the serial have evolved in a moderately
convincing manner. When he arrived in Ambridge in the 1960s,
he was a Brummie with a 'past', always hearing things on the
semi-criminal grapevine. Respectability descended with marriage
to barmaid Polly Mead of the Bull, cut short by Polly's untimely
death. Another relationship, with teacher Kathy, followed,

again ending in marriage, but also more storyline-filling tears when sexy, 'shower-scene' Jolene eventually captured Sid's heart for a third time. Now in late middle age (he's 63), the tearaway's long evolved into a bit of a reactionary. Vanessa Whitburn supervised the greying of Sid.

> He still has a jovial, jack-the-lad quality – but he's homophobic, he prefers things to stay as they are, he loves the fact that Jolene is sexy but she mustn't take it too far, certainly not with strangers. You know, Sid's a bit on the conservative side when it comes to those sorts of things, whereas he probably wouldn't have been when he was a young man.

Alan Devereux has been playing Sid for over forty years, and it's one of the extraordinary features of the serial just how many of its cast reach back several decades. New personalities appear quite regularly, but Whitburn likes to make sure there are never more than fifty speaking characters at any one time. Norman Painting famously goes back to the very first pilot episode as Phil Archer, as does June Spencer, who's been Peggy (with a break in the 1950s) ever since. Likewise, Patricia Greene (known to all the cast as Paddy) has been Phil's long-suffering wife Jill since he married her following the death of his first wife Grace in the fire of 1955 (scheduled, as all *Archers* addicts know, as a spoiler for ITV's first transmission – ah, those *were* the radio days). Felicity Finch, no arriviste herself, has a very soft spot for this sense of antiquity, recalling her own arrival in the village two decades ago.

> I remember when I first came in and I went past the shop and there was a card in the window and Mollie [Harris – 'Martha'] was renting out a room; she had a card up in the shop – but then I went to Mrs Antrobus and stayed there. And of course Mrs Antrobus, you don't hear from her now – it's very clear that she's in some kind of sheltered housing.

Marjorie Antrobus fell silent – because actress Margot Boyd retired – and became one of the *Archers* cohort of 'silent' characters. It may be a function of a radio soap, living in the imagination, that these 'silent' characters amuse listeners so much. Shane the barman and Jack Woolley's chauffeur Higgs were two such and Vanessa Whitburn has strict views about giving them a voice. 'I'm not keen on silent characters eventually speaking,' she affirms. 'If a character has been established as silent for quite a few years, I think you cast them at your peril, myself.' What really annoys her is outside directors who work briefly on the show and don't quite 'know the rules'.

> They'll decide to give them sort of a mumble, off. I hate that and I try to cut it out if I can, but sometimes I can't cut it out on the edit, so then it has to stay. But, no, I don't think it's right, because we all know what these people sound like!

So much so, in fact, that not long ago Vanessa developed an extensive storyline featuring *only* silent characters; a sort of rather satisfying virtual existential fantasy. It featured a relationship between the two ancient retainers at Lower Loxley Hall, Titcombe and Eileen Pugsley, '"Mrs Pugsley" as she was known. We looked in the archives and she hadn't had a first name, so we invented one because we were now going to marry her to Titcombe.'

> The idea was that she was divorced, but her husband was still alive; she'd had great difficulty with the divorce and so she felt she shouldn't marry again whilst he was still alive. Then he died and she was free to marry Titcombe!

And that's the joy of radio. A few words of dialogue in a script, a good dollop of imagination on the part of the programme team and the listener, and a bit of reality – or at least of *Ambridge* reality – takes wing. It's part of why, when she was controller, Helen Boaden so enjoyed working closely with the *Archers* team. 'One of the best days I ever had in Radio 4,' she remembered with just a touch of the wonderment of the visitor to Universal Studios, 'was spending a day with the scriptwriters of *The Archers* as they went through storylines. I knew it really,

A fling too far?

When Ruth Archer had her moment of madness with cowman Sam Batton in 2006, it was, as so often, a massive publicity coup. Another big landmark for this serial was coming up – the 15,000th episode – so what better than a bit of front-page copy? And editorials, no less; and a buzz of incredulity that spread briefly across the Radio 4-listening classes and beyond, because this was Ruth and David, the stalwart centre of the Ambridge scene, heirs to Phil and Jill at Brookfield, and thus before *them* to Dan and Doris, the original Ambridge royalty. Out of character, cried many; how could good-as-gold, loyal Ruth think of two-timing steady old David? As many an unbelieving listener responded: 'Ooh nooo!'

So what was the verdict of the Radio 4 professionals? First off, former controller and *Archers* aficionado, Helen Boaden:

> I have had a few problems, frankly! Because I think Ruth was too down to earth to get involved and I don't think David had neglected her that badly. It certainly seemed to come out of the blue. So I'm afraid I turned into a grumpy old woman thinking, 'Well I'm sorry! Ruth wouldn't say that!'

really well because I'd listened for so many years, and apparently after I'd gone one of them said, "Gawd, she knows a lot, doesn't she?"'

This intimacy is a real feature of the strange and very different world that radio soaps inhabit. It's a sort of semi-reality where we're more or less happy to accept the conventions and let the fiction lie unquestioned, although we're all in on the joke. Marion Greenwood remembers a bizarre example from 2002 of reality and fiction merging into a sunny joke by members of the audience . . .

who, at the Countryside Alliance march, had a poster saying 'Jennifer! Brian's the father of Siobhan's child!'; they were marching with these banners! And you just think, 'That's wonderful',

'Utterly improbable!' cried critic Gillian Reynolds, quite exasperated at the idea; she smelled a publicity rat: 'We've got a 15,000th episode coming up, let's create a situation. Now that's the deathwish! No. Rubbish!' Maybe, but it certainly got the fans talking – on the *Archers* messageboard, for example: 'I kept seeing these references to "WR",' says former Radio 4 publicist Marion Greenwood, 'and found out that it meant "Whingeing Ruth". And they spin off into all sorts of really violent arguments about how David is treating Ruth.'

Meanwhile, Vanessa Whitburn was reporting that Felicity Finch was booed by angry listeners when they held the public celebrations for the serial's 15,000th edition. Yet she points out that, after the anger, the audience responded with more sympathy as the ebb and flow of the fallout progressed:

> And I think there's a wisdom in that: be careful when you judge because life is complex, and things sometimes take time to unravel. So there is a wisdom there – and it's the wisdom of the everyday. *The Archers* constantly says that in all sorts of ways.

because of that sense of humour, the sense of actually knowing the difference between reality and fantasy, but mixing them up in that wonderful way. That's the really good side of Radio 4. Just makes me laugh every time I think of it.

The script meetings Helen Boaden was referring to are where the big storylines of *The Archers* get initiated. Each month, Whitburn gathers her ten writers (such as the ultra-experienced Mary Cutler and Joanna Toye), producers and researchers round the table for eight hours of thrashing out the potential stories, testing them out on one another:

Everybody has a shared ownership of the programme; no one is asked to write things they don't know about or they haven't helped evolve. So if they're writing a 'peak moment', a 'peak week', they have helped to evolve the stuff that ran up to that.

As we've seen already, in common with all soaps more 'stuff' has gone on in Ambridge over the years than in a dozen average Midlands villages; Vanessa Whitburn says she's running roughly twice or even three times the number of storylines at any one moment than her predecessor was in the 1970s. Much of the long-running material grows out of the lives of the characters: Nelson's wine bar, Jaxx Caff, Tom Archer's sizzling sausages, Jack's Alzheimer's, all these are the gentle run-of-the mill doings against which the big horrors play out. It's these slow-burn social stories that lie alongside the lurid which are, in Felicity Finch's view, what makes the serial still relevant, powerful drama, week-in, week-out.

> I feel one of the reasons that *The Archers* has survived is because of the juxtaposition of the everyday story, literally, of country folk – you know, like the village fete – with stories that are to do with very serious social issues. In the time *I've* been in the programme, we've dealt with depression, anorexia, breast cancer, GM crops, racism in the countryside . . . large numbers of people said that they learned more about GM crops from Tom trashing a field of GM crops than they ever did by watching the news or reading the newspapers!

Fact to fiction

One big story *The Archers* could hardly have failed to run back at the beginning of the millennium was the foot and mouth outbreak. This was when real agriculture impinged on the fictional farmers of Ambridge. From its inception, of course, the serial was a vehicle for carrying careful messages about farming methods, about inoculation against TB, foul-pest, swine vesicular disease (remember Phil's outbreak in 1974?), about new farming technology. In fact I seem to remember an interminable running story right through the 1960s about a revolutionary new milking parlour at Hollow Tree (or was it Brookfield?) . . . These messages were often not-too-craftily woven in – 'What's all this I hear, Phil, about a new subsidy that the government's just announced . . .?'

But when, in 2001, the real foot and mouth crisis struck, the disaster proved a godsend for the fiction. 'Well done *The Archers* for writing foot and mouth disease into last week's scripts. It has quite restored my faith, recently severely tried,' cheered Gillian Reynolds from the columns of the *Telegraph*. 'Symptoms of the virulent soap-opera affliction, plot sag, have now been averted, thanks to signals from the real world . . .' Felicity Finch, as Ruth, was in the middle of it:

> They were almost rewriting it every day; all the time trying to reflect exactly what farmers were going through. And I remember hearing that farmers took great solace from that, from hearing us reflecting the misery and the awfulness of it and the tensions, the not knowing how long you were going to have to be in quarantine for.

And Felicity, an actress not a farmer, remember, does well to remind us that the contemporary debate has brought the issues that bestride the serial week-in, week-out closer to listeners' interests and preoccupations: 'Farming, over the last ten years or so, has become so much more in the forefront of the news in our minds, whether it's been to do with foot and mouth or BSE, TB, the quality of the food that we eat, whether it's local food, organic food . . .' Now, she says, she can't look at a field of hay without thinking, 'Yeah, yeah, we've just been doing that!'

But, wait, here's a revelation: Ruth Archer Allergic to Farming – Shock!

> The funniest thing is, when I was about fourteen, somebody asked me to visit him for a day at his farm. And I spent the whole day inside because I was allergic to everything! Streaming eyes! Red blotches all over my face! And I couldn't go outside! So even now I don't actually know how I would be on a farm!

A matter of timing

In 1998, controller James Boyle took his life in his hands and changed the schedule for *The Archers*. For generations, the programme's repeat had run at 1.45 pm after *WATO*; now he decided he must change it. Boyle's problem was that the very strength of the serial meant that the millions who hung around to catch it after *The World at One* tended to take the closing sig tune as the natural moment to quit Radio 4 for the afternoon. 'People were just streaming away, and the reason for shifting it to two o' clock was to make sure that those who were able to stay (and we knew in detail from the research that they were there) would stay, listen to *The Archers* and then give [*The Afternoon Play*] a try. You dangle *The Archers* in front of them and then extend the mood.'

There were protests, there were letters; but it worked.

It was the thing that brought in most letters of protest. I would say about 1,500 letters came in to say 'This is outrageous. I can't listen to *The Archers* at two o'clock!' But by God, a huge number of people could, and did!

So, after nearly sixty years of death, doom and dairying, apart from the obvious appeal of great, compelling stories told with style and conviction, what is the particular element about *The Archers* – other than the Everest one: because it simply is there in the schedule six days out of seven – that keeps five million listeners, still one heck of an audience, agog. Gillian Reynolds reckons it's the quality of the cast: 'They're all such *good* actors in that show!' For Marion Greenwood, it's the care with which big storylines are set up: 'They would have started planting the seed two years before.' Felicity Finch, for her part, thinks it's more fundamental altogether,

I don't think people quite realise how quickly their imaginations are working and the pictures are building in their head. I heard Trevor Harrison who plays Eddie Grundy saying the other day that when he hears it, he actually *sees* the cows in the cowshed and the tractor crossing the field. If he's in a scene, he'll still see the pub in his head, even though he knows he's in front of the microphone . . . It sounds odd, but I find myself doing exactly the same thing. I don't question it, and I can see the cows, I can see the cowshed, I can see Brookfield kitchen, and I think that the listener builds these amazing pictures – it's the old cliché saying that radio's better than TV because the pictures are better.

As for the editor, in the hot seat for over sixteen years herself, Vanessa Whitburn believes the spell of *The Archers* is yet more elusive still:

It's like good poetry: the sum is greater than the parts. You can pin down the parts (and that's what I spend a lot of my time doing) but in the end the whole is a bit of a mystery. It has to be modern, but it has to be resonant of the past – as does Radio 4.

CHAPTER TEN
7.15 pm: After dark

'Programmes for Settled Listening' is how *Radio Times* described the evening schedule on Radio 4 in its curtain-raising guide to the complexities of Tony Whitby's 1970 schedule. Exactly what 'unsettled' listening might be isn't revealed, but this description goes to the very heart of one of Radio 4's perpetual dilemmas. Radio on the move, radio while you're cooking, boiling kettles, cleaning your teeth – living a life, in fact – is not the most perfect way to communicate information and ideas; nor indeed to enjoy the benefits of beautifully and expensively executed stereophonic plays and features. So, the traditional wisdom has been, sit-down-and-listen radio is best placed when listeners can, well, sit down and listen; i.e. in the evening.

But here's the paradox. Radio 4's primetime – in common with all UK stations – is in the morning and, to a lesser extent, the afternoon; and this has been the case for a lot longer than Radio 4 has been around. However, once the evening with its more 'settled' regime takes over, we all tend to turn to the box for entertainment and information, and radio listening nose-dives: you don't acquire viewing figures (as until recently) of 15 million for big BBC1 hits without sucking in the audience from somewhere else. So settled *listening* is a minority sport.

Increasingly, portable audio downloads ('podcasts'), delivered into the listener's ears through noise-defeating headphones, are opening up 'settled-listening' oases even in the midst of our busy-busy twenty-first-century lives. However, for the moment the controller's dilemma is as I've described it, and it informs much of the debate around what the evenings on Radio 4 should consist of, how they should be shaped.

The other problem with these wonderful programmes that Tony Whitby wanted his audience to listen to so carefully is that they cost a great deal of money. Radio dramas are the most expensive programmes on Radio 4, and if you have a whole evening of drama, as Whitby did on Monday September the 14th 1970, it isn't going to come cheap. That evening, thirty minutes of detective serial was followed directly by something altogether meatier, a World Theatre presentation of a play by the great German dramatist Heinrich von Kleist. In total, two and a half solid hours featuring substantial casts, and heard by how many? Veteran drama director Ned Chaillet reckons popular evening plays in the 70s had an audience of perhaps a quarter of a million; Kleist probably struggled to get that. When set against the three, four or even five million who heard *Today*, it didn't constitute particularly good economic sense for the network. 'Therefore you start looking at how much you're paying for the daytime and for the night; and "the money should go to where the biggest audience is" became the logic,' sighs Chaillet, a little regretfully.

Back in 1970, Radio's Director of Programmes, Gerry Mansell was exuding confidence in his controller's new evening pattern. Out went almost all the music that had riddled the old Radio 4 and in came 'drama, documentaries, discussions, which television, by its nature, cannot provide', he told *Radio Times*. 'At least half our audience in the evening are people who have television in their homes, but who choose radio.' Ian Trethowan, the future DG, then running Radio, added, 'We believe that we can bring maybe hundreds of thousands back to the more attractive programmes we hope to present.'

So what sort of shape did Radio 4's evening have forty years ago? Well, as you'll by now guess, the pre-1970 version was markedly different from what replaced it. There was lots of music – full live orchestral concerts were common – and even when there wasn't a concert, listeners had at least an hour's worth of music to enjoy every evening, including the much-loved weekly selection box called *Music to Remember*. Around the music were clustered documentaries, short plays, a bit of comedy and fifteen-minute talks in an apparently fairly random pattern. To navigate your way round this line-up, a copy of *Radio Times* was essential, the only fixed weekday points being the end of *The Archers* at 7.00 pm and the *Ten O'Clock* news magazine at, yes, ten. Beyond that the schedule did become a little bit more predictable, with *Book at Bedtime* at two minutes past eleven, followed by more *Music at Night*.

It was to the heart of the evening that Tony Whitby brought some fresh, ordered thinking. Henceforth Mondays would be drama, Tuesdays, features and talks; Wednesday had the *Midweek Play*, plus a book programme and *This Island Now* about life in town and country; Thursdays were science nights with *New Worlds* (presented by Paul Vaughan, later to become the great stalwart of the arts show *Kaleidoscope*, of which more anon). Friday evening now centred around *Any Questions?* just as today, with Radio 4 inheriting the programme's live origination from Radio 2.

Enquiring minds

And then came *Analysis*. Still going strong nearly forty years later, *Analysis* was born with Whitby's schedule on April the 10th 1970 and was one of the most significant current affairs programmes it brought into being. 'Now there's a strange programme; started in one era, survived how long?' Radio historian Gillian Reynolds has watched *Analysis*'s reputation grow: 'When I think of the ideas that have come to me through that over the years!'

First up on the new show was the Chancellor of the Exchequer Roy Jenkins and his forthcoming budget. With future controller Ian McIntyre in the presenter's chair, and a ferocious young intellect George Fischer as producer, the new programme could be depended on to have plenty of intellectual rigour. 'George Fischer and Ian McIntyre,' sighs Gillian Reynolds, 'and the hallmark astringent thinking! And the script goes through eight or nine drafts; that shows in the quality of the thought. One of the contributors, Frances Cairncross, actually told me that every time she did it, it was *such* hard work it gave her mouth ulcers!'

Ian McIntyre, whom we've met as the controversial Radio 4 controller who took an axe to *Today*, was then still magnificent in front of the microphone, his incisive style a model of the explicative journalism that has always been the hallmark of *Analysis*. Clear, thoughtful, without frills or distracting actuality; simply the line of beauty in argument by the people who mattered. An example at random, from February 1974: 'Under Plainer Cover' looked at censorship and artistic freedom. It starred, amongst others, for the liberal tendency publisher John Calder, and for the pro-censorship lobby Mrs Mary Whitehouse; the producer (as of many editions) was future controller Michael Green. Green much admired Ian's style and clarity of thinking, as did Gillian Reynolds:

> He 'had thoughts'. Ian was a great broadcaster, on *Analysis*, on various series like *Divided by a Common Language*; I remember him on the SALT talks – very good on strategic arms limitation. A stunning writer and a really, really good presenter.

Unsurprisingly, given its prominent place within the new current-affairs-conscious shape of Radio 4, *Analysis* came in for a fair degree of attention from BBC mandarins. Radio Review Board was slightly cool about the programme's second edition, 'The Nixon Doctrine', though it had been well chaired, they felt, and the high quality of Ian McIntyre's presentation remains a theme through several examinations. Thus *Analysis* very soon hit its stride with an impressive cast of contributors and high-octane subjects, as in May 1971 when the programme tackled the long drawn-out post-colonial drama in Zimbabwe ('Rhodesia: the View from Salisbury'). For this edition, *Analysis* secured what Gerry Mansell declared was 'in the nature of a scoop', an interview with the country's premier, Ian Smith. Ian Trethowan told Review Board, 'It was the best interview he had ever heard Mr Smith give' and Tony Whitby went one better, praising it as 'simply the best documentary Radio 4 had done'.

In nearly forty years of broadcasting the programme has taken on hundreds of different subjects, at home and abroad, with dozens of different presentational voices, amongst whom, besides McIntyre, David Wheeler, Peter Hennessey, John Eidinow and Michael Charlton were some of the best known. It's true that, sometimes, *Analysis* could – and can – sound dry as dust, a dull subject unfolding in a plodding way. But far more often, and particularly in the hands of the illuminating Mary Goldring, it was a wonder. 'Mary Goldring's voice I remember quite distinctly,' says Gillian Reynolds; 'You felt as if she was the neighbour coming in with an eye as to the exact state of your sofas and she would notice where the cobwebs were, but not in any accusatory way.' Goldring would usually start her programmes with a simple premise, perhaps a scene which she'd describe, and then slowly, slowly wind us in, like a fisherman reeling in his catch; for me the perfect combination of the lucid *Analysis* argument and compelling storytelling – and the hallmark of a great radio journalist.

While *Analysis* has continued to probe issues in its cerebral fashion for well over three decades, another significant programme in the Radio 4 evening has been tackling them in quite a different manner, and for nearly as long. By 1977, Tony Whitby was dead, shockingly prematurely of cancer, and Ian McIntyre had surrendered his presenter's chair for that of Radio 4's controller. His erstwhile producer, Michael Green, meanwhile was hatching an idea. 'I had long thought what the network lacked,' he told me, 'was journalism through revelations, through storytelling.' He talked of creating 'a *Panorama* of radio, where people actually got dust on their boots and went out and saw things, came back and weighed up the evidence and said, "Well, this is what I think."'

The programme he created and edited was *File on Four*, a bastion of investigative journalism on Radio 4 (complete with its distinctively un-current-affairs signature tune fanfare). The other vital characteristic of the new programme was that it was produced not from the London news hub, but from the Manchester studio. Cue a severe outbreak of metropolitan snobbery: 'I learned about Broadcasting House politics very rapidly,' smiles Green.

I remember Douglas Muggeridge who was Deputy Managing Director at the time saying: 'Well dear boy, if you want to go anywhere, you've surely got to go via Heathrow?' That was the sort of attitude; that it was inconceivable that you could make serious journalism out of a place called Manchester.

A team of three producers and a couple of brilliant young reporters, David Henshaw and Steve Bradshaw, worked on the show which was initially anchored by the Oxford economist Peter Oppenheimer, 'and the programme suddenly took off; people welcomed it. I think we made some good journalism,' says Michael Green with justified satisfaction.

That was part of that new departure that characterised the network as a whole: let's go and sniff some other air and see what's going on out there, rather than asking people to come in to us. I mean television had been at it for years and radio had been rather left behind. But then radio started to catch up in a big way.

'*File on Four* is the most intense programme-making experience I've ever had.' The speaker is Helen Boaden, now the BBC's Director of News, but formerly a reporter in Manchester. It was the programme that made her reputation as an investigative journalist and then, when she became its editor, as a remarkable leader. 'It's incredibly relentless because what might take *Panorama* eight weeks, you're often doing in ten days. And yet the quality and depth of your research has to be every bit as good.'

The breakthrough edition of *File on Four* for the future controller came early in her time on the show. It was the 1980s and Helen had noticed reports of 'this funny thing that was beginning to develop in Africa' known locally as 'slim' disease. Together with her producer John Drury, Boaden travelled to Uganda and Kenya to investigate what were the first reported manifestations of AIDS. 'People didn't really know what was happening. Uganda was trying to deal with it, whereas Kenya was trying to suppress it and pretend it wasn't happening.' Helen Boaden's *File on Four* programme about the origins of

AIDS won her a Sony Gold Award and a great deal of broadcasting kudos.

> I remember saying to the man whose job it was on his little moped to distribute the condoms: 'And how many condoms do you have?' and he said, 'Oh, forty', and I said, 'And how many men are in this area?' And it was something like 40,000. That's where I began to learn how to really do evidential journalism.

Afghanistan under the Soviet Union, BSE, problems in Britain's gaols, witness intimidation, the Lockerbie trial . . . the list of big running stories, domestic and international, that have caught the attention of *File on Four* (and prize juries: the show has over forty gongs to its name) is some sort of rough index of the major preoccupations of the last quarter of a century. 'It completely formed me as a journalist,' says Boaden. 'The question I learned from *File on Four* is "Where is your evidence?" Indeed, when I left and they threw me a wonderful party, in the middle of the goodbye card was a note that just said in big letters AND WHERE IS YOUR EVIDENCE?'

Into the heart of the evening

These days, the tenor of Radio 4's evening can on occasion stretch away from *The Archers* in a succession of increasingly gloomy and serious programmes that feel almost too guilty for words. 'There's a bit too much lecturing going on for me,' groans Gillian Reynolds, and certainly the dedicated listener to Radio 4 can on occasion enjoy a procession of programmes on, for instance, AIDS in Ukraine, the innocent victims of germ-tests, plus some pretty near-the-knuckle stuff from fringe theatre with Mark Lawson all within the space of ninety tough minutes (and that's a real example from early 2006).

Not that *Front Row* is usually quite such a testing listen. It's sharply focused modern arts journalism with a brief that's eclectic, accessible and distinctly non-metropolitan. Here the Arctic Monkeys rub shoulders with Leni Riefenstahl, Joni

Mitchell with Marty Wilde, while Sylvie Guillem dances and Delius's little seen opera *Koanga* gets reviewed. With Mark Lawson at the heart of the arts action alongside John Wilson and Kirsty Lang, the successor to the veteran *Kaleidoscope* (see page 278) has grown to be one of the key critical reference points for arts journalism.

And when Mark, John or Kirsty has rung down the safety curtain, Radio 4's other evening affliction begins to show its first symptoms: Repeat-itis. It was James Boyle in 1998 who, recognising the reality of dwindling audiences, finally took the brutal decision to move big money out of the evening and offer, in the time-honoured weasel words, 'another chance to hear' (i.e. repeat) programmes. Thus after *Front Row*, the morning's *Woman's Hour* serial drama gets a second outing. Likewise, at the other end of the evening, the last half hour before *The World Tonight* consists, on four nights a week, of repeat offerings from the morning's 9.00 am shows.

In between, just as in Tony Whitby's day, it's that mix of serious stuff that's often very powerful but that might intimidate a peaktime, more take-it or leave-it listener. Michael Green used to call them sometimes 'sit-down-and-worry programmes' and others have referred to them rather unflatteringly as 'hard-chair' listens, and it's true that both *Analysis* and *File on Four* are part of that mid-evening pattern, but so too are some of the often grim yet riveting documentaries made for the *It's My Story* personal-narrative series.

These days the nine o'clock strip across the week is occupied by science programmes of one sort or another, with many of the great names of forty years of radio science, like Peter Evans and Geoff Watts, still turning up to mingle with newer voices such as Dr Mark Porter. James Boyle was responsible for finding a settled home for so many of these traditionally nomadic pro-grammes, and in doing so undoubtedly gave real shape, purpose and intellectual stiffening to the evenings on the network. It seems daft now that Boyle was the man whom the press cease-lessly and completely wrongly accused of 'dumbing down' Radio 4.

The best response to 'dumbing down' was by [*WATO* presenter] Nick Clarke who walked in and said to one of our commissioners, 'I listened to the new Radio 4 schedule last night and my brain nipped' – he'd been listening to the science programmes and the repeat of *In Our Time* and he said, 'How can *anyone* say it's dumbed down?'

Dumb-down James Boyle never did. In fact it's astonishing quite how much brain-nipping science, medical and natural history programming Radio 4 still does; and not just at 9.00 pm. Afternoons have *Material World*, *Home Planet* and *Check Up*, while in the mornings you find the regular natural history slots. For those reared on a diet of *Blue Planet*s and *Planet Earth*s, the pedigree of Radio 4's natural history programmes may well surprise.

Older listeners will remember *The Living World*, with Derek Jones, a veteran West Country broadcaster, who spent many years grubbing around on 'radio nature trails' in which he would narrate in hushed tones the inner rustlings and twitterings of woods, usually situated not far from the Natural History Unit's Bristol home. And longer ago still, C. Gordon Glover presented an unashamedly romantic, poetical nature programme called *The Countryside in Summer* or *Autumn* or *Winter* etc., which was heralded by one of the most exquisite signature tunes Radio 4 ever broadcast. I still recall with huge pleasure those seasonal reports (like Eric Simms's on birds) on every aspect of rural life, not unlike the 'country notes' that still appear in the broadsheets, thirty or more years since Glover finally closed his cottage door.

Now let's face it, men grovelling about in muddy woods listening to the distant sound of the nightjar doesn't sound much like broadcasting magic. Yet it was. Sir David Attenborough and his amazing producers may be able to take us deep under the oceans and high above the plateaux of the world to wonder, but radio takes us into the reality of the experience. Because while television we watch, radio we *feel*. And if James Boyle bid farewell to *The Living World* and *The Natural History Programme*, who can forget the remarkable programmes not so

very long ago about the awakening of the spring as it travelled
north with the warming sun across Europe, or the 'Migration'
series of 2003 that tracked on *Today* and elsewhere the journeys
of the whooper and Bewick swans from Russia, when, for a
moment, the fate of Bewicks Andrei and Anatoli became almost
a national obsession.

Arty time

But it was not always thus. There was a time when science and
arts programming were forced into an arranged marriage, but
ended up glaring at one another and soon divorced, having to
find their own discrete berths in the schedule.

The story, inevitably, begins with Tony Whitby scratching his
head about what to do with his arts programming. His first
attempt was *Options* (funny how arts programmes often go for
abstract titles – *Kaleidoscope*, *Arena* (on television) and, as we
shall soon see, *Scan*). The presenter was Antony Jay, for whom
the stardom of co-writing *Yes Minister* was still ten years away.
Options started well, with a thumbs-up from Whitby, but less
than a year on, a decision was taken, apparently as the result of
changes in arts coverage on Radio 3, to rethink.

Thus, in October 1971, was born *Scan*, with, in the producer's chair, Philip French, today the *Observer*'s distinguished
film critic. Internal BBC reaction to *Scan* was a little mixed, with
the controller of Radio 3 banging on rather relentlessly about
the superficial treatment of an item on Buñuel, and another
department head lamenting that the programme had been
'rather chatty'. Given that much of the rest of the show was
given over to discussing the cinema of Ingmar Bergman, I'd say
a degree of chattiness was probably no bad thing.

Also working on *Scan* (and *Options*) was Rosemary Hart,
who more than any other editor shaped Radio 4's arts coverage
for two and a half decades. In 1971 she found herself trotting
off to New York with her colleague Patricia Brent and presenter
Gillian Reynolds, who remembers 'doing amazing things . . . like
the first *Godfather* movie and the movie of *Cabaret* and *Follies*,

the Sondheim show'. But it was a London musical opening that's seared *Scan* into Rosemary's memory: her presenter on this occasion was the then film critic of the London *Evening Standard*, Alexander Walker:

> There was a revival of *Hair*, and it advertised that the cast took their clothes off in the middle of it. On this particular day, which was very cold, they didn't take their clothes off, and Alex said, 'Absolute outrage!' And he said, 'We're going to complain because it's against the Trades Descriptions Act.' We trolled round to the Stage Door where he complained bitterly to the manager, and I've never been so embarrassed in my entire life!

But *Scan*, too, wasn't long for the schedule, because plans were being hatched that would lead to one of Radio 4's most successful long-runners, the arts show *Kaleidoscope*. Rosemary Hart, its creative genius, recalls the slightly odd way it began: 'Tony Whitby . . . said, "I want a marriage of arts and science. It's ridiculous this divide, they should come together."' *Scan* was therefore abandoned and in 1973, with a menu that, as requested, bizarrely featured both science and art, *Kaleidoscope* took shape.

Hart gathered round her a small group of highly talented producers with the appropriate breadth of skills: Alan Haydock and Miriam Newman represented the arts, while shouting for science was Michael Bright; 'and he brought with him Paul Vaughan whom he'd been producing,' Rosemary remembers. Vaughan, equally at home presenting the science show *New Worlds* as the arts, was to become perhaps the best known of *Kaleidoscope*'s presenters, but all would become, to one degree or another, household names of arts broadcasting over the next quarter century: Ronald Harwood (who did the first edition), Michael Oliver, Waldemar Januszczak, Tony Palmer, Paul Allen, Edward Mullins, Natalie Wheen, Jackie Gillott, Mark Steyn and others.

Kaleidoscope, being a child of the 1970s, was born with a Radiophonic Workshop signature tune, though this slipped away as fashions changed. So eventually did the science, though, as Rosemary Hart remembers with a degree of resignation, not immediately.

> We struggled on for a year with this mix, but it was an impossible marriage because it didn't satisfy the sciences or the arts. For example, I remember we had a programme which had a review of the latest production of *Hamlet*, with something called 'aggressive anemones'. Which was hopeless! Or hip replacements: I can remember very well the doctor coming in with all these bones and describing the operation live on air, followed by a review of a *Carry On* film.

It had to stop. 'At the end of a year, I went to Tony Whitby and said, "This is really not working." So after just over a year we off-loaded science and a new science programme was born.'

One of the innovations *Kaleidoscope* introduced was to broadcast live, and late, in order to encompass first-night reviews, though, like so many programmes that aren't locked down by other factors to a particular time of day, it had a tendency to roam around the schedule when the controller wanted to make a change. Very quickly, a good review on *Kaleidoscope* became as much a hallmark of success as excellent notices in the papers, and quotations from reviews labelled 'BBC *Kaleidoscope*' began to appear on billboards. Another measure of the affection in which it was held was that it soon acquired its own internal faux-insulting soubriquet, 'Ka-loadacrap'.

The first live coverage of the Booker prize, the first arts show to report from China, Sir Laurence Olivier on Ralph Richardson, and Graham Greene on Graham Greene were a few of the many coups the programme pulled off. Greene, says Rosemary Hart, would only do the interview on tape, and at dead of night. 'And I'd read that he was very keen on whisky, so I took down a bottle of scotch, the very best I could purchase, and we did this brilliant interview. And then we sat in the studio until past midnight drinking this bottle of scotch and just chatting . . .' But scoops and stars didn't always work out so smoothly. On one occasion, *Kaleidoscope*'s technology and that of the brand new stage machinery at the Apollo Victoria Theatre

A shelf full of books

When I first arrived as a producer at Radio 4, talk was all of a new programme. Now there are few thrills in broadcasting like starting a brand new show: ideas fly about, pilot programmes are made, played and critically flayed and then remade better. The show whose early maelstrom moments I found myself parachuted into was Radio 4's long-running literary magazine *Bookshelf*. The editor Helen Fry determined she wanted a 'no-brow' programme, and 'from classics to comics' was how *Radio Times* first described it. The presenter was a young Irish broadcaster, Frank Delaney, today himself a prolific writer, who brought immediate style and charm to the new show. Heralded by its bouncy guitar-picking signature tune, *Bookshelf* became an instant success.

Covering far more than just the latest outpourings from the big publishing houses, *Bookshelf* rediscovered classics that had slipped from view, as well as literally from time to time catching up with the world of comics, like the *Beano*. One of the programme's early strengths was the freedom given to us producers to follow our own instincts: I remember a special edition we recorded in Paris for Easter 1982 – at what in those pre-Starbucks days was such a novelty, a café-bookshop called Mille Feuilles (the waiter told us he loved comic books) – and memorable interviews with Joseph Heller (my battered copy of *Catch-22* has Heller's *Bookshelf* autograph on the title page), J.G. Ballard and Iris Murdoch amongst many others. 'I remember meeting some people who were my heroes,' says fellow producer Alastair Wilson, 'Stan Barstow, John Braine, Alan Sillitoe – you know, not inconsiderable people.' Wilson's maverick approach ensured

in London collided to disastrous and very public effect. It was 1984 and the show was Andrew Lloyd Webber's rollerskating locomotive fantasy *Starlight Express*.

I think it was the first time we'd used the radio car, which only had to beam the signal from Victoria to Broadcasting House; but you had to raise the antenna. Anyway the reviewer came

Bookshelf's pedigree by taking listeners down literary byways rarely explored by other book programmes:

> I remember doing a couple of programmes where we were dealing with what was meant to be 'hot property' on the London publishing machine, and I thought, 'I'm going to do what I think!' So I got Michael Foot in to talk about Hazlitt, I got Michael Foot in to talk about Swift . . .

Personally, what I loved most of all was the opportunity to make what we called 'author profiles' – thirty-minute literary biographies. So, for example, with a later presenter, Hunter Davies, we discovered the real-life characters behind Arthur Ransome's children's classic *Swallows and Amazons*. The memory of sailing out to 'Wild Cat Island' on Coniston Water aboard a tiny dinghy will never leave me; especially when a peculiarly splashy wave soaked a protesting Hunter to his underpants.

The last man to sit in the presenter's chair was Libby Purves's erstwhile 'instant' poet on *Midweek* Nigel Forde (see Chapter Three). Nigel and I had some delicious literary experiences, my favourite being a feature we made about the epistolary farewells of those sent to the guillotine in the French Revolution. On another occasion, Forde travelled round the country on that authorial progress that is the publicity tour. *Bookshelf*'s subject was the literary lion and intellect Anthony Burgess, who wasn't particularly keen to go along with what his publishers were asking: 'I mean, he was very affable to them, but he just wanted to talk about music, so we sat in taxis together discussing music.'

☞

hurtling into the radio car and we said, 'How was it?' 'It was great. Except that, at the very end, all the singers' mics went down.'

The item was broadcast, no doubt some passing comment was made about the microphone glitch, and Hart thought nothing more about it until . . .

But the edition that Forde remembers with greatest fondness was, perhaps inevitably for a poet, when he persuaded the notoriously reticent Ted Hughes to do a turn on the show. The recording was to take place at Hughes's home.

> I was terrified. But he was lovely! He was very kind, very affable, very smiley, not at all the grim Yorkshireman that he's painted. He made some conditions: 'You dawn't describe this house; you dawn't talk about the rooms, how you get here, anything like that.'

The subject was ostensibly a work in progress about Shakespeare. However, as the minutes ticked into hours, inevitably the talk turned to Hughes's work (which he'd originally forbidden Forde to mention) and yet another precious moment of literary broadcasting emerged blinking and unexpected on to Radio 4.

Bookshelf itself lasted about a decade and a half, and by the end it had lost a lot of its early zip, but for many of those years it was about as good as radio book programmes get – funny, sad, inventive and enquiring. I for one have it to thank for many of my happiest moments in radio journalism.

I was coming up on the train the following morning and I saw headlines on a paper which said BBC OBLITERATES SOUND OUTPUT FROM 'STARLIGHT EXPRESS'!

The theatre was apparently using the same radio frequency for its microphones as – legitimately – the BBC was using to transmit back to base from the radio car. 'So once we started to transmit, they cancelled each other out. But the horror of having obliterated the end of *Starlight Express*! We were just pleased to have got a signal all the way from our little car up to Broadcasting House!'

Kaleidoscope survived for a quarter of a century, seeing off in its time five controllers. Yet a change of face at the top, Rosemary Hart reports, was always greeted with trepidation: 'It was always a battle; one dreaded the establishment of another controller because you knew the programme was vulnerable. You know, "How many people are really going to be interested in a nightly dose of arts when there are so many other things happening?"' In the end, *Kaleidoscope* eventually went dark in 1998, though not through cultural philistinism, but rather as the result of the same sort of schedule refreshment that had brought it into being a quarter century earlier: James Boyle just decided he wanted a different style of arts programme with a more popular cultural agenda, and *Front Row* was hatched.

Letters, questions and mazes

Today, besides *Front Row* there's a book programme and a film programme, plus *Saturday Review* (another Boyle innovation) offering regular formal arts criticism, music and arts documentary slots and all in all, frankly, very little fear on Radio 4 of cultural underexposure or retrenchment.

What we have lost, however, are the measured tones and even more measured views of Alistair Cooke on a Friday evening, offering the wisdom of the long perspective on the world. *A Point of View*, which replaced Cooke's eternal *Letter from America* when he died in 2004, is often good. However, Cooke was a peerless broadcaster and a courteous man – even, from atop his lofty pedigree when I invited him to appear on *Word of Mouth*, genuinely delighted to be voted by listeners the finest user of spoken English.

I mentioned earlier his extraordinary piece of reportage of the bomber crash on the Empire State Building, and few who have heard it will forget his 1968 eyewitness account of the assassination of Robert Kennedy at the Ambassador Hotel, Los Angeles. On June the 5th that year Cooke reported for *Ten O'Clock* (precursor to Whitby's *World Tonight*) how he had stood in an anteroom at the hotel and heard shots from the ballroom where Kennedy was giving his victory speech in the California Primary elections, and then watched police bundling the assassin, Sirhan Sirhan away. In a year that had two months earlier seen Martin Luther King cut down in his prime, should Americans, asked Cooke in his *Letter from America* the following Friday, accept mass guilt for the series of assassinations?

If as a journalist he stood so often at the shoulder of history, Cooke also had the technical ability of a master of radio storytelling to be able to deploy brilliantly the elements of his reportage. His classic trick was to start a small story element running and then wind in another parallel, usually bigger idea; these often unlikely bedfellows he would then bring into the same frame, such that each amplified the other in one glorious truth. 'He'd start off with the Franklin stove,' remembers Gillian Reynolds, 'and end up with the state of the dollar; and your eye would follow both of these rockets climbing the air and then they would burst together, and there was that feeling of assurance of being at home in his company.'

A glance back through the *Letter from America* files reveals both the panoptic quality of Cooke's vision of America, and also that magical parable-telling technique at work. So here's the unexpurgated drama of the Watergate crisis played out like a soap opera through the *Letters*, but spiced with wit: as in May 1973, with President Nixon baffling the world with his statements about the break-in at the Democratic HQ, Alistair Cooke indulges in a brief aria about 'the American tendency to use long words unnecessarily, or to disguise mental confusion' – and this was three decades *before* Donald Rumsfeld. Also peppering the grand observations are shards of his own life which he unshowily used to point up, for example, the disunited state of America: once, he says, he loved to go for walks round Washington but – 'quaint idea' – today it's become too dangerous. Cooke somehow managed to make these regular reference points among his own fascinations – a master-surgeon profiled (he was much absorbed with medics), a golfing holiday described – appear not at all self-regarding, but rather, simply, part of his own lens on America, and thus perfectly justified.

Not surprisingly, perhaps, Cooke's biographer was another deeply cultured man of radio, Nick Clarke, whose death in 2006 robbed Radio 4 of a likewise measured, considered voice of experience and wit: two grave losses to the thoughtful analysis of the contemporary world within two and a half short years.

Alongside his regular duties on *The World at One*, which he anchored for fifteen years, Nick Clarke was Jonathan Dimbleby's regular deputy on that absolute cornerstone of Radio 4's Friday evening schedule, *Any Questions?*

As with so many of the network's oldest properties – the 'listed buildings' that Radio 4 HQ sometimes call them – *Any Questions?* has evolved gently. The basic format has hardly changed: 'a spontaneous discussion', as *Radio Times* always used to describe it, by four panellists who are asked questions by a live audience in town halls, churches, schools and colleges across the UK and occasionally abroad. The questions are always posed live and panellists are never warned in advance of the subjects the producer will choose.

Any Questions? (the interrogative is part of the title) started as a Light Programme fixture on Friday nights, with its weekend repeat across on the Home. But as the better-defined networks spawned by *Broadcasting in the Seventies* took shape, its natural home was clearly on Radio 4. The programme had started life as long ago as 1948 in the then West of England Home Service, being nationally networked from 1950; it had nonetheless always retained a whiff of the cowshed about it, not least in the character of one of its long-serving regulars, the Dorsetshire rural writer Ralph Wightman. The first 'Travelling Question-Master' was a former newsreader, Freddy Grisewood, and when Radio 4 started, there were regulars who appeared if not quite week-in week-out, then frequently enough for their social views and political standpoint to become familiar to listeners. Baroness Mary Stocks represented the left, Lord Bob Boothby spoke for the colourful wing of the Tory party, dyspeptic Australian writer and journalist Russell Braddon was the voice of the reactionary while Wightman's agricultural tones offered home-spun wisdom that used to make my hair curl.

Grisewood retired from the programme at the age of seventy-nine just as Radio 4 was getting into its stride and immediately the network and the production team started moves to shift its style and tone: Head of Programmes (South West) told Review Board that he thought it 'desirable to lose the rural image'. The team had made fewer bookings in village halls, choosing town venues instead; 'One broadcast,' he added, 'would be from a Butlin's holiday camp' no less. But who would succeed dear old Freddy? Names were mooted, and by the end of January that year one name was topping the list; he was by today's criteria not the obvious choice, yet, as a replacement who would help shift the programme from the village hall to the heart of urban telly-watching England, disc-jockey David Jacobs was not a bad bet ('that urbane charmer who *never* flaps' *Radio Times* called him). He was also more available now for a weekly gig as his BBC1 pop-review show *Juke Box Jury*, that had been on air since the late fifties, had just played its last (ding) hit and (squawk) miss.

Reading between the lines of the Review Board notes, it's clear people worried that the great and the good might feel a little uncertain in the hands of a man who was also the voice of the Eurovision Song Contest and *Pick of the Pops*. As it turned out, David Jacobs's sheer professionalism swept all before him and he was to anchor the show with suave good humour, even when a near riot broke out with Enoch Powell on the team, for sixteen years. Since then, there have been no more attempts to install ex-disc-jockey chairmen and a brief spell with *Today*-man John Timpson was followed by unquestionably the most dynamic period of the programme's nearly sixty years' existence, under Jonathan Dimbleby.

A sort of *Any Questions?* without the audience is in some ways the stamp of a comparatively recent evening creation (at least alongside Jonathan's show) that has made a firm mark on Radio 4. *The Moral Maze* has the authority of Michael Buerk – ex-correspondent, ex-*Nine O'Clock News* anchor – to give it weight. It's also got a cast of robust if sometimes catty opinion-formers and promoters at hand to poke about in the ethical issues of the day. Another hit from the Michael Green era, it's a programme that, when it first appeared in those pre-James Boyle schedules in 1990, felt fresh and original, with controversialists like Janet Daley, and even notorious diarist MP Alan Clark making headlines, and a cast of sharp-thinking regulars like the *Guardian* columnist Edward Pearce and academic Roger Scruton. The programme's argumentative nature was so refreshing that 'listening to this radio discussion programme has become de rigueur' affirmed an article in 1993. 'Why have expensive dinner parties, with shattered crockery and friendships, when you have *The Moral Maze?*' It was a contrivance, naturally, and flourished in its predictable dog-fights between right and left, liberals and conservatives.

Sadly, like so many shows that stay firmly rooted in their original format and don't jump on the evolutionary escalator, *Moral Maze* has become somewhat lost in the schedule. It started as a nine o'clocker and has now symbolically drifted away to the mid- and late evening. Nearly two decades after it first fizzed into the Radio 4 schedule, critic Gillian Reynolds is fed up with it: 'It's got about as much to do with morality as a chocolate teapot! I simply can't stand it! And a maze it isn't. Because everybody knows the way in and the way out and I find that kind of phoney controversialism . . . I really can't be doing with it.'

And so to bed

The World Tonight was for many years the last word on current events on Radio 4. There would be a late summary just before closedown, but Douglas Stuart's gentle and reflective late-night way with news was the final offering on the world agenda for the day. It was the last main piece in the current affairs pattern that Tony Whitby created and, as Review Board noted in May 1970 shortly after it began, 'It was intended to be leisurely and to deal with the news of the day in greater depth than was possible elsewhere.' Some, though, thought Stuart too laid back even for those listeners themselves about to take up a horizontal posture. With the advent of *Newsnight* on BBC2 ten years later, the unique place of the radio late-evening current affairs round-up was somewhat eclipsed, though today, under presenter Robin Lustig, its expansive coverage allows for more depth and scrutiny, with a very strong record in overseas stories, notably a clutch of recent prize-winning reports on China.

Current affairs aside, as late-evening slips deeper into night, Radio 4's preoccupations reflect, not surprisingly, the gradual rounding up of thoughts, drawing lines under events and a gentle move towards closedown. Controller Mark Damazer says he'd love to turn the network into a 24-hour vehicle if the money were available, but for now the tide of programming, like the audience, is slipping away fast. Time for bed and a little literature before we put out the light.

Readings are something that work so well on radio. Television needs to *do* something with the visuals all the time, but radio, the medium of intimacy, can work wonders with the slimmest of resources: powerful words and the right voice. 'The thing that really decided me to go back to Radio 4 after I'd been in television for a long time [was] Cyril Cusack reading *Madame Bovary* absolutely beautifully.' Monica Sims was in many ways loath to make the journey back from children's TV when invited to become controller of Radio 4, but that one performance decided her: 'I thought, "If Radio 4 can do readings like that, it's really worth doing." ' It was a work of art, I thought, as some readings can be, and that's what made me go, [and] think well I *will* try it. So I tried it and then I stayed!'

Unsurprisingly, the simplicity (and relative cheapness) of broadcasting that involves merely one adapter, one reader, one producer and one assistant to prepare the scripts and help with a bit of copyright clearance is always going to appeal, especially when the effect on the listener can be so powerful. From the very beginning, speech radio has found plenty of space for fiction and non-fiction readings, classic and contemporary. Today, of course, there's Oneword, a commercial channel (these days part of Channel 4 Radio) that features a good many books amongst wider speech programming, but it's the Radio 4 favourites over many, many decades that have built up a huge audience for books on the wireless. *Morning Story* (originally a Light Programme fixture), *Story Time*, the *Woman's Hour* story, *Book at Bedtime* and *The Late Book* are just some of the favourites that have come and gone down the years. *Story Time* disappeared under David Hatch ('I thought there were enough stories already'), and an afternoon reading at 3.30 pm arrived with James Boyle's new schedule in 1998.

'*Book at Bedtime* has been all over the schedule,' observes former Radio 4 publicity chief Marion Greenwood. Too true. When it started in 1949, the bedtime listen was at 11.00 pm (and on the Light Programme); it then oscillated as late as 11.45 at one stage, and then back to eleven under Tony Whitby. By 1973 it had slipped forward to 10.15 then, when complaints arrived that it was too early, the book was on its travels again, ending up at 10.45. This movable feast slid back to its original 11.00 berth in 1983, but by Michael Green's time it had slipped forward again to 10.15. 'And I'd not been in the chair for very long,' recalls Green, the great evolver of the Radio 4 schedule, 'when I said, "Well, we're in the late 80s now. [That] strikes me as being a little on the early side!"' So the books were moved along the Radio 4 schedule shelf once again to a quarter to eleven where they could, as Green also wanted, be a bit more daring: 'The later we go the slightly broader the range of books we might be able to read.'

'A Bonk at Bedtime' was the *Sun*'s response to the programme's first outing in its latest slot – to kick off the new autumn schedule for 1989, Green had dared to broadcast D.H. Lawrence's sexually explicit novel *Lady Chatterley's Lover*. It was a signal, says Green: 'You could say that those who'd had their cocoa and got upset by the more risqué stuff could turn off now. You're allowed to switch off now!' *Ulysses* by James Joyce joined *Lady Chatterley* between the bedtime covers and the controller confesses he wasn't too upset by the jokey headlines: 'I mean good for a laugh, but also people say[ing] actually, this network, it's not quite the maiden aunt we thought it was.'

Raunchy books, spooky playlets (do you remember *Just Before Midnight*?) and, these days, late-night risqué comedy have populated the closing hours of Radio 4's schedule, particularly since James Boyle's revamp ten years ago. With audiences a fraction of the morning peak available to listen, the network can afford to be more daring, commissioning projects like the experimental summer audio anthologies *White Nights* that I produced in 2006; or the interactive drama *The Dark House*, in which the scenario was in part determined by listeners; or the biggest comedy hit Radio 4 has had in a few years, the Paul Whitehouse spoof phone-in *Down the Line*, which proved once more the network's amazing ability to make a huge splash as national newspapers devoted a host of headlines and special articles to its inventive genius. It's clear that, even at dead of night, there's little danger of Radio 4 hiding away under some broadcasting boulder as in many ways it did in 1967.

All this, and I haven't even mentioned the *Shipping Forecast* and 'Sailing By' – but before we get to them, we've got to head deep into the maze of the Radio 4 weekend . . .

CHAPTER ELEVEN
Something for the weekend

Weekends are funny times for broadcasters. They're the traditional, biggest moment for running landmark programming and, paradoxically, for many people precisely the time for *not* staying around to watch the telly or listen to the radio at all. Also being the moment when for most people work comes to a juddering halt, the normal scheduling rules don't apply, or apply rather differently. How for instance do you capture a listening audience that wants to be out looking for MDF furniture down at the superstore, when you'd actually prefer them to be lingering over another cup of freshly filtered coffee, *Excess Baggage* and the Saturday morning documentary?

Then again, how do you get people to stay indoors on a sunny spring Sunday to bend an ear to *Gardeners' Question Time* when the grass will have grown an extra millimetre by the time they've finished? So weekends do feel different on Radio 4; today they're a mix of specialised leisure programming in keeping with the supposedly more relaxed pace of weekend life, but also a useful repository for all those repeats and fag-ends of programmes that need stowing somewhere.

The way we spend our weekends has changed pretty radically over the four decades; the passing in 1994 of legislation to permit shops to open on Sundays meant that for many Britons, the Lord's day would henceforth mean jumping into the car to join the long queues heading for warehouse malls and out-of-town sofa centres, DIY stores and fashion emporia. Radio 4 has had to acknowledge the fact. Reflect, too, just how relatively simple Saturdays and Sundays could be forty years ago: family visits perhaps, a drive in the country possibly, lots of gardening and, yes, plenty of DIY even then; but no internet surfing, no mobile phoning, no comedy clubbing; discos, certainly, but not really many dance clubs; a trip to the flicks on a Saturday night of course, though fewer people were going to the pictures at the back end of the 1960s than ever.

Television was rampant, with audiences of over twenty million for the great sit-coms of the era: those people sitting on sofas with eyes glued to the screen weren't out on the town. Nor were they listening to Radio 4 for that matter.

And was it any wonder: while TV was offering the chills of *Dr Who*'s second encounter with the Cybermen, summer 1967's *Saturday Night Theatre* on the wireless raised the curtain on such walnut-veneered classics as J.B. Priestley's *Eden End* or a three-part adaptation of R.F. Delderfield's novel of Derbyshire farming life, *A Horseman Riding By*. Frankly, it wasn't a difficult choice for most people. Indeed, listeners might even have been tempted away from their radios altogether by the attractions of a touring exhibition called 'Colour Television Comes to Town' ('the most ambitious meet-the-people exercise ever attempted by the BBC . . .') that criss-crossed the country from Croydon in London to Birmingham, Leeds, Manchester, Newcastle and Glasgow.

Much of the rest of Saturday's Home Service offering wasn't that exciting either: a warren of news briefings, religious homilies, press round-ups, farming, *From Our Own Correspondent*, *Yesterday in Parliament*, *The Week in Westminster* (still today, oddly enough, a Saturday morning fixture), some gardening and of course a regulation dollop of Christianity in the form of *The Daily Service*; not to mention a hefty segment of teach yourself Chinese, Spanish or German. It wasn't, to be honest, a very alluring mix. Only as the Saturday lunch was beginning to sizzle did dad come in from the garage to check up on the latest car news in *Motoring and the Motorist* with Bill Hartley in the Jeremy Clarkson role.

Also featuring on the lunch menu were the first glimmers of box-office appeal, with a dose of entertainment – of sorts – following the one o'clock news: in summer 1967 it was the agonising comedy version of *Any Questions?* called *Does the Team Think?* in which 'Professor' Jimmy Edwards teamed up with other ageing comics to answer embarrassing audience questions put to them by McDonald Hobley. *Desert Island Discs* – still a weekend favourite – came next (a young Roy Hudd was the castaway on July the 8th), and then (unthinkable for the modern Radio 4), it being the end of Wimbledon fortnight, the rest of the afternoon on this particular Saturday was entirely taken up with tennis; commentators Max Robertson and Maurice Edelston watched John Newcombe and Billie Jean King run out the winners. (There again, all the *real* tennis excitement that summer was actually over on BBC2 who were screening the championships in colour for the first time.)

By the time the *Broadcasting in the Seventies* reforms take effect, Saturday is beginning to look a lot fresher and tidier. *Today* dominates the early schedule followed by a much more coherent mix of information programmes, though the daunting slab of further education still sits fairly and squarely across the mid-morning (but now given a modern-sounding identity, *Study on 4*). Later on, there's also a fresher, more urban feel to *Any Questions?* at lunchtime; Hackney is the venue and the team is markedly less rustic.

On the other hand, the Saturday evening pattern of music-plus-drama would stay much the same for decades, as in July 1971 Tony Whitby announced 'from 7.30 to 8.30 a programme of popular serious music records [with] the title "These You Have Loved".' *Start the Week*er Richard Baker was the host and for years to come this compilation of evergreen classical favourites remained a mellow fixture of the schedule. *These You Have Loathed*, as we all knew it, proved an extraordinarily resilient plant as the encroaching speech concreted over more and more of the output, with its replacement *Baker's Dozen* essentially the same show with a new name; when Richard eventually departed, Brian Kay's *Music In Mind* filled a similar role.

Songs, seagulls and celebrity

One of Radio 4's programmes which is defined by its music, though rarely contains more than about fifteen minutes of it in

Saturday-night savvy

His *Radio Times* photograph shows a young man with a hint of a smile playing about his lips, the strangely high angle emphasising the receding hair-line, the dome of his forehead, and masking those gleaming eyes. This picture, published around the time of Radio 4's birth, offers little hint of the flamboyance of the man who was Brian Redhead – no beard, no playful irony about the expression, not a trace of the man's exuberance. Yet all these characteristics were clearly evident to listeners who in 1967 had already made a firm favourite of Redhead's weekend spot in the old Home Service schedule, after the ten o'clock evening news on Saturdays. The programme was *A Word in Edgeways*.

Edgeways was a discussion programme, a format beloved of speech radio mandarins because it's cheap and relatively simple: a trio of guests, plus a presenter, locked up in a studio for forty-five minutes, chatting away on a prescribed theme. Overheads are minimal – just a few train fares and taxis – and Bob's your broadcasting uncle. True enough – except, not really. You only have to cast an ear to the many *un*successful and leaden-footed discussions that have also limped their way through the Radio 4 schedules over the years to realise that. This one, however, was rather special, and those who remember it do so with almost universal affection.

Tony Whitby inherited *Edgeways* from his predecessor and now his Director of Programmes, Gerard Mansell, and so it's perhaps unsurprising that he didn't feel quite the same way about his adoptive child as those he'd himself sired. It wasn't, he confessed to

total, is the domain these days of Kirsty Young, but was first inhabited by Roy Plomley who, in 1942, invented one of radio's longest-running and elemental formats. *Desert Island Discs* represents much of what Radio 4 is all about: a deceptively simple formula for eliciting information, stories and surprising biographical detail about someone the audience is fascinated by. It's always been a highspot of the schedule, and has long

Review Board, 'among his favourites', citing Brian Redhead's 'note of self-satisfaction' (see Chapter Two). Yet Whitby knew when he had a hit on his hands and averred that Redhead was 'a very good broadcaster and the strength of the programme'. The weekly conversations were discursive, combative and pretty intellectual. A cast of mostly men in those less equal times (though women took over one edition in June 1971) discussed, according to *Radio Times*, 'topical matters – and some less topical'.

Typical subjects included 'patriotism', 'the business community and the Church', 'whether contemporary arts are only for the few', 'immigrant housing and integration', 'whether sport has become a national obsession' and 'the aims and advantages of a university education'. Led by Redhead, it was a little like a piece of chamber music, played every Saturday night by a group of expert minds. In many ways, the contemporary parallel is with Melvyn Bragg's *In Our Time* – it was, broadly speaking, a programme of ideas: 'It was like entering yourself for a marathon,' remembers occasional contributor Gillian Reynolds. 'You had to have the stamina physically, because it exhausted you to do it.'

Edgeways was resolutely a Manchester programme and Brian, a proud man of the north. Not surprising then that often the guests also had northern accents, but all were, in the words of Michael Green who produced the show, 'such polymaths that they could cope with almost anything you put to them'. There were regular performers such as architectural specialist Dr Patrick Nuttgens of York University and the Dean of Liverpool, Dr Edward Patey, and those who just appeared a handful of times like Reynolds:

☞

occupied a weekend slot – and though these days it also appears on a Friday morning, it *feels* to me like an essential part of the weekend selection box.

Stars, really big Hollywood and West End stars, have always been one of the show's big draws, but it's the format that makes the whole thing tick, the rigorous adherence by each of its presenters (there have only ever been four) to a handful of

Brian would think out an idea in stages or structure an idea so that he could hop from one bit to another, and bring things in; and you had to be *very* astute to follow where he was going. You had to concentrate really, really hard. I remember doing one about travel with Ray Gosling and Laurens van der Post – I mean call that unusual casting! But when you finished it, boy! was your head spinning!

As producer, Michael Green had to feed Redhead's capacious intelligence.

He was masterly. I used to just provide him with raw material, but the moment he spotted a hare running somewhere he would go after it and my raw material was sort of dumped on the table. And that was the magic of it. You never quite knew where you were going to end up.

Jenny Abramsky, now radio's boss, listened to the programme when she was a student and loved it: 'When you're at university you play with words . . . and how you can use them in different ways as you try and impress your lecturer; and suddenly you'd listen to Brian Redhead and it was just wonderful! I came from a family where people talked around a dinner table; Brian made you feel you were part of that dinner table: a terrific programme!'

'An unrehearsed intellectual adventure' was Brian's apt description of his approach to *Edgeways*, recalls Green.

simple questions: Which eight pieces of music and why? Which of those pieces in particular? And finally, what book and above all what luxury would you take with you to the island? These disingenuous queries offer an almost perfect springboard for revelation and anecdote; each edition bookended, without exception, by Eric Coates's composition 'By the Sleepy Lagoon' (with regulation seagulls) that has always introduced the programme.

The first 'castaway' (which, in the sense of 'guest', has entered the language thanks to *DID*) was the émigré Austrian entertainer Vic Oliver. Roy's style with his guests was gentlemanly

I remember we did one programme about 'politeness'; can you imagine! But it was the most extraordinary conversation about politeness as a form of lying – it went down tracks, unimaginable tracks, for forty-five minutes, and I remember sitting back and thinking this programme had come out of nowhere almost.

Review Board continued to carp about Redhead's style: 'he tended to talk too much', his 'enthusiasm seemed manufactured', and despite the fact that *A Word in Edgeways* was quintessentially *his* programme, doubts were even expressed, by Tony Whitby no less, over whether it wouldn't fare better under a different chairman. Yet, as he pointed out in another Review Board session, '*A Word in Edgeways* [has] a distinct style of its own, quite unlike any other part of Radio's speech output.' It was this, he felt, that made it a valuable property; 'probably irreplaceable', agreed Gerry Mansell.

Eventually, though not until it was well past its twenty-first birthday, this Saturday night ritual was replaced, and, not many years later, in 1994, its irrepressible host himself died. However, the spirit of *Edgeways* lives on to this day – in Andrew Marr's *Start the Week* and, perhaps most clearly, in *In Our Time* – enquiring, curious and with a distinct capacity for erudition, but also for wit.

In one sense, it's a definition of Radio 4 itself.

and discreet (they always met for lunch ahead of the recording), but he was rigorously firm when applying the rules. While his unchallenging approach ('his complete inability to conduct an interview', as one commentator described it) never much appealed to me, I loved the way Roy was so hot on the luxuries: no inanimate objects – 'I can't take my little puppy?' 'No!' Grand pianos, another favourite request (you could shelter underneath) were likewise disallowed: 'It has to be an upright', would come Roy's reply.

Desert Island Discs has never aspired to inquisitorial probing (though Sue Lawley once had a much-discussed go at Gordon

Brown's sexuality), but it can elicit some powerful confessional material: John Peel, for example, admitted that he missed his father more some time afterwards than when he had died 'because there are more things now which have happened I'd have liked him to have known about – doing this programme being one of them'.

Plomley himself died suddenly in May 1985 after forty-three years as gatekeeper of the island's guest-list. According to *The Times* 'finding a replacement has been a bit like naming a new Pope'. It was a race with many runners and riders – Peter Ustinov, Richard Baker (again!), John Mortimer, Johnny Morris, Robert Robinson, Steve Race, John Timpson, Nigel Rees, even Simon Bates were mooted – but on January the 5th 1986, it was Michael Parkinson whose Yorkshire tones greeted listeners as the Sleepy Lagoon faded away behind him; his first guest, film director Alan Parker. 'I hope I will be able to do it as well and as long as [Roy] did,' said Parky, ahead of his first programme. He immediately set about changing things: out went the polite lunches, out went the bland interviewing style. As one journalist observed, 'Now things are clearly going to be a little grittier.' Not for long, however: after two years, he was off.

'I actually thought that Parkinson did it very, very well,' said David Hatch, who was the controller in charge of selecting him. 'It needed a change of direction from the comfortableness of dear Roy.' However, there were tensions: Plomley's widow, Diana, was reportedly uneasy with the show's sharper new style and David Hatch revealed there was friction in the production office. 'But if you follow somebody like Roy Plomley you're gonna get beaten up. It takes a couple of turns before the next person's all right. It's the one after, you know, who survives.' And so it proved, with Sue Lawley, erstwhile host of television news and *Nationwide* and a relative stranger to radio, turning into what would be hailed as the perfect presenter.

Marion Greenwood, then Radio 4 publicity chief, was in charge of making sure that all went according to plan on recording day. Some celebrities, she recalls, were very protective of their privacy, like the Hollywood legend who arrived 'in this black coat with a big collar, dark glasses and her hat pulled on' and insisted on drawing the curtain across in front of the studio glass before she took it all off. She didn't want anyone in the production team to see that she'd not bothered with make-up. However, the most memorable encounters, Greenwood says, were those that defied the screen-god image, as when Australian star Nicole Kidman was cast away ('who came all by herself – no entourage – looked absolutely fantastic, tall, willowy, completely awesome skin'), and then, on the way out of the studio, was involved in one of those bizarre meetings that usually only happen in fictional 'What if?' articles:

> There was David Attenborough coming down the corridor to record the Christmas edition: Nicole Kidman and David Attenborough meeting in the corridor and each of them overwhelmed by meeting the other one, with David Attenborough going 'Heh! heh!' and with Nicole Kidman going 'It's David Attenborough!' – just wonderful!

Two other programmes from the very earliest days of Radio 4 still make it alongside *DID* into the modern Saturday morning – though in slightly different places. *From Our Own Correspondent* and *The Week in Westminster* are classic formulas, with the content constantly evolving rather than the actual shape or purpose of the programmes, though the replacement of a staff announcer by the colourful Kate Adie on *FOOC* and the arrival of parliamentary broadcasting have both made the shows actually *sound* very different from their equivalents from 1967. It would, however, take another seven years for someone to think of running a financial-advice programme on a Saturday lunchtime. Now *Money Box* is itself a veteran of thirty years, having started in 1977, together with its famous signature by Instant Sunshine ('Don't let money stew; with profit in view / What you must do, is tune to . . . *Money Box*') and presenter Louise Botting.

Finally, in this catalogue of the old but gold, after lunch along troops another survivor of 40+ years, a regular 'catch-up' programme that sits, substantially unaltered for generations like a rather unlovely yet utilitarian piece of municipal architecture, slap bang in the middle of the afternoon. It's been around since the 1960s when it was called *Home This Afternoon* but changed its title under Tony Whitby to the prosaic but more precise *Weekend Woman's Hour* – he well knew the value of a strong brand like *Woman's Hour* and wasn't going to waste the opportunity to capitalise on it.

Peel appeal

Whitby's successor but six, James Boyle, built some new structures in front of the 6.00 pm news – in our information-rich world, *Saturday PM* seems now a no-brainer – and it was also he who radically altered Saturday evenings with the invention of *Saturday Review* and *The Archive Hour*.

His biggest innovative success though came in the morning. Standing in the way of change, however, were a trio of gnarled old Radio 4 oak trees. Thus in 1998 Boyle took an axe first to *News-stand*, the review of the weekly press, and then sharpened his blade to get rid of the long-established bargain-break consumer travel shows like *Going Places* or *Breakaway*. (The sound of cheeky chappie Bernard Falk and his annoyingly memorable sig tune – 'We'll do the Breakaway, get hot and shake away' – is one Radio 4 memory I'm personally not particularly keen to dwell on.) Nor did listeners now want a very metropolitan, sophisticated Shaftesbury-Avenue-stage-door-gossipy chat-show on a breezy Saturday morning when they were off to the superstore or the golf club: so *Loose Ends* would move to cocktail hour where it more comfortably belonged.

More to the point, Boyle also had the ideal property waiting in the wings, fully developed, piloted and ready to run, with even a Sony Gold Award to its name. It was called *Offspring* and was a programme for and about families. Michael Green who'd commissioned it, sees what it became – *Home Truths* with John Peel – as a perfect example of Radio 4's 'capacity to re-invent itself on the one hand, while being quite rooted in the past'.

At the time, John Peel, with his record of original and unconventional music broadcasting, was an offbeat choice for presenter of a programme on family life ('an unlikely booking,' says Green). Yet Peel was a devoted family man, and his former Radio 1 audience, for whom thirty years before he'd been a heroic rebel, now found him maturing, as they themselves became middle-aged, into a clever, affectionate, laid-back, funny commentator on his own and their home lives. Yet, as Michael Green recalls, 'When I was asked whether I would commission *Offspring* in a short series, I was full of doubt. You know, was John from Radio 1 the right guy for this? Well, let's give it a whirl. And six weeks later we realised it *was* the right thing.'

Home Truths became a monster hit for Radio 4, winning four Sony awards in 1999, gave the network a huge nearly two-million listener boost at the top of the weekend, and offered Peel a whole new broadcasting idiom to tap into. Andy Kershaw, friend and associate of John's, admitted the show was 'cloying, sentimental and indulgent', but it was familiar and familial, and it struck a big chord: items on car boot sales rubbed shoulders with terminal illness, a women's barbershop choir with the septuagenarian father of triplets and other extraordinary personal tales of disaster and heroism. All human life is there, used to proclaim the *News of the World*, and *Home Truths*, with its jaunty sig tune (one of the few on Radio 4 in the modern era) did much to espouse the same spirit.

When out of an autumn day death came to Peel in October 2004 at the age of sixty-five, the programme was doomed. 'Relentlessly professional, his trademark was a slightly weary but amused, deadpan style,' wrote the *Daily Telegraph* in its obituary of Peel. Certainly his tone and approach was a great part of his success on the show, and David Stafford, Michael Rosen and Tom Robinson who took over from him on a rota basis, all of them top-notch presenters in their own field, couldn't quite match the appeal of Peel. For once it's not too great a cliché to say that John Peel *was Home Truths* and when he died, the end was almost inevitable.

Sunday observance

Radio 4 from its inception has, as I've noted already, had an inordinate sense of the Church of England about it. Not for nothing was Lord Reith a devout Christian, and the Sunday schedule that the new network inherited from the Home Service was run through, like Blackpool-rock lettering, with a broad strand of Christian devotion. Growing ecumenism across the decades has led to *Thought for the Day* developing a distinctly diverse roster of spiritual opinions to animate *Today*, and many of the other religious interludes that peppered the early schedule have quietly disappeared, though *Bells on Sunday* (admittedly truncated) is still a treasured Radio 4 oddity. (Who in their right mind would actually even think of transmitting a sequence of change-ringing each week, other than this very special network?) But throughout, *The Sunday Service* has remained a bulwark of Christian worship. What James Boyle did in 1998 was to get the faithful on their knees early.

Boyle is a great pragmatist and realised that most Radio 4 listeners were no longer practising Christians; broadcasting a religious office at just the moment they were dawdling over the Sunday papers was thus not a clever move. So the service had to shift, earlier. It was radical, it wasn't popular with the traditionalist wing of the audience, but it was right. And the invention of *Broadcasting House*, a clever mix of news, comment and, above all, irony and wit, with Eddie Mair hosting, was inspired.

A garden is a lovesome thing

Sunday mornings have traditionally been dominated by doings in Ambridge. The omnibus *Archers* repeat has been the centrepiece and biggest draw, from the earliest days when it went out at 9.30 am ahead of the service, to today's placing (reflecting perhaps a more snoozy setting of the alarm) of ten o'clock. Another big Sunday shift by Boyle was the banishing of *Pick of the Week* from its juicy morning showcase to the early evening (see Chapter Three), but if Margaret Howard's voice was long associated with Radio 4's Sunday, for an earlier generation of listeners Sunday meant the walnut tones of Franklin Engelmann. Given that Engelmann died only five years after the birth of Radio 4, and was in truth more a Home Service survivor, he managed to lay his hand on three of the new network's most celebrated and long-lived properties.

Franklin was the voice of *Brain of Britain*, (entitled when he and it started, *What Do You Know?*), of *Down Your Way* (finally axed in 1992) and of *Gardeners' Question Time*, the latter two being core Sunday programming from the first days of Radio 4. It's hard today to imagine one single personality being able – or indeed permitted – to anchor *three* big shows simultaneously on the network, two of them on the same day.

Franklin Engelmann had the posh voice and clipped vowels (and equally well-tended moustache) typical of BBC announcers of the 1950s and 60s ('a brown voice' Gillian Reynolds calls it, 'not a totally dark chocolate voice – it's got raisins in it!'): starchy, but not unbending – just rather bland. Ideal, in fact for bland programmes such as *Down Your Way* that offered tourist-board quaintness when the team fetched up in yet another market town to talk to the mayor, the oldest inhabitant and a representative of some bizarre and antique craft. I have to admit that its freewheeling signature tune ('London Landmarks: the Horseguards, Whitehall' by Haydn Wood) became for me one of those instant signals to reach for the off-button, even when in 1972 Brian Johnston took over the travelling and light interviewing duties.

On *Gardeners' Question Time* Engelmann would occasionally allow a warmer side to show, creakily cracking a smile when quizzing some unfortunate questioner about a pernicious pyracantha or a clematis that was reluctant to bloom – and of course his formality made a fine contrast with the trio of wise experts who turned up for Radio 4's first Sunday schedule on October the 1st 1967: 'Fred Loads of Lancaster, Bill Sowerbutts of Ashton-under-Lyne and Professor Alan Gemmell of Keele University'. Those voices! How many regular broadcasters did

A little bit of a pirate

Gerald Priestland was, until his death in 1991, one of Radio 4's latterday stars. Not a star, you understand, in the conventional sense: Gerald eschewed the cheap and glitzy in favour of the literate and the literary – but he enjoyed the limelight and didn't shrink from it.

In his later years, when he became BBC Religious Affairs Correspondent, he was a weekend favourite on Radio 4, presenting a weekly Saturday morning 'letter' called *Yours Faithfully*. Yet again, as I've shown throughout this book, it was the medium's intimacy that connected so personally the speaker to his audience, because Priestland articulated thoughts that pass through all our minds in a way that had meaning, good sense and – yes – sentiment. His wife described him as 'a very emotional person' and he had a strong romantic streak, calling himself once a 'soft-boiled' journalist. When he was Roy Plomley's Desert Island castaway, amongst other pieces, he chose the sublime and sensuous Bach cantata 170, *Vernügte ruh* ('Contented rest, beloved inner joy') which, he said, meant for him 'all shall be well, and all manner of things shall be well'.

Priestland was a commentator who'd sprung from a career as a newsman; who put in many years as a correspondent in Delhi and above all Washington, but who, like Alistair Cooke and, in another era, Fergal Keane, felt that simply reporting bald facts was not enough. '*Real* reporting, real corresponding,' he once told an interviewer, 'is always the passing on of personal experience personal understanding at first hand. And you have to convey this in such a way that it stimulates the listener.'

Gerald Priestland was a big man – physically mountainous at 6' 7", and with a big personality to match: sheer news reporting would

Radio 4 boast in the 1960s and 70s with accents as broad as these three? The avuncular Fred, the estate head gardener, wise-cracking Bill, the professional grower, and the breezy Scottish academic, Alan – for thirty years together they were often more of a comedy act than garden advisers.

Indeed, this knockabout quality that the audience loved

never contain him. Television called, and Priestland was commissioned to offer a short commentary tailpiece to the *Nine O'Clock News*, though it wasn't a great success. Then, when BBC2 started, it was again the unfortunate Gerald who found himself desperately answering the incessant phone calls from the TV studio gallery amid a complete power blackout in west London that killed the whole first evening's transmission – except the embarrassed output of his news-desk.

In Tony Whitby's current affairs plan of 1970, Priestland was chosen as anchor of Radio 4's new 7.00 pm show, *Newsdesk*. His experience and flair for observation and individuality were what endeared him to the controller, and were in marked contrast to the more traditionally detached style of Douglas Stuart on *The World Tonight*. Stuart has made no secret of his personal dislike of Priestland's approach (he called him 'a pompous pontificator') which was undoubtedly opinionated and could at times be pompous. It wasn't helped by the tone that Gerald gradually adopted, his voice increasingly taking on as he aged the rolling orotund echo of the pulpit.

Friends and colleagues found Priestland difficult and 'a total maverick', a powerful personality – 'not a very mellow person, really', Gerald's close friend and successor in the Religious post Rosemary Hartill called him. Another friend described him in his determination to go his own way as 'a little bit of a pirate'.

But for all his swagger, his self-confidence, the inner Priestland was beset with doubt, and suffered agonies of depression: 'Nobody who hasn't been in there,' he said, 'can really understand the lonely unreachable hell of it.' When, with the aid of sustained medical help and a newfound (Quaker) faith, he recovered, Gerald went on to

☞

didn't go down well at Review Board. In March 1971 *GQT* came in for a drubbing: the cast never varied and often dispensed inaccurate information, they moaned. Snootily, the head of Documentaries and Talks observed that 'when their inadequacies became apparent even to themselves they fell back on music-hall jokes'. But this was just a passing squall in the

306 AND NOW ON RADIO 4

become Religious Correspondent in 1977. *Yours Faithfully* followed, with an amazing regular postbag, especially when he wrote with deep understanding of the depression which led to the suicide of his former *Newsdesk* colleague, Jackie Gillott.

Six hundred letters arrived in response to that one short talk alone, and when he set out on the huge religious documentary series *Priestland's Progress*, he moved for a while near the top of the Radio pantheon, coming second in Radio 4's annual man of the year competition (beaten by the Prince of Wales). Few who heard it will forget the rather lovely theme music that heralded his *Progress*, a whistled tune inspired by 'He Who Would Valiant Be'. Priestland himself composed it, cleverly threading the tune of Bunyan's hymn through his own melody: it spoke for the man – a personal whistle, one man's journey of discovery, a pilgrim's progress through faith. He even had the right surname.

Gerald had lived hard as a journalist, consuming his favourite Bushmills whisky in large quantities, and paid the price with his health, suffering a stroke which almost, but not quite, robbed him of the power to broadcast. An agonisingly moving last talk, his speech slurring a little from the disability, deeply touched listeners with its sheer honesty about pain and Priestland's serene acceptance of what was shortly to come to him: 'I have had the feeling,' he said, 'of being crushed under a rock till I could see only one crack of light – and that was the love of God: the absolute certainty, when everything else had been taken from me, that God loved me.'

GQT garden which continued to flourish. Clay Jones and then Dr Stefan Buczacki took the chair in succession to Franklin Engelmann, and the simple winning formula, with minor modifications, carries on to this day, with Eric Robson in the hot seat. Although the programme has not been without its own attacks of severe wilt, as when the whole team resigned and signed up to Classic FM in 1994 in protest about production changes, *GQT* has been on the air in one form or another since 1947 and is yet another of Radio 4's listed buildings, with a big summer party in 2007 to mark its sixtieth birthday.

James Boyle didn't move *GQT*, which has been at 2.00 pm since time immemorial, but he did much to neaten up the rather undisciplined shape of Sunday. He created the 'literature hour' in the afternoon and invented a *Westminster Hour* politics show after the 10.00 pm news. Additionally, in a flash of realisation, James decided – a small, yet audience-pulling detail – on a little splurge of cash at the top of the evening to buy another box of soap powder: 'God, I hadn't remembered that Sunday night is just a paste-together of repeats – let's make it more exciting! Let's have another episode of *The Archers*!'

Another long-running Sunday favourite that seasonally occupies half of the 'literature hour' and 'which does more to move the spirit on Sunday evenings than any God-slot', as Sue Arnold put it in the *Observer*, is the poetry request programme, *Poetry Please*. It has many fans, not least Gillian Reynolds: 'I remember one a few years ago that was the most wonderful exegesis of a Louis MacNeice poem, and every image in it was so clear to me. I did not want to listen to anything else for a good ten minutes after I'd heard that.' The idea for *Poetry Please* is claimed by Monica Sims, who told me she was on a train journey with her deputy, Richard Wade, when it suddenly occurred to her that while Radio 4 covered most areas of life, there was no dedicated space for poetry: '"Radio's full of request programmes; we've never had people requesting poems." He said, "We can try it, see how it works" – and *Poetry Please* is still part of the output and I'm glad it's still there.'

Another anthological programme that's 'still there', and was originally created to offer a bit of glamour at the end of Sunday evening, takes us neatly once more, as we approach the closing passages of this book, to the very beginning of the Radio 4 story. It's a programme that has much in common with *Poetry Please*, being produced in Bristol and featuring a fair slug of verse of one sort and another. *With Great Pleasure*, like so many of Radio 4's most resilient shows, features the simplest of simple formats: a celebrity introduces a personal anthology of readings and extracts, given before an adoring audience.

Cleverly, too, it's timeless, because to refresh it all the producer needs to do is bring in, say, the odd star of the comedy circuit like Shazia Mirza or Pauline McLynn or Jo Brand (all of whom have guested in recent series) and the choice of extracts and the byplay with the audience will do the rest.

Back in 1969, Tony Whitby, visionary as ever, had been pondering his empty slots. 'I urgently need offers,' he wrote to all his production heads ten days before Christmas 1969, in the vain hope they'd come up with something before the party hats went on. Top of his list of 'major available Radio 4 evening spaces' was Sunday at 10.10 pm, a 'Personal Anthology Audience Show' – 'In which a well known public figure introduces a selection of prose and poetry (and perhaps archive speech) which has meant something to him (or her), linking it with personal narrative and reminiscence.'

Thus was born, fully formed in the controller's mind, the as yet unnamed *With Great Pleasure.*

> There could be one or perhaps two readers. A wide variety of anthologists of greatly varying tastes is essential . . . A sense of occasion must be created.

Whitby's suggested sample guest-list for a first series is a mix of politicians like Horace King (Speaker of the House of Commons), actors such as Eric Porter (heart-throb of TV's *Forsyte Saga,* still fresh in viewers' minds), Enid Bagnold the novelist (apparently a strange choice until you realise that she'd just published her autobiography) and one 'soldier': Montgomery. No comedians, though, back in 1969.

There was one small difference from today's programme, however, that's perhaps instructive. The total cost (including fees for the celebrity and the actors) was: '£175 (approx)'.

CHAPTER TWELVE

12.00 midnight: Night lines

There's a pause; a distant rumble of traffic, an engine accelerating briefly above the hum, perhaps a heehawing police car, distantly; and then the clangour of bells striking midnight – one day ebbs; a new day, a new year is rung in. This nightly passage is marked on Radio 4 (unless repair-work is under way in the tower) by 'the bongs', popularly known as 'Big Ben', the most famous chime in the world. These then usually slide away, faded discreetly under the voice of the newsreader, except, that is, for the transition from New Year's Eve to New Year's Day when all twelve strokes are heard (or not, of which more shortly). Indeed, Big Ben's inherent solemnity is only intensified by being associated routinely with death and crisis, as the traditional herald to news bulletins and moments of national mourning on radio and television. Even in these days of computer tickers, breaking news alerts displayed on screens of every type, size and function, of 24-hour availability of updated information, that moment at midnight (and also, earlier, at six) when the onward flow of talk on Radio 4 pauses, when the network breathes in to chime the hour, still has the resonance of history and the gravity of the news it so often heralds.

It's no surprise, therefore, that any unexpected change, break-down or cock-up in that solemn routine also draws the ears and the eyes of the nation. I've mentioned elsewhere Sue MacGregor's celebrated 'crashing' of the pips on her very last *Today*; similarly, the non-appearance, perhaps because of a particularly hard frost, of one of Ben's bongs rarely goes unremarked. 'You want to say, "how can people be interested in it?" but they are!' sighs Marion Greenwood, formerly of the Radio 4 press office. She knew full well what to expect when on one occasion there was a problem with the mechanism and the decision was taken that the midnight chime wouldn't be transmitted. 'I had news crews from around the world wanting to go up St Stephen's tower to record earlier bongs, because we weren't going down at midnight.'

Worse was to follow on New Year's Eve 2002, when the nation (or at least that fraction tuned to Radio 4) stood with glasses of bubbly poised, this listener included, to await the heralding of 2003 from St Stephen's tower – and nothing materialised. Nada. Not the faintest hoot of a klaxon, squeak of a footie-whistle or even the distant hilarity of party-mood Westminster. Dead air; thirty seconds of it; as one paper remarked the next day, an *eternity* in radio. And then a fumbled and embarrassed apology from continuity. It was a minuscule mistake – someone had failed to switch something somewhere – but a very, very public one and the press had a field day, jokily alleging plots and conspiracies and having a good laugh at the BBC in the process.

In broadcasting, mistakes like these happen, there's a degree of fuss, and then in general they're forgotten; but there's a more serious point here because, as I said earlier, it is that ringing in of the hour – and particularly when the full chime and twelve strokes are heard – that has been the accompaniment to big international developments that have occurred on the stroke of midnight (like Britain's accession to the EU in 1973), or to the announcement of wars declared, and remembered in cenotaph ceremonial, or to disasters reported. All are wrapped up in the mythology of Big Ben's chimes.

News is just coming in . . .

And at that moment when a huge story breaks, the burden of finding the right tone, the appropriate degree of formality, falls to the newsreader who has to pick up off the back of the fading bell – to sure-footed professionals like, amongst others, Harriet Cass, Peter Donaldson and Charlotte Green. Charlotte was on duty on the evening of December the 21st 1988, when Radio 4 announced, in a news flash, the crash of Pan Am flight 103 from Heathrow to JFK. That the cause was a terrorist bomb wouldn't emerge for days, but in those first hours even the basic facts were exceedingly sketchy. 'That was my very first news flash,' she recalls, 'and it seemed to be relatively hopeful that people had survived and that only one person had died. Of course the true story emerged throughout the night and that was truly shocking.' It's the newsreader's professional duty at this point to convey neither a false sense of hope nor any note of personal distress, whatever images are playing out in his or her imagination: 'You have to keep that in check; and actually that's almost inhuman in a way because the human response is to be emotionally almost overwhelmed because it was so dreadful. But you have to keep all that tied up.'

On that pre-Christmas Wednesday evening, BBC parties were still in full swing round Broadcasting House, but in the news studio Charlotte had to communicate the information as it trickled in:

> . . . local people remembering the sheer horror and fear of this huge fuselage on fire just dropping on to their town, and homes and people being vaporised and nothing left at all. And also bodies still strapped in their aircraft seats landing in the fields, completely unmutilated but just still strapped into their seats. That again had a profound impact on me. But the important thing is that you concentrate on getting the story across and remaining authoritative and getting the right tone; it's hard, but I think it's training.

These days BBC correspondents reporting from war zones are given substantial help with psychological stress in the face of the appalling scenes that they have to report. Yet the studio-based newsreader, too, though not staring the reality in the face, has to maintain a similar calm detachedness while following the grim details of a developing story, the imagination working overtime.

Inevitably, it's when the hurly-burly of the newsroom is left behind that the true horror of a disaster like Lockerbie, or the

Kegworth air crash that Green found herself reporting just six weeks later, makes itself felt. 'When you go home you let it out then, and it *is* awful. I needed people to talk to and actually go over it – over and over it in great detail – in order to sort of get it out of my system in a way. It was profoundly shocking.' But, and this footnote won't be surprising for anyone who has ever set foot in a newsroom, the black humour of news-watchers – itself in part a psychological safety valve – will always surface: 'Because there was this awful link with me and dreadful air crashes, for about a year afterwards, every time I came in for a late shift, up would go the cry, "Oh, nobody get on a plane tonight. Charlotte's reading the news."'

The newsroom is the heart of radio during the night-time hours, preparing bulletins for all the networks that, unlike Radio 4, remain on air. 'Although the ship, the BBC's great ship, goes on and on all through the night, a lot of the building goes to sleep. But the newsroom doesn't.' These words are from Sir Richard MacCormac who's spent more time than most studying the ways radio people operate, as he was responsible for the key design of the new Broadcasting House with its vast newsroom which, it's hoped, will by the end of the decade draw all the BBC's news resources together in central London. 'In that sense it's like the engine-room; it just keeps going sort of thudding onwards twenty-four hours a day.'

Radio's HQ in Portland Place, awaiting the newsroom's return, tends these days to be a quiet place at night, the familiar smiling daytime faces behind the reception desk replaced now by outsourced overnight security. Once, the eighth floor 'staff restaurant' was a place where some came at night to ponder programmes (one Radio 4 colleague told me he had his best ideas there), to linger over coffees gazing out northwards at the dark mass of Hampstead, the glare of lights along Marylebone Road. Now the canteen that served night-shift staff for forty, fifty years, and the old extension that housed it, have been demolished. But the original 1932 building remains, buffed up and unrecognisable in many ways to those who've worked in it for generations, like Laurie Taylor, who's been broadcasting on and off there for over three decades.

There is a very, very funny thing about Broadcasting House, about the corridors of Broadcasting House, about the feeling of Broadcasting House. So many people say, 'This is where this used to be' or, 'This is where that used to be' – I mean these are people who've been twenty or thirty years so they know . . . the history of the place. The very building for them is full of memories.

Over in west London, the *Today* office is, at this end of the day, still pretty dead. The morning rush hasn't yet started: 'It's very deserted at night and very limited in places to get any food. It does breed a spirit of camaraderie, though, amongst those that are there,' reports Mike Thomson, who's often there putting the finishing touches to his latest package on Africa; 'because when you go through the night shift together, everyone has their times when you think, "Oh woe is me! Where is life? What am I doing here? This is horrible!' and, you know, that gets shared around a bit. People having to try to go to sleep in undignified positions.'

Announcers, like *Today* reporters, no longer do overnight shifts – it saves a lot of licence-payers' money – so the midnight bulletin (thirty minutes long and Radio 4's 'journal of record') plus the surrounding continuity presentation are their last duties of the day. As the end of broadcasting on the network approaches, their presence often becomes more felt, more appreciated by the listening audience. 'My God,' exclaims Libby Purves, 'one must never underestimate the sheer emotional security blanket that is the Radio 4 announcer.' In the post-midnight moments, when listeners are perhaps seeking elusive sleep, these conductors of the network offer an intimacy that uniquely radio provides, talking directly to you. 'Peter Donaldson's voice, Dilly Barlow's voice, Charlotte Green's voice, Brian Perkins – those guys! The modesty, the sense of service, the sense of reason – they are calm voices of reason.'

Most days, Sundays excepted (when, these days, there's a repeated documentary or discussion), the tone of the final half hour, before the network joins the very different terrain of BBC World Service, is resolutely intimate. The *Late Book* is a small-scale offering, a single voice in your ear, before a return to

Continuity and the comforting voice of the announcer who takes the network through its final, not inconsiderable flourish.

Sea fever

It is, of course, entirely utilitarian: a sequence of music and speech that alerts listeners to the impending bulletin, which itself then offers vital information to those at sea. Prosaically, it consists of a piece of music called 'Sailing By', followed by the *Shipping Forecast*. And yet, just as *Farming Today*'s audience consists (as James Boyle discovered) largely of town-dwellers hankering after a rural *ideal*, so many who regularly catch the closedown sequence on Radio 4 (Ronald Binge's tune and the ritual recitation of 'the shipping forecast, issued by the Meteorological Office, on behalf of the Maritime and Coast-guard Agency . . .') are not sailors, but resolute landlubbers.

> The sea is calm tonight.
> The tide is full, the moon lies fair
> Upon the Straits; – on the French coast the light
> Gleams and is gone; the cliffs of England stand,
> Glimmering and vast, out in the tranquil bay.

Matthew Arnold's poem 'Dover Beach' perfectly encapsulates the spirit in which many Radio 4 listeners embrace the *Shipping Forecast*: gazing into the depths of the night, a seascape of indigo swept by a distant lighthouse beam . . . Sandettie Light Vessel automatic . . . St Catherine's Point automatic . . . Machrihanish automatic. I, like thousands who've never used a shipping forecast in anger, nonetheless love its mantra-like quality, the power of the words to evoke images. It's also a distant echo of the romance that many still feel for the radio pirates of the 1960s aboard their storm-tossed ships, with whom I began this book.

Once the observations were made manually by human beings, stationed in lonely postings on ships and rocks, and although those 'automatic' tags belie the mechanical nature of today's data collection, the romance of the sea still transcends the prosaic reality. 'It's the nearest thing to poetry that I ever get to read (or *did* ever get to read) on the radio – wonderful cadences' recalls Charlotte Green, who as a newsreader no longer these days has the forecast among her regular duties. 'I must admit I have a special affinity with the *Shipping Forecast*. I love it – and it seemed to touch a chord in people because a lot of people would write and say that they particularly liked me reading it and the way I read it.'

'There are warnings of gales in Thames, Dover, FitzRoy, Trafalgar, Sole, Fastnet, Shannon. The General synopsis at two-three-double-oh: Low, Tyne, 994: expected south Norway, 1000, by oh-seven-double-oh tomorrow. Atlantic low, 999 moving steadily east; expected Sole 990 by same time . . .'

It was Charlotte Green's reading of the forecast that once inspired a photographer to take a remarkable sequence of portraits of the locations mentioned in the bulletin; but the reality of Dogger, Faeroes, Valentia island and the rest is nothing compared with the images that are conjured in the mind of the listener. 'It is a mantra, it is people listening, probably at their most vulnerable, last thing at night, and it just imbues itself into their psyche,' according to Charlotte's colleague Peter Donaldson. So writers have dreamed up fantasies round the name Malin – surely some evil necromancer – and who but the strange people of the north dwell in North Utsire and South Utsire? Each name brings with it a sailor's trunk full of associations from our own and our nation's histories: *Viking, Trafalgar, Fastnet, Fair Isle* . . . and I can't hear *Lundy* without seeing an old 'half-puffin' coin, currency on that tiny island in the Bristol Channel, that lurked for years at the bottom of my piggy-bank.

Southwesterly five or six, becoming cyclonic seven or gale eight. Rough or very rough. Rain then showers. Moderate or poor . . .

No lesser poets than Seamus Heaney, in 'The Shipping

Forecast' ('Dogger, Rockall, Malin, Irish Sea: / Green, swift upsurges, North Atlantic flux . . .') and Carol Ann Duffy ('Prayer') have used the ringing cadences of the bulletin ('Darkness outside. Inside, the radio's prayer — / Rockall. Malin. Dogger. Finisterre.'). The bands Blur ('This is a Low') and Radiohead ('In Limbo') likewise have been inspired by the forecast's incantatory lines. Inevitably, the forecast has also been the source of much comic imitation, by Stephen Fry amongst many, and a brilliant parody version of the forecast, composed for a *Broadcasting House* item on the clogged state of Britain's roads and read of course by Charlotte Green, brought a clamour of requests for copies: it ends

> Malin: head-gasket blown. Severe. A new low. Burst vessel, silly automatic Vauxhall. Rage. Severe wails, perhaps violent storm off in a strop later. Tears. Tantrum. And that completes the Traffic Forecast.

And yet we would perhaps do well to listen to Peter Donaldson, one of Radio 4's finest jokers and until his retirement the network's Chief Announcer, who recalls the more playful side of the shipping forecast, as undisclosed to the listener romantically dreaming at home of Dogger Bank and fog on the Tyne . . . His story is of a former announcer colleague, Eugene Fraser. Eugene was a supreme announcer, but also enjoyed practical jokes, especially where the *Shipping Forecast* was concerned: 'He used to come into the studio when you were reading [it] and set fire to the bottom. So you had to speed up to get to it before the fire did. He was the biggest practical joker there was, the most mischievous. But we did have fun in those days.'

Musical sails

The harbinger for the *Shipping Forecast* is a piece of music entitled 'Sailing By', which, according to Donaldson, has nothing to do with ships ('it was the incidental music for a film about

balloons'). It was composed by British light music composer
Ronald Binge whose 'Elizabethan Serenade' was also a firm
favourite of those old Radio 4 music anthologies like *Baker's
Dozen*. 'Sailing By' is much loved as a night-time lullaby, though
personally I have to confess to a certain antipathy to its soupy
string tone, a feature of Binge's compositional style. It sailed on
to Radio 4's airwaves as a timing buffer for the *Shipping
Forecast* (which must start on the dot of midnight-forty-eight)
when Radio 4 acquired the BBC's Long Wave frequency in
1978.

The piece has its fan club (it included prisoner Myra Hindley)
and its detractors ('drunken strings, a seedy wire brush on
cymbal, guitar limply strummed and those watery flutes rising
and falling conspire to cast you adrift into an Ancient Mariner
void . . .' wrote one journalist). James Boyle, the great schedule
reformer, has an unusually soft spot for the piece: 'I find it
enchanting and no one else does.'

> When 'Sailing By' comes on I feel as if all's right with the world,
> that another day has been successfully completed as a listener.
> And when folks said to me, 'Why don't you just get rid of it?' I
> felt, 'Why don't we just *not*!'

Three years before Boyle took his seat in the controller's
office, a storm force 10 had broken out over a plan to axe the
tune. Marion Greenwood was the press officer in the firing line:
'I don't think we had quite expected the huge great onslaught
that there was, because it was just this bit of music!' The move
wasn't just a whim on the part of the controller, Michael Green.
He needed to make some space (and save some cash – £30,000
in royalties no less) to schedule his *Late Book*, and the fixed
timing of the forecast (in those days fifteen minutes earlier at
midnight-thirty) made it all just too tight to have 'Sailing By' as
well, Greenwood remembers.

> People said it's what put them to sleep and made them feel safe
> and secure, and it was their dead husband's favourite piece of
> music, so how could we do this . . .? In fact I remember somebody

writing in saying could she have a copy for his funeral? But we just had to tough it out because in order to get the book on you had to lose something.

So the tune disappeared from weekdays, only putting in a weekend appearance. Inevitably yet another schedule shake-up then meant, along with another row ('seamen are angry that BBC Radio 4 is to change the timing of its late-night shipping forecast . . .') that 'Sailing By' could sail back again.

And so to bed. But not quite. Those melodic ships (or possibly balloons) have sailed by, the deep-low-southeast-Iceland has filled a little, and Charlotte Green is alone in a studio with a microphone. The National Anthem, still transmitted at closedown on Radio 4, is poised to roll and the time is ticking towards one am when the rather different sound of BBC World Service will appear on the Radio 4 wavelength. Over on Five Live, they're about to be *Up All Night*, but Radio 4 is ringing down the safety curtain on its domain for another day; Ambridge sleeps.

But for now . . . a few words before closedown, please, Charlotte: 'I always made a point of signing off with a very personal message, not in any way cloying or sentimental; just that I hoped that they'd enjoyed the evening and what they'd listened to and I wished them *a peaceful night*.' Those words, spoken in Charlotte's gentle, slightly husky tones, chimed especially with listeners in these moments between waking and sleep, a benison for going gentle into this good night . . .

And that was something, that one phrase, that seemed to resonate with people. I got an awful lot of letters from people saying that, often very lonely people. My voice and other announcers' voices were the only ones coming into their homes often all day, every day. And that struck a chord with them – 'a peaceful night'. It made me realise how very many lonely people there are for whom Radio 4 is a lifeline.

And not only for the lone and the lonely. It's also a whole world of experience to savour and sample for fertile imaginations waiting to be stimulated by the ideas, facts and fictions that throng Radio 4's programmes. It may have its duff moments, its creaky old formats; it may often annoy and delight in equal measure, but it remains, forty years on, still the most idiosyncratic and listened to speech network in the world. It's still, astonishingly, the most popular radio station *bar none* in London, and its national audience figures are stable at nearly ten million listeners a week. Long before he became controller, the youthful James Boyle was one:

> Radio 4 was part of my life ambition if you like. It was one of the things that taught me to understand, gave me knowledge, and it was one of the things that formed me and taught me to be ambitious . . . Radio 4 was one of the voices in our household that taught me to look up and out and beyond . . .

Nearly thirty years before Boyle became controller, the network's other great creative reformer Tony Whitby, a man formed by television but with a zeal for the senior service, wrote: 'In the realm of ideas, radio operates with uncluttered lucidity: in the realm of the imagination, it soars where other media limp.'

Finally, what about a seasoned professional in front of the mic? What keeps John Humphrys, Sony Radio Academy news journalist of 2007, getting up in the (small hours of the) morning? Is it still fun?

> Yes, I wouldn't be doing it if it weren't; I would have stopped it long ago. I've kept thinking about stopping it every year, every time my contract comes up I think about stopping it, and I realise I'd be sitting there at ten past eight one morning, and hearing Jim or whoever interviewing somebody and thinking, 'Bloody hell, I wish I were doing that!' So I keep going on. As Churchill said, 'Keep buggering on.'

We're nearly done. Closedown is upon us. In a sunlit, north-facing room in Hobart, Tasmania, Tony is clicking at his keyboard; it's just coming up to noon. Tony's a PhD student in his twenties, but has never been to Europe, let alone to the UK.

He's a proud Tasmanian, yet, thanks to the internet, he loves
Terry Wogan and keeps an ear tuned for what's going on
literally half a world away. It's his way of defeating what some
Australians refer to as the 'tyranny of distance'. This morning
he's been surfing bbc.co.uk, and now he's stumbled upon slash-
Radio 4. A click on 'Listen Live' and the strains of Ronald
Binge's 'Sailing By' modulate into the litany of the *Shipping
Forecast*.

Outside the window, in the curiously Scottish-looking
harbour, boats bob tranquilly at anchor in the summer heat
under the watchful bulk of Mount Wellington:

> Lands End to St David's Head, including Bristol Channel: North,
> five to seven, occasionally gale eight; backing west, four or five
> later. Rain or showers. Moderate or poor, becoming good . . .

And somewhere deep in Tony's imagination a picture dimly
takes shape . . .

Index